ELEMENTS OF
Literature
SECOND COURSE

The Holt Reader
An Interactive WorkText

Instruction in Reading Literature and Informational Materials

Standardized Test Practice

HOLT, RINEHART AND WINSTON
A Harcourt Education Company
Austin • Orlando • Chicago • New York • Toronto • London • San Diego

CREDITS

Supervisory Editors: Juliana Koenig, Fannie Safier

Managing Editor: Mike Topp

Administrative Managing Editor: Michael Neibergall

Senior Product Manager: Don Wulbrecht

Editors: Susan Kent Cakars, Crystal Wirth, Michael Zakhar

Copyediting Supervisor: Mary Malone

Copyeditors: Elizabeth Dickson, *Senior Copyeditor;* Christine Altgelt, Joel Bourgeois, Emily Force, Julie A. Hill, Julia Thomas Hu, Jennifer Kirkland, Millicent Ondras, Dennis Scharnberg

Project Administration: Elizabeth LaManna

Editorial Support: Bret Isaacs, Brian Kachmar, Erik Netcher

Editorial Permissions: Ann B. Farrar, Kimberly Feden, David Smith

Design: Bruce Bond, *Design Director, Book Design*

Electronic Publishing: Nanda Patel, JoAnn Stringer, *Project Coordinators;* Sally Dewhirst, *Quality Control Team Leader;* Angela Priddy, Barry Bishop, Becky Golden-Harrell, Ellen Rees, *Quality Control;* Juan Baquera, *Electronic Publishing Technology Services Team Leader;* Christopher Lucas, *Team Leader;* Lana Kaupp, Kim Orne, Susan Savkov; *Senior Production Artists;* Ellen Kennedy, Patricia Zepeda, *Production Artists;* Heather Jernt, *Electronic Publishing Supervisor;* Robert Franklin, *Electronic Publishing Director*

Production/Manufacturing: Michael Roche *Senior Production Coordinator;* Belinda Barbosa Lopez, *Senior Production Coordinator;* Carol Trammel, *Production Manager;* Beth Prevelige, *Senior Production Manager*

Contents

PART 2 Reading Informational Materials

PART 3 Standardized Test Practice

Literature

Informational Materials

Skills Contents

Literary Skills

Reading Skills for Literary Texts

Reading Skills for Informational Texts

To the Student

A Book for You

Imagine this. A book full of stories you want to read and informational articles that are really interesting. Make it a book that actually tells you to write in it, circling, underlining, jotting down responses. Fill it with graphic organizers that encourage you to think a different way. Make it a size that's easy to carry around. That's *The Holt Reader: An Interactive WorkText*—a book created especially for you.

The Holt Reader: An Interactive WorkText is designed to accompany *Elements of Literature*. Like *Elements of Literature*, it's designed to help you interact with the literature and informational materials you read. The chart below shows you what's in your book and how the book is organized.

PART 1 Reading Literature	PART 2 Reading Informational Materials	PART 3 Standardized Test Practice
Literary selections from *Elements of Literature*	Informational texts topically or thematically linked to literary selections	Standardized test practice of literature and informational reading

Learning to Read Literary and Informational Materials

When you read informational materials like a social studies textbook or a newspaper article, you usually read to get the facts. You read mainly to get information that is stated directly on the page. When you read literature, you need to go beyond understanding what the words mean and getting the facts straight. You need to read between the lines of a poem or story to discover the writer's meaning. No matter what kind of reading you do—literary or informational—*The Holt Reader: An Interactive WorkText* will help you practice the skills and strategies you need to become an active and successful reader.

Setting the Stage: Before You Read

In Part 1, the Before-You-Read activity helps you make a personal connection with the selection you are about to read. It helps you sharpen your awareness of what you already know by asking you to think and write about a topic before you read. The more you know about the topic of a text, of course, the easier it is to understand the text. Sometimes this page will provide background information you need to know before you read the text.

Interactive Selections from *Elements of Literature*

The literary selections in Part 1 are many of the same selections that appear in *Elements of Literature,* Second Course. The selections are reprinted in a single column and in larger type to give you the room you need to mark up the text.

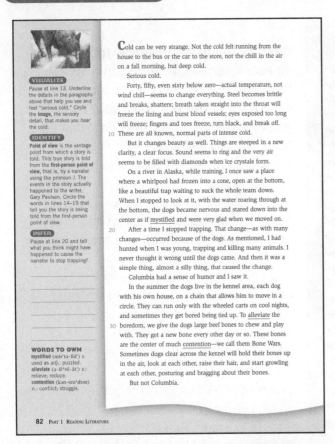

VISUALIZE
Pause at line 13. Underline the details in the paragraphs above that help you see and feel "serious cold." Circle the **image**, the sensory detail, that makes you *hear* the cold.

IDENTIFY
Point of view is the vantage point from which a story is told. This true story is told from the **first-person point of view**, that is, by a narrator using the pronoun *I*. The events in the story actually happened to the writer, Gary Paulsen. Circle the words in lines 14–19 that tell you the story is being told from the first-person point of view.

INFER
Pause at line 20 and tell what you think might have happened to cause the narrator to stop trapping?

_____
_____
_____
_____
_____

WORDS TO OWN
mystified (mis'tə-fīd') *v.* used as *adj.*: puzzled.
alleviate (ə-lē'vē-āt') *v.*: relieve; reduce.
contention (kən-ten'shən) *n.*: conflict; struggle.

Cold can be very strange. Not the cold felt running from the house to the bus or the car to the store, not the chill in the air on a fall morning, but deep cold.

Serious cold.

Forty, fifty, even sixty below zero—actual temperature, not wind chill—seems to change everything. Steel becomes brittle and breaks, shatters; breath taken straight into the throat will freeze the lining and burst blood vessels; eyes exposed too long will freeze; fingers and toes freeze, turn black, and break off.
10 These are all known, normal parts of intense cold.

But it changes beauty as well. Things are steeped in a new clarity, a clear focus. Sound seems to ring and the very air seems to be filled with diamonds when ice crystals form.

On a river in Alaska, while training, I once saw a place where a whirlpool had frozen into a cone, open at the bottom, like a beautiful trap waiting to suck the whole team down. When I stopped to look at it, with the water roaring through at the bottom, the dogs became nervous and stared down into the center as if mystified and were very glad when we moved on.
20 After a time I stopped trapping. That change—as with many changes—occurred because of the dogs. As mentioned, I had hunted when I was young, trapping and killing many animals. I never thought it wrong until the dogs came. And then it was a simple thing, almost a silly thing, that caused the change.

Columbia had a sense of humor and I saw it.

In the summer the dogs live in the kennel area, each dog with his own house, on a chain that allows him to move in a circle. They can run only with the wheeled carts on cool nights, and sometimes they get bored being tied up. To alleviate the
30 boredom, we give the dogs large beef bones to chew and play with. They get a new bone every other day or so. These bones are the center of much contention—we call them Bone Wars. Sometimes dogs clear across the kennel will hold their bones up in the air, look at each other, raise their hair, and start growling at each other, posturing and bragging about their bones.

But not Columbia.

Usually Columbia just chewed on his bone until the meat was gone. Then he buried it and waited for the next bone. I never saw him fight or get involved in Bone Wars and I always
40 thought him a simple—perhaps a better word would be primitive—dog, basic and very wolf-like, until one day when I was sitting in the kennel.

I had a notebook and I was sitting on the side of Cookie's roof, writing—the dogs are good company for working—when I happened to notice Columbia doing something strange.

He was sitting quietly on the outside edge of his circle, at the maximum length of his chain. With one paw he was pushing his bone—which still had a small bit of meat on it— out and away from him, toward the next circle.
50 Next to Columbia was a dog named Olaf. While Columbia was relatively passive, Olaf was very aggressive. Olaf always wanted to fight and he spent much time arguing over bones, females, the weather—anything and everything that caught his fancy. He was much scarred from fighting, with notched ears and lines on his muzzle, but he was a very good dog—strong and honest—and we liked him.

Being next to Columbia, Olaf had tried many times to get him to argue or bluster, but Columbia always ignored him.

Until this morning.
60 Carefully, slowly, Columbia pushed the bone toward Olaf's circle.

And of all the things that Olaf was—tough, strong, honest— he wasn't smart. As they say, some are smarter than others, and some are still not so smart, and then there was Olaf. It wouldn't be fair to call Olaf dumb—dogs don't measure those things like people—but even in the dog world he would not be known as a whip. Kind of a big bully who was also a bit of a doofus.

When he saw Columbia pushing the bone toward him, he
70 began to reach for it. Straining against his chain, turning and trying to get farther and farther, he reached as far as he could

EVALUATE
In lines 37–42, the narrator says that he had thought that Columbia was more simple or primitive than the other dogs because Columbia went his own way and didn't fight or get involved in the Bone Wars. Based on your **prior experience** with animals, do you agree with this conclusion? Why or why not?

_____
_____
_____
_____
_____

PREDICT
Pause at line 59. What do you think is going to happen between Columbia and Olaf?

_____
_____
_____

INFER
Underline the reason that the narrator says, "It wouldn't be fair to call Olaf dumb" (lines 64–65). What does this reason tell you about the narrator's **perspective** on dogs, that is, the way he understands or judges them, at this point in his story?

Strategies to Guide Your Reading: Side Notes

Notes in the side column accompany each selection. They guide your interaction with the text and help you unlock meaning. Many notes ask you to circle or underline in the text itself. Others provide lines on which you can write. Here are the kinds of notes you will work with as you read the selections: identify, retell, infer, predict, interpret, evaluate, visualize, and build fluency.

Identify asks you to find information (like the name of a character or a description of the setting) that is stated directly in the text. You will often be asked to circle or underline the information in the text.

Retell asks you to restate or explain in your own words something that has just happened.

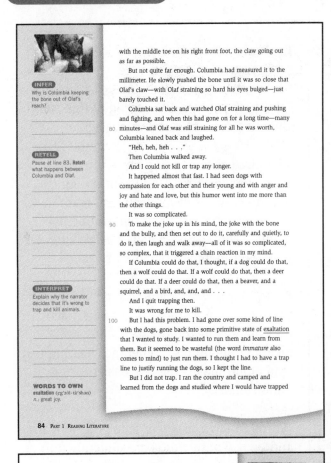

Why is Columbia keeping the bone out of Olaf's reach?

_____

_____

Pause at line 83. **Retell** what happens between Columbia and Olaf.

_____

_____

_____

_____

_____

Explain why the narrator decides that it's wrong to trap and kill animals.

_____

_____

_____

_____

_____

_____

WORDS TO OWN
exaltation (ĕg'zôl-tā'shən) n.: great joy.

with the middle toe on his right front foot, the claw going out as far as possible.

But not quite far enough. Columbia had measured it to the millimeter. He slowly pushed the bone until it was so close that Olaf's claw—with Olaf straining so hard his eyes bulged—just barely touched it.

Columbia sat back and watched Olaf straining and pushing and fighting, and when this had gone on for a long time—many
80 minutes—and Olaf was still straining for all he was worth, Columbia leaned back and laughed.

"Heh, heh, heh . . ."

Then Columbia walked away.

And I could not kill or trap any longer.

It happened almost that fast. I had seen dogs with compassion for each other and their young and with anger and joy and hate and love, but this humor went into me more than the other things.

It was so complicated.
90 To make the joke up in his mind, the joke with the bone and the bully, and then set out to do it, carefully and quietly, to do it, then laugh and walk away—all of it was so complicated, so complex, that it triggered a chain reaction in my mind.

If Columbia could do that, I thought, if a dog could do that, then a wolf could do that. If a wolf could do that, then a deer could do that. If a deer could do that, then a beaver, and a squirrel, and a bird, and, and, and . . .

And I quit trapping then.

It was wrong for me to kill.
100 But I had this problem. I had gone over some kind of line with the dogs, gone back into some primitive state of exaltation that I wanted to study. I wanted to run them and learn from them. But it seemed to be wasteful (the word _immature_ also comes to mind) to just run them. I thought I had to have a trap line to justify running the dogs, so I kept the line.

But I did not trap. I ran the country and camped and learned from the dogs and studied where I would have trapped

if I were going to trap. I took many imaginary beaver and muskrat but I did no more sets and killed no more animals. I
110 will not kill anymore.

Yet the line existed. Somehow in my mind—and until writing this I have never told another person about this—the line still existed and when I had "trapped" in one area, I would extend the line to "trap" in another, as is proper when you actually trap. Somehow the phony trapping gave me a purpose for running the dogs and would until I began to train them for the Iditarod, a dog-sled race across Alaska, which I had read about in _Alaska_ magazine.

But it was on one of these "trapping" runs that I got my
120 third lesson,[1] or awakening.

There was a point where an old logging trail went through a small, sharp-sided gully—a tiny canyon. The trail came down one wall of the gully—a drop of fifty or so feet—then scooted across a frozen stream and up the other side. It might have been a game trail that was slightly widened or an old foot trail that had not caved in. Whatever it was, I came onto it in the middle of January. The dogs were very excited. New trails always get them tuned up and they were fairly smoking as we came to the edge of the gully.
130 I did not know it was there and had been letting them run, not riding the sled brake to slow them, and we virtually shot off the edge.

The dogs stayed on the trail, but I immediately lost all control and went flying out into space with the sled. As I did, I kicked sideways, caught my knee on a sharp snag, and felt the wood enter under the kneecap and tear it loose.

I may have screamed then.

The dogs ran out on the ice of the stream but I fell onto it. As these things often seem to happen, the disaster snowballed.
140 The trail crossed the stream directly at the top of a small frozen waterfall with about a twenty-foot drop. Later I saw the

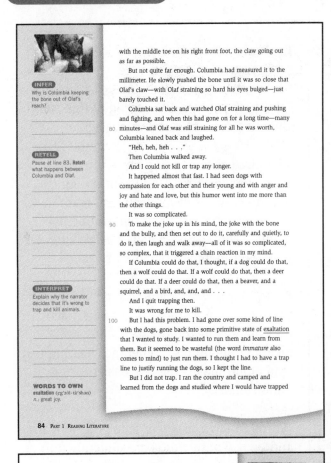

What do you think the narrator means by "phony trapping" (line 115)?

_____

_____

_____

Use the space below to draw a picture of the trail described in lines 121–129. Draw and label the _gully_, the _frozen stream_ at the bottom of it, and the _trail_ going down and across the stream, and up to the other side of the gully.

Sketch of Trail

_____

1. **my third lesson:** The first lesson is described in the two previous chapters of _Woodsong._

Infer asks you to make an **inference,** or an educated guess. You make inferences on the basis of clues writers give you and on experiences from your own life. When you make an inference, you read between the lines to figure out what the writer suggests but does not say directly.

Predict asks you to figure out what will happen next. Making predictions as you read helps you think about and understand what you are reading. To make predictions, look for clues that the writer gives you. Connect those clues with other things you've read, as well as your own experience. You'll probably find yourself adjusting predictions as you read.

Interpret asks you to explain the meaning of something. When you make an interpretation of a character, for example, you look at what the character says or does, and then you think about what the character's words and actions mean. You ask yourself why the character said those words and did those things. Your answer is the interpretation. Interpretations help you get at the main idea of a selection, the discovery about life you take away from it.

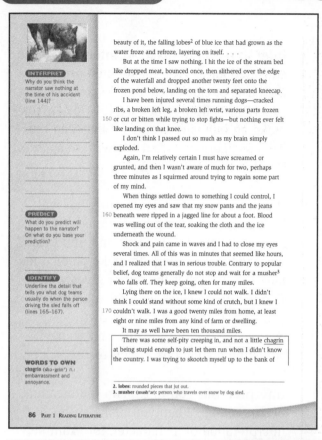

INTERPRET
Why do you think the narrator saw nothing at the time of his accident (line 144)?

PREDICT
What do you predict will happen to the narrator? On what do you base your prediction?

IDENTIFY
Underline the detail that tells you what dog teams usually do when the person driving the sled falls off (lines 165–167).

WORDS TO OWN
chagrin (shə·grin') n.: embarrassment and annoyance.

beauty of it, the falling lobes[2] of blue ice that had grown as the water froze and refroze, layering on itself. . . .

But at the time I saw nothing. I hit the ice of the stream bed like dropped meat, bounced once, then slithered over the edge of the waterfall and dropped another twenty feet onto the frozen pond below, landing on the torn and separated kneecap.

I have been injured several times running dogs—cracked ribs, a broken left leg, a broken left wrist, various parts frozen or cut or bitten while trying to stop fights—but nothing ever felt like landing on that knee.

I don't think I passed out so much as my brain simply exploded.

Again, I'm relatively certain I must have screamed or grunted, and then I wasn't aware of much for two, perhaps three minutes as I squirmed around trying to regain some part of my mind.

When things settled down to something I could control, I opened my eyes and saw that my snow pants and the jeans beneath them were ripped in a jagged line for about a foot. Blood was welling out of the tear, soaking the cloth and the ice underneath the wound.

Shock and pain came in waves and I had to close my eyes several times. All of this was in minutes that seemed like hours, and I realized that I was in serious trouble. Contrary to popular belief, dog teams generally do not stop and wait for a musher[3] who falls off. They keep going, often for many miles.

Lying there on the ice, I knew I could not walk. I didn't think I could stand without some kind of crutch, but I knew I couldn't walk. I was a good twenty miles from home, at least eight or nine miles from any kind of farm or dwelling.

It may as well have been ten thousand miles.

There was some self-pity creeping in, and not a little chagrin at being stupid enough to just let them run when I didn't know the country. I was trying to skootch myself up to the bank of

_____

2. **lobes:** rounded pieces that jut out.
3. **musher** (mush'ər): person who travels over snow by dog sled.

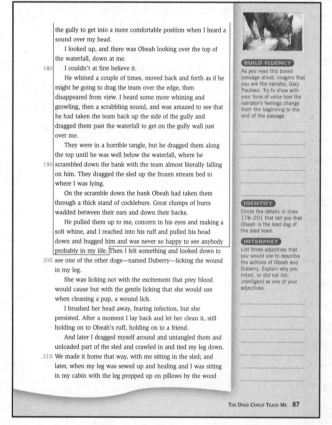

the gully to get into a more comfortable position when I heard a sound over my head.

I looked up, and there was Obeah looking over the top of the waterfall, down at me.

I couldn't at first believe it.

He whined a couple of times, moved back and forth as if he might be going to drag the team over the edge, then disappeared from view. I heard some more whining and growling, then a scrabbling sound, and was amazed to see that he had taken the team back up the side of the gully and dragged them past the waterfall to get on the gully wall just over me.

They were in a horrible tangle, but he dragged them along the top until he was well below the waterfall, where he scrambled down the bank with the team almost literally falling on him. They dragged the sled up the frozen stream bed to where I was lying.

On the scramble down the bank Obeah had taken them through a thick stand of cockleburs. Great clumps of burrs wadded between their ears and down their backs.

He pulled them up to me, concern in his eyes and making a soft whine, and I reached into his ruff and pulled his head down and hugged him and was never so happy to see anybody probably in my life. Then I felt something and looked down to see one of the other dogs—named Duberry—licking the wound in my leg.

She was licking not with the excitement that prey blood would cause but with the gentle licking that she would use when cleaning a pup, a wound lick.

I brushed her head away, fearing infection, but she persisted. After a moment I lay back and let her clean it, still holding on to Obeah's ruff, holding on to a friend.

And later I dragged myself around and untangled them and unloaded part of the sled and crawled in and tied my leg down. We made it home that way, with me sitting in the sled; and later, when my leg was sewed up and healing and I was sitting in my cabin with the leg propped up on pillows by the wood

BUILD FLUENCY
As you read this boxed passage aloud, imagine that you are the narrator, Gary Paulsen. Try to show with your tone of voice how the narrator's feelings change from the beginning to the end of the passage.

IDENTIFY
Circle the details in lines 178–201 that tell you that Obeah is the lead dog of the sled team.

INTERPRET
List three adjectives that you would use to describe the actions of Obeah and Duberry. Explain why you listed, or did not list, *intelligent* as one of your adjectives.

Evaluate asks you to form opinions about what you read. For example, you might see the following note at the end of a story: "How satisfying is the ending of this story? Give two reasons for your answer."

Visualize asks you to picture the characters, settings, and events being described in a selection. As you read, look for details that help you make a mental picture. Think of visualizing as making your own mental movie of a selection.

Build Fluency asks you to read a poem or passages from a story. It lets you practice phrasing, expression, and reading in meaningful chunks. Sometimes hearing text read aloud makes the text easier to understand.

Words to Own lists words for you to learn and own. These words are underlined in the selection, letting you see the words in context. The words are defined for you right there in the side column.

The Dogs Could Teach Me

Narrator's Reaction Chart

"The Dogs Could Teach Me" is told from the **first-person point of view.** As Gary Paulsen tells his story, he reveals his innermost reactions to the events that occur.

After you read "The Dogs Could Teach Me," fill in the event column with major events from the story. Then, fill in the second column with Paulsen's reactions—his inner thoughts and feelings.

Event	Narrator's Reaction

THE DOGS COULD TEACH ME 89

After You Read: Graphic Organizers

After each selection, **graphic organizers** give you a visual way to organize, interpret, and understand the reading or literary focus of the selection. You might be asked to chart the main events of the plot or complete a cause-and-effect chain.

The Dogs Could Teach Me

Vocabulary and Comprehension

A. Complete each sentence with a word from the Word Bank.

Word Bank
mystified
alleviate
contention
exaltation
chagrin

1. At first, Gary Paulsen was _____ by Columbia's unusual behavior.

2. The beauty of the natural world makes many people feel a sense of _____ .

3. To reduce or _____ the pain caused by cold temperatures, dogs huddle together.

4. The phrase "a bone of _____" means a disagreement about a particular subject.

5. If you make a foolish mistake, you will probably feel _____ and embarrassment.

B. Show your understanding of words in the Word Bank by answering the following questions.

1. What might cause <u>contention</u> between a person and a dog?

_____

_____

2. How would you <u>alleviate</u> someone's fear of dogs?

_____

_____

3. How would a dog show <u>chagrin</u>?

_____

_____

90 PART 1 READING LITERATURE

After You Read: Vocabulary and Comprehension

Vocabulary and Comprehension worksheets at the end of literary selections check your knowledge of the Words to Own and your understanding of the selection.

PART 2 Reading Informational Materials

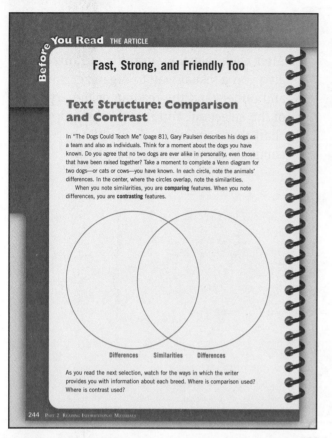

Focus on Skills: Before You Read

The Before-You-Read page in Part 2 teaches skills and strategies you'll need to read informational materials like textbooks, newspaper and magazine articles, and instructional manuals. You'll learn how to recognize text structure, find the main idea, and determine an author's perspective or point of view on these Before-You-Read pages.

Interactive Informational Texts

The informational texts in Part 2 are linked by theme or by topic to the literature selections that appear in *Elements of Literature,* Second Course and *The Holt Reader: An Interactive WorkText,* Second Course. For example, the text you see on the example pages reproduced here comes from an informational text on sled dogs that you might want to read after you've finished "The Dogs Could Teach Me," Gary Paulsen's retelling of two experiences he had with sled dogs that changed the way he thought about animals. The informational selections are printed in a single column and in larger type to give you the room you need to mark up the text.

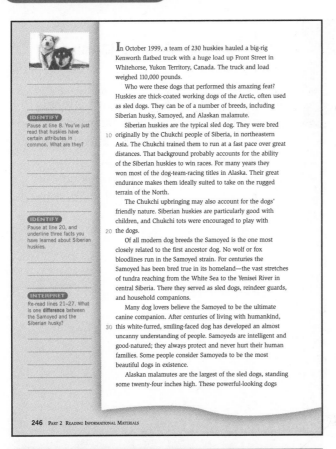

In October 1999, a team of 230 huskies hauled a big-rig Kenworth flatbed truck with a huge load up Front Street in Whitehorse, Yukon Territory, Canada. The truck and load weighed 110,000 pounds.

Who were these dogs that performed this amazing feat? Huskies are thick-coated working dogs of the Arctic, often used as sled dogs. They can be of a number of breeds, including Siberian husky, Samoyed, and Alaskan malamute.

10 Siberian huskies are the typical sled dog. They were bred originally by the Chukchi people of Siberia, in northeastern Asia. The Chukchi trained them to run at a fast pace over great distances. That background probably accounts for the ability of the Siberian huskies to win races. For many years they won most of the dog-team-racing titles in Alaska. Their great endurance makes them ideally suited to take on the rugged terrain of the North.

The Chukchi upbringing may also account for the dogs' friendly nature. Siberian huskies are particularly good with children, and Chukchi tots were encouraged to play with 20 the dogs.

Of all modern dog breeds the Samoyed is the one most closely related to the first ancestor dog. No wolf or fox bloodlines run in the Samoyed strain. For centuries the Samoyed has been bred true in its homeland—the vast stretches of tundra reaching from the White Sea to the Yenisei River in central Siberia. There they served as sled dogs, reindeer guards, and household companions.

Many dog lovers believe the Samoyed to be the ultimate canine companion. After centuries of living with humankind, 30 this white-furred, smiling-faced dog has developed an almost uncanny understanding of people. Samoyeds are intelligent and good-natured; they always protect and never hurt their human families. Some people consider Samoyeds to be the most beautiful dogs in existence.

Alaskan malamutes are the largest of the sled dogs, standing some twenty-four inches high. These powerful-looking dogs

IDENTIFY
Pause at line 8. You've just read that huskies have certain attributes in common. What are they?

IDENTIFY
Pause at line 20, and underline three facts you have learned about Siberian huskies.

INTERPRET
Re-read lines 21–27. What is one **difference** between the Samoyed and the Siberian husky?

246 PART 2 READING INFORMATIONAL MATERIALS

Strategies to Guide Your Reading: Side Notes

As in Part 1, **notes** in the side column accompany each selection. They guide your interaction with the text and help you unlock meaning. Many notes ask you to circle or underline in the text itself. Others provide lines on which you can write. Here are the kinds of notes you will work with as you read the informational materials in Part 2: identify, retell, infer, predict, interpret, evaluate, visualize, and build fluency. See pages xii–xiv for an explanation of each note.

Fast, Strong, and Friendly Too

Compare-and-Contrast Chart

Compare and **contrast** the characteristics of the four breeds of dog you've just read about by filling in the chart below. Look back through the article and the notes you took as you read to help complete the chart.

Breed of Dog	Where Bred	Appearance	Demeanor	Abilities
Siberian husky				
Samoyed				
Alaskan malamute				

248 PART 2 READING INFORMATIONAL MATERIALS

After You Read: Graphic Organizers

After each selection, a **graphic organizer** gives you a visual way to organize, interpret, and understand the selection. These organizers focus on the strategy introduced on the Before-You-Read page. You might be asked to collect supporting details that point to a main idea or to complete a comparison chart.

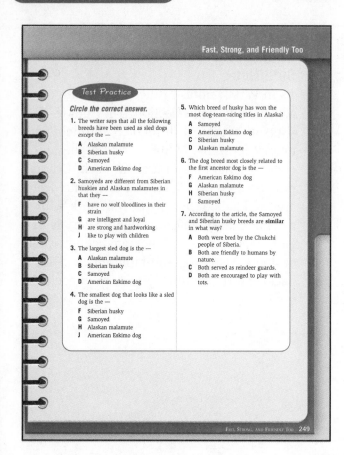

Fast, Strong, and Friendly Too

Test Practice

Circle the correct answer.

1. The writer says that all the following breeds have been used as sled dogs *except* the —
   A Alaskan malamute
   B Siberian husky
   C Samoyed
   D American Eskimo dog

2. Samoyeds are different from Siberian huskies and Alaskan malamutes in that they —
   F have no wolf bloodlines in their strain
   G are intelligent and loyal
   H are strong and hardworking
   J like to play with children

3. The largest sled dog is the —
   A Alaskan malamute
   B Siberian husky
   C Samoyed
   D American Eskimo dog

4. The smallest dog that looks like a sled dog is the —
   F Siberian husky
   G Samoyed
   H Alaskan malamute
   J American Eskimo dog

5. Which breed of husky has won the most dog-team-racing titles in Alaska?
   A Samoyed
   B American Eskimo dog
   C Siberian husky
   D Alaskan malamute

6. The dog breed most closely related to the first ancestor dog is the —
   F American Eskimo dog
   G Alaskan malamute
   H Siberian husky
   J Samoyed

7. According to the article, the Samoyed and Siberian husky breeds are **similar** in what way?
   A Both were bred by the Chukchi people of Siberia.
   B Both are friendly to humans by nature.
   C Both served as reindeer guards.
   D Both are encouraged to play with tots.

FAST, STRONG, AND FRIENDLY TOO **249**

After You Read: Reading Check and Test Practice

Reading Check and Test Practice worksheets at the end of informational selections check your understanding of the selection with short-answer and multiple-choice questions. The multiple-choice questions are similar to the ones you'll answer on state and national standardized tests.

STANDARDIZED TEST PRACTICE   LITERATURE

DIRECTIONS
Read the two stories. Then, read each question that follows on page 321 and circle the best response.

The Dog and the Wolf
Aesop (sixth century B.C.)

One cold and snowy winter the Wolf couldn't find enough to eat. She was almost dead with hunger when a House Dog happened by.

"Ah, Cousin," said the Dog, "you are skin and bones. Come, leave your life of roaming and starving in the forest. Come with me to my master and you'll never go hungry again."

"What will I have to do for my food?" said the Wolf.

"Not much," said the House Dog. "Guard the property, keep the Fox from the henhouse, protect the children. It's an easy life."

That sounded good to the Wolf, so the Dog and the Wolf headed to the village. On the way the Wolf noticed a ring around the Dog's neck where the hair had been rubbed off.

"What's that?" she asked.

"Oh, it's nothing," said the Dog. "It's just where the collar is put on at night to keep me chained up. I'm used to it."

"Chained up!" exclaimed the Wolf, as she ran quickly back to the forest.

Better to starve free than to be a well-fed slave.

The Puppy
Aleksandr Solzhenitsyn (twentieth century)

In our backyard a boy keeps his little dog Sharik chained up, a ball of fluff shackled since he was a puppy.

One day I took him some chicken bones that were still warm and smelled delicious. The boy had just let the poor dog off his lead to have a run round the yard. The snow there was deep and feathery; Sharik was bounding about like a hare, first on his hind legs, then on his front ones, from one corner of the yard to the other, back and forth, burying his muzzle in the snow.

He ran toward me, his coat all shaggy, jumped up at me, sniffed the bones—then off he went again, belly-deep in the snow.

I don't need your bones, he said. Just give me my freedom. . . .

—*translated by* Michael Glenny

1. In the fable "The Dog and the Wolf," the Wolf decides to go to the village with the House Dog because she —
   A is hungry
   B wants an easier life
   C wants to be chained up
   D likes children

2. What does the Wolf notice on the way to the village?
   F Children playing happily
   G Well-fed people
   H A ring on the Dog's neck
   J The Dog limping

3. In "The Puppy," where is the little dog, Sharik, usually kept?
   A Chained in the yard
   B In a doghouse
   C In the living room
   D In the boy's bedroom

4. What do the House Dog and Sharik have in common?
   F They both are chained at times.
   G They both run away from home.
   H They both are starving.
   J They both hate their masters.

5. What do both the Wolf and Sharik want more than food?
   A Love
   B Freedom
   C Security
   D Fame

6. Which of the following sentences *best* expresses the **theme** that both the fable from ancient Greece and the story from modern-day Russia have in common?
   F Nothing is worth more than freedom.
   G Playing is more fun than eating.
   H It is worth being chained up in order to be fed.
   J One can never have both food and freedom.

7. In the first paragraph of "The Puppy," the writer uses the word shackled. Using context clues, you can guess that *shackled* means —
   A punished
   B chained up
   C fed
   D fenced in

Putting Your Skill as a Reader to the Test
The last part of this book gives you practice in reading and responding to the kinds of literary and informational selections you read in Parts 1 and 2. The selections and multiple-choice questions are similar to the ones you'll see on state and national standardized tests.

PART 1 READING LITERATURE

Raymond's Run

Make the Connection

"If You Only Knew…"

Squeaky Parker, the main character in "Raymond's Run," relies on her first impression to evaluate others. As the story goes on, she finds out that people can be full of surprises. Has your first impression of someone ever turned out to be wrong? Think of a friend, relative, or teacher who has surprised you. Write his or her name at the top of the graphic organizer below. Then, write down your first impression of the person and what you learned about him or her over time.

Person

At first I thought

Then I realized

Raymond's Run

Toni Cade Bambara

IDENTIFY

What is the narrator's main responsibility in life? Underline where you find out what it is.

win the
race

IDENTIFY

Who is telling you this story? Underline her name.

INFER

Pause at line 19. Write down three words that describe what you know about Squeaky's **character** so far?

fast
tought
skinny

IDENTIFY

Who is involved in the main **conflict** of the story? Write their names.

Squeaky
Gretchen

I don't have much work to do around the house like some girls. My mother does that. And I don't have to earn my pocket money by hustling; George runs errands for the big boys and sells Christmas cards. And anything else that's got to get done, my father does. All I have to do in life is mind my brother Raymond, which is enough.

Sometimes I slip and say my little brother Raymond. But as any fool can see he's much bigger and he's older too. But a lot of people call him my little brother cause he needs looking after 10 cause he's not quite right. And a lot of smart mouths got lots to say about that too, especially when George was minding him. But now, if anybody has anything to say to Raymond, anything to say about his big head, they have to come by me. And I don't play the dozens[1] or believe in standing around with somebody in my face doing a lot of talking. I much rather just knock you down and take my chances even if I am a little girl with skinny arms and a squeaky voice, which is how I got the name Squeaky. And if things get too rough, I run. And as anybody can tell you, I'm the fastest thing on two feet.

20 There is no track meet that I don't win the first-place medal. I used to win the twenty-yard dash when I was a little kid in kindergarten. Nowadays, it's the fifty-yard dash. And tomorrow I'm subject to run the quarter-meter relay all by myself and come in first, second, and third.

The big kids call me Mercury[2] cause I'm the swiftest thing in the neighborhood. Everybody knows that—except two people who know better, my father and me. He can beat me to Amsterdam Avenue with me having a two-fire-hydrant headstart and him running with his hands in his pockets and whistling. But that's 30 private information. Cause can you imagine some thirty-five-year-old man stuffing himself into PAL[3] shorts to race little kids? So as far as everyone's concerned, I'm the fastest and that goes for Gretchen, too, who has put out the tale that she is

---

1. **play the dozens:** trade insults (slang).
2. **Mercury:** in Roman mythology, messenger of the gods, known for his speediness.
3. **PAL:** Police Athletic League.

going to win the first-place medal this year. Ridiculous. In the second place, she's got short legs. In the third place, she's got freckles. In the first place, no one can beat me and that's all there is to it.

I'm standing on the corner admiring the weather and about
40 to take a stroll down Broadway so I can practice my breathing exercises, and I've got Raymond walking on the inside close to the buildings, cause he's subject to fits of fantasy and starts thinking he's a circus performer and that the curb is a tightrope strung high in the air. And sometimes after a rain he likes to step down off his tightrope right into the gutter and slosh around getting his shoes and cuffs wet. Then I get hit when I get home. Or sometimes if you don't watch him he'll dash across traffic to the island[4] in the middle of Broadway and give the pigeons a fit. Then I have to go behind him apologizing to all the old people sitting around trying to get some sun and getting all
50 upset with the pigeons fluttering around them, scattering their newspapers and upsetting the waxpaper lunches in their laps. So I keep Raymond on the inside of me, and he plays like he's driving a stage coach which is OK by me so long as he doesn't run me over or interrupt my breathing exercises, which I have to do on account of I'm serious about my running, and I don't care who knows it.

Now some people like to act like things come easy to them, won't let on that they practice. Not me. I'll high-prance down 34th Street like a rodeo pony to keep my knees strong even if it
60 does get my mother uptight so that she walks ahead like she's not with me, don't know me, is all by herself on a shopping trip, and I am somebody else's crazy child. Now you take Cynthia Procter for instance. She's just the opposite. If there's a test tomorrow, she'll say something like, "Oh, I guess I'll play handball this afternoon and watch television tonight," just to let you know she ain't thinking about the test. Or like last week when she won the spelling bee for the millionth time, "A good thing you got 'receive,' Squeaky, cause I would have got it

---

4. **island:** traffic island, a car-free area in the middle of a road.

IDENTIFY

Underline the three reasons why Squeaky thinks she's going to beat Gretchen this year.

_____

_____

_____

_____

_____

_____

_____

_____

_____

_____

_____

_____

BUILD FLUENCY

Imagine you are Squeaky as you read this passage aloud. Try to capture Squeaky's tone of voice, especially when she is quoting Cynthia Procter. Read the passage twice: See if you read more smoothly the second time.

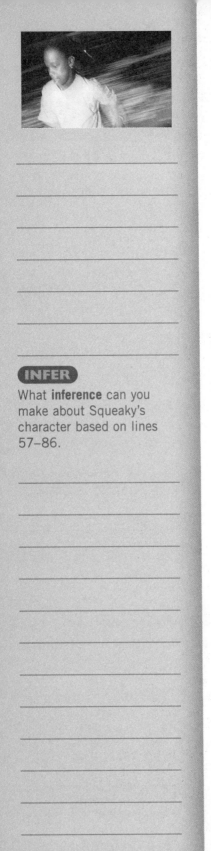

INFER

What **inference** can you make about Squeaky's character based on lines 57–86.

wrong. I completely forgot about the spelling bee." And she'll
70 clutch the lace on her blouse like it was a narrow escape. Oh,
brother. But of course when I pass her house on my early
morning trots around the block, she is practicing the scales on
the piano over and over and over and over. Then in music
class she always lets herself get bumped around so she falls
accidentally on purpose onto the piano stool and is so surprised
to find herself sitting there that she decides just for fun to try
out the ole keys. And what do you know—Chopin's[5] waltzes
just spring out of her fingertips and she's the most surprised
thing in the world. A regular prodigy. I could kill people like
80 that. I stay up all night studying the words for the spelling bee.
And you can see me any time of day practicing running. I never
walk if I can trot, and shame on Raymond if he can't keep up.
But of course he does, cause if he hangs back someone's liable
to walk up to him and get smart, or take his allowance from
him, or ask him where he got that great big pumpkin head.
People are so stupid sometimes.

So I'm strolling down Broadway breathing out and breathing
in on counts of seven, which is my lucky number, and here
comes Gretchen and her sidekicks: Mary Louise, who used to
90 be a friend of mine when she first moved to Harlem from Baltimore
and got beat up by everybody till I took up for her on account
of her mother and my mother used to sing in the same choir
when they were young girls, but people ain't grateful, so now
she hangs out with the new girl Gretchen and talks about me
like a dog; and Rosie, who is as fat as I am skinny and has a
big mouth where Raymond is concerned and is too stupid to
know that there is not a big deal of difference between herself
and Raymond and that she can't afford to throw stones. So they
are steady coming up Broadway and I see right away that it's
100 going to be one of those Dodge City scenes[6] cause the street
ain't that big and they're close to the buildings just as we are.

---

5. **Chopin's:** Frédéric François Chopin (shō·pan′) (1810–1849), Polish composer
   and pianist.
6. **Dodge City scenes:** showdowns like those in the television western *Gunsmoke,*
   which was set in Dodge City, Kansas. In a typical scene, a marshal and an outlaw face off with pistols on an empty street.

First I think I'll step into the candy store and look over the new comics and let them pass. But that's chicken and I've got a reputation to consider. So then I think I'll just walk straight on through them or even over them if necessary. But as they get to me, they slow down. I'm ready to fight, cause like I said I don't feature a whole lot of chit-chat, I much prefer to just knock you down right from the jump and save everybody a lotta precious time.

110   "You signing up for the May Day races?" smiles Mary Louise, only it's not a smile at all. A dumb question like that doesn't deserve an answer. Besides, there's just me and Gretchen standing there really, so no use wasting my breath talking to shadows.

"I don't think you're going to win this time," says Rosie, trying to signify[7] with her hands on her hips all salty, completely forgetting that I have whupped her behind many times for less salt than that.

"I always win cause I'm the best," I say straight at Gretchen
120 who is, as far as I'm concerned, the only one talking in this ventriloquist-dummy routine. Gretchen smiles, but it's not a smile, and I'm thinking that girls never really smile at each other because they don't know how and don't want to know how and there's probably no one to teach us how, cause grown-up girls don't know either. Then they all look at Raymond who has just brought his mule team to a standstill. And they're about to see what trouble they can get into through him.

"What grade you in now, Raymond?"

"You got anything to say to my brother, you say it to me,
130 Mary Louise Williams of Raggedy Town, Baltimore."

"What are you, his mother?" sasses Rosie.

"That's right, Fatso. And the next word out of anybody and I'll be *their* mother too." So they just stand there and Gretchen shifts from one leg to the other and so do they. Then Gretchen puts her hands on her hips and is about to say something with her freckle-face self but doesn't. Then she walks around me

---

7. **signify:** act boastful or insult someone (slang).

IDENTIFY
Underline Squeaky's ideas for settling her **conflict** with Gretchen and her friends.

PREDICT
Pause at line 109. What do you think will happen when Squeaky and Raymond meet Gretchen and her friends?

_____

_____

_____

_____

_____

INFER
Why does Squeaky call her conversation with the other girls a "ventriloquist-dummy routine" (line 121)?

_____

_____

_____

_____

INFER
Why doesn't Squeaky allow Raymond to answer Mary Louise's question (lines 129–130)?

_____

_____

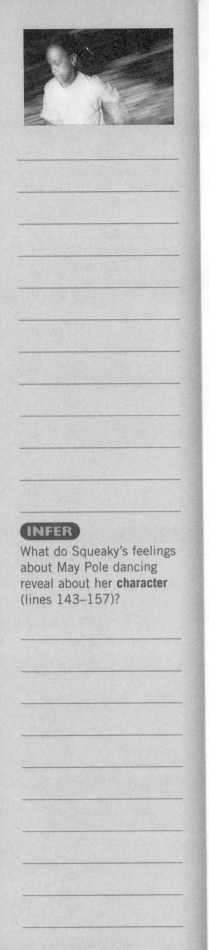

looking me up and down but keeps walking up Broadway, and her sidekicks follow her. So me and Raymond smile at each other and he says, "Gidyap" to his team and I continue with my
140 breathing exercises, strolling down Broadway toward the ice man on 145th with not a care in the world cause I am Miss Quicksilver[8] herself.

I take my time getting to the park on May Day because the track meet is the last thing on the program. The biggest thing on the program is the May Pole dancing, which I can do without, thank you, even if my mother thinks it's a shame I don't take part and act like a girl for a change. You'd think my mother'd be grateful not to have to make me a white organdy dress with a big satin sash and buy me new white baby-doll
150 shoes that can't be taken out of the box till the big day. You'd think she'd be glad her daughter ain't out there prancing around a May Pole getting the new clothes all dirty and sweaty and trying to act like a fairy or a flower or whatever you're supposed to be when you should be trying to be yourself, whatever that is, which is, as far as I am concerned, a poor black girl who really can't afford to buy shoes and a new dress you only wear once a lifetime cause it won't fit next year.

I was once a strawberry in a Hansel and Gretel pageant when I was in nursery school and didn't have no better sense
160 than to dance on tiptoe with my arms in a circle over my head doing umbrella steps and being a perfect fool just so my mother and father could come dressed up and clap. You'd think they'd know better than to encourage that kind of nonsense. I am not a strawberry. I do not dance on my toes. I run. That is what I am all about. So I always come late to the May Day program, just in time to get my number pinned on and lay in the grass till they announce the fifty-yard dash.

I put Raymond in the little swings, which is a tight squeeze this year and will be impossible next year. Then I look around
170 for Mr. Pearson, who pins the numbers on. I'm really looking for Gretchen if you want to know the truth, but she's not

---

8. **Quicksilver:** another name for mercury, a silver-colored liquid metal that flows rapidly.

INFER

What do Squeaky's feelings about May Pole dancing reveal about her **character** (lines 143–157)?

around. The park is jam-packed. Parents in hats and corsages and breast-pocket handkerchiefs peeking up. Kids in white dresses and light-blue suits. The parkees unfolding chairs and chasing the rowdy kids from Lenox[9] as if they had no right to be there. The big guys with their caps on backwards, leaning against the fence swirling the basketballs on the tips of their fingers, waiting for all these crazy people to clear out the park so they can play. Most of the kids in my class are carrying bass
180 drums and glockenspiels[10] and flutes. You'd think they'd put in a few bongos or something for real like that.

Then here comes Mr. Pearson with his clipboard and his cards and pencils and whistles and safety pins and fifty million other things he's always dropping all over the place with his clumsy self. He sticks out in a crowd because he's on stilts. We used to call him Jack and the Beanstalk to get him mad. But I'm the only one that can outrun him and get away, and I'm too grown for that silliness now.

"Well, Squeaky," he says, checking my name off the list and
190 handing me number seven and two pins. And I'm thinking he's got no right to call me Squeaky, if I can't call him Beanstalk.

"Hazel Elizabeth Deborah Parker," I correct him and tell him to write it down on his board.

"Well, Hazel Elizabeth Deborah Parker, going to give someone else a break this year?" I squint at him real hard to see if he is seriously thinking I should lose the race on purpose just to give someone else a break. "Only six girls running this time," he continues, shaking his head sadly like it's my fault all of New York didn't turn out in sneakers. "That new girl should
200 give you a run for your money." He looks around the park for Gretchen like a periscope in a submarine movie. "Wouldn't it be a nice gesture if you were . . . to ahhh . . . ."

I give him such a look he couldn't finish putting that idea into words. Grown-ups got a lot of nerve sometimes. I pin

---

9. **Lenox**: Lenox Avenue, a major street in Harlem (now called Malcolm X Boulevard).
10. **glockenspiels** (gläk'ən·spēlz'): musical instruments with flat metal bars that are struck with small hammers and produce bell-like sounds. Glockenspiels are often used in marching bands.

INTERPRET
Re-read Squeaky's description of the May Day crowd (lines 172–181). How do you think she feels about the people in the crowd? Underline parts of the text that support your opinion.

IDENTIFY
Why is Mr. Pearson called "Jack and the Beanstalk"? Underline the part of the text where you find out.

INFER
Why would Mr. Pearson suggest that Squeaky lose the race on purpose?

INFER

What does Squeaky mean when she says she is "so burnt" (line 205)?

_____

_____

_____

_____

_____

_____

_____

_____

_____

INTERPRET

Underline Squeaky's observation of Gretchen as the race is about to begin. Why is this detail significant?

_____

_____

INTERPRET

Why do you think Raymond is lining up along with the runners (lines 233–235)?

_____

_____

number seven to myself and stomp away, I'm so burnt. And I go straight for the track and stretch out on the grass while the band winds up with "Oh, the Monkey Wrapped His Tail Around the Flag Pole," which my teacher calls by some other name. The man on the loudspeaker is calling everyone over to the
210 track and I'm on my back looking at the sky, trying to pretend I'm in the country, but I can't, because even grass in the city feels hard as sidewalk, and there's just no pretending you are anywhere but in a "concrete jungle" as my grandfather says.

The twenty-yard dash takes all of two minutes cause most of the little kids don't know no better than to run off the track or run the wrong way or run smack into the fence and fall down and cry. One little kid, though, has got the good sense to run straight for the white ribbon up ahead so he wins. Then the second-graders line up for the thirty-yard dash and I don't even
220 bother to turn my head to watch cause Raphael Perez always wins. He wins before he even begins by psyching the runners, telling them they're going to trip on their shoelaces and fall on their faces or lose their shorts or something, which he doesn't really have to do since he is very fast, almost as fast as I am. After that is the forty-yard dash which I used to run when I was in first grade. Raymond is hollering from the swings cause he knows I'm about to do my thing cause the man on the loudspeaker has just announced the fifty-yard dash, although he might just as well be giving a recipe for angel food cake
230 cause you can hardly make out what he's sayin for the static. I get up and slip off my sweat pants and then I see Gretchen standing at the starting line, kicking her legs out like a pro. Then as I get into place I see that ole Raymond is on line on the other side of the fence, bending down with his fingers on the ground just like he knew what he was doing. I was going to yell at him but then I didn't. It burns up your energy to holler.

Every time, just before I take off in a race, I always feel like I'm in a dream, the kind of dream you have when you're sick with fever and feel all hot and weightless. I dream I'm flying
240 over a sandy beach in the early morning sun, kissing the leaves of the trees as I fly by. And there's always the smell of apples,

just like in the country when I was little and used to think I was a choo-choo train, running through the fields of corn and chugging up the hill to the orchard. And all the time I'm dreaming this, I get lighter and lighter until I'm flying over the beach again, getting blown through the sky like a feather that weighs nothing at all. But once I spread my fingers in the dirt and crouch over the Get on Your Mark, the dream goes and I am solid again and am telling myself, Squeaky you must win,

250 you must win, you are the fastest thing in the world, you can even beat your father up Amsterdam if you really try. And then I feel my weight coming back just behind my knees then down to my feet then into the earth and the pistol shot explodes in my blood and I am off and weightless again, flying past the other runners, my arms pumping up and down and the whole world is quiet except for the crunch as I zoom over the gravel in the track. I glance to my left and there is no one. To the right, a blurred Gretchen, who's got her chin jutting out as if it would win the race all by itself. And on the other side of the

260 fence is Raymond with his arms down to his side and the palms tucked up behind him, running in his very own style, and it's the first time I ever saw that and I almost stop to watch my brother Raymond on his first run. But the white ribbon is bouncing toward me and I tear past it, racing into the distance till my feet with a mind of their own start digging up footfuls of dirt and brake me short. Then all the kids standing on the side pile on me, banging me on the back and slapping my head with their May Day programs, for I have won again and everybody on 151st Street can walk tall for another year.

270   "In first place . . ." the man on the loudspeaker is clear as a bell now. But then he pauses and the loudspeaker starts to whine. Then static. And I lean down to catch my breath and here comes Gretchen walking back, for she's overshot the finish line too, huffing and puffing with her hands on her hips taking it slow, breathing in steady time like a real pro and I sort of like her a little for the first time. "In first place . . ." and then three or four voices get all mixed up on the loudspeaker and I dig my sneaker into the grass and stare at Gretchen who's staring back,

INFER
Why has Squeaky decided she likes Gretchen "a little for the first time" (lines 275–276)?

we both wondering just who did win. I can hear old Beanstalk
280 arguing with the man on the loudspeaker and then a few others
running their mouths about what the stopwatches say. Then I
hear Raymond yanking at the fence to call me and I wave to
shush him, but he keeps rattling the fence like a gorilla in a
cage like in them gorilla movies, but then like a dancer or
something he starts climbing up nice and easy but very fast.
And it occurs to me, watching how smoothly he climbs hand
over hand and remembering how he looked running with his
arms down to his side and with the wind pulling his mouth
back and his teeth showing and all, it occurred to me that
290 Raymond would make a very fine runner. Doesn't he always
keep up with me on my trots? And he surely knows how to
breathe in counts of seven cause he's always doing it at the
dinner table, which drives my brother George up the wall. And
I'm smiling to beat the band cause if I've lost this race, or if me
and Gretchen tied, or even if I've won, I can always retire as a
runner and begin a whole new career as a coach with Raymond
as my champion. After all, with a little more study I can beat
Cynthia and her phony self at the spelling bee. And if I bugged
my mother, I could get piano lessons and become a star. And
300 I have a big rep[11] as the baddest thing around. And I've got
a roomful of ribbons and medals and awards. But what has
Raymond got to call his own?

    So I stand there with my new plans, laughing out loud by
this time as Raymond jumps down from the fence and runs
over with his teeth showing and his arms down to the side,
which no one before him has quite mastered as a running style.
And by the time he comes over I'm jumping up and down so
glad to see him—my brother Raymond, a great runner in the
family tradition. But of course everyone thinks I'm jumping up
310 and down because the men on the loudspeaker have finally
gotten themselves together and compared notes and are
announcing "In first place—Miss Hazel Elizabeth Deborah
Parker." (Dig that.) "In second place—Miss Gretchen P. Lewis."

---

11. **rep:** reputation (slang). People often create slang by clipping off parts of words.

IDENTIFY

What is Raymond doing when Squeaky realizes he could become a runner?

INTERPRET

Pause at line 302. Underline two details from the previous paragraph that show Squeaky has changed.

And I look over at Gretchen wondering what the "P" stands for. And I smile. Cause she's good, no doubt about it. Maybe she'd like to help me coach Raymond; she obviously is serious about running, as any fool can see. And she nods to congratulate me and then she smiles. And I smile. We stand there with this big smile of respect between us. It's about as real a smile as girls
320 can do for each other, considering we don't practice real smiling every day, you know, cause maybe we too busy being flowers or fairies or strawberries instead of something honest and worthy of respect . . . you know . . . like being people.

IDENTIFY

Underline the words from the text that tell you that Squeaky's and Gretchen's smiles are different from Gretchen's earlier smile (page 7, line 121).

EVALUATE

Are you satisfied with the conclusion of the story? Do you feel that Squeaky's **conflict** with Gretchen has been resolved?

_____

_____

_____

_____

_____

_____

_____

_____

_____

_____

_____

_____

_____

_____

_____

Conflict Chart

A **conflict** is a struggle of some kind. Fill in the chart below to show the different kinds of conflicts Squeaky faces. In the last column, tell how each conflict is resolved by the story's end. (Are they all resolved?)

Squeaky's conflicts	Description of problem	How it is resolved
With other kids		
With Gretchen		
With Mr. Pearson		
Within her own heart and mind		

Vocabulary and Comprehension

A. Replace the underlined words from Squeaky's dialect with words or phrases from standard English.

1. I'll <u>high-prance</u> _____ down the street like a rodeo pony.

2. Squeaky almost tried to avoid the girls, but decided she was being

<u>chicken</u> _____ .

3. The park was <u>jam-packed</u> _____ with people.

4. Raphael Perez wins by <u>psyching</u> _____ the other runners.

B. Answer each question below.

1. What qualities is Squeaky best known for?

_____

_____

2. Why does Squeaky have to take care of her older brother?

_____

_____

3. How does Squeaky feel just before a race?

_____

_____

4. Why does Squeaky want to be Raymond's track coach?

_____

_____

Mrs. Flowers

Make the Connection

A Lifeline for You

In this selection, taken from her autobiography, Maya Angelou describes a woman who threw her a lifeline and changed her life forever. Who has thrown you a lifeline? Think about the person who has had the most and best influence on you so far. It could be someone you know personally, or someone that you've heard or read about. Fill in the lines on the Lifeline Award below:

Lifeline Award

To:

_____

in admiration and gratitude for

_____

_____

_____

_____

Background

"Mrs. Flowers" is from a volume of Maya Angelou's autobiography. When Angelou (born Marguerite Johnson) was a little girl, her parents separated. She and her brother, Bailey, were sent to Stamps, Arkansas, to live with their grandmother (called Momma), who owned a general store. A year before meeting Mrs. Flowers, Marguerite had been violently assaulted by a friend of her mother's. In reaction she became depressed and withdrawn, and she stopped speaking.

Mrs. Flowers

FROM I Know Why the Caged Bird Sings

Maya Angelou

IDENTIFY

Underline the words in the first sentence that tell how the narrator felt before she met her "lifeline."

_____

_____

INFER

Imagery is writing that uses descriptive language that appeals to the senses. Circle three images in lines 5–16 that describe Mrs. Flowers. What do these images suggest about the kind of person she is?

_____

_____

_____

_____

_____

_____

INFER

In your own words, tell what it means for a person to be "the measure of what a human being can be."

_____

_____

_____

_____

_____

_____

_____

WORDS TO OWN
taut (tôt) _adj.:_ tightly stretched.
benign (bi·nīn′) _adj.:_ kind.

For nearly a year, I sopped around the house, the Store, the school, and the church, like an old biscuit, dirty and inedible. Then I met, or rather got to know, the lady who threw me my first lifeline.

Mrs. Bertha Flowers was the aristocrat of Black Stamps. She had the grace of control to appear warm in the coldest weather, and on the Arkansas summer days it seemed she had a private breeze which swirled around, cooling her. She was thin without the taut look of wiry people, and her printed voile[1] dresses
10 and flowered hats were as right for her as denim overalls for a farmer. She was our side's answer to the richest white woman in town.

Her skin was a rich black that would have peeled like a plum if snagged, but then no one would have thought of getting close enough to Mrs. Flowers to ruffle her dress, let alone snag her skin. She didn't encourage familiarity. She wore gloves too.

I don't think I ever saw Mrs. Flowers laugh, but she smiled often. A slow widening of her thin black lips to show even, small white teeth, then the slow effortless closing. When she
20 chose to smile on me, I always wanted to thank her. The action was so graceful and inclusively benign.

She was one of the few gentlewomen I have ever known, and has remained throughout my life the measure of what a human being can be.

One summer afternoon, sweet-milk fresh in my memory, she stopped at the Store to buy provisions. Another Negro woman of her health and age would have been expected to carry the paper sacks home in one hand, but Momma said, "Sister Flowers, I'll send Bailey up to your house with these
30 things."

She smiled that slow dragging smile, "Thank you, Mrs. Henderson. I'd prefer Marguerite, though." My name was beautiful when she said it. "I've been meaning to talk to her, anyway." They gave each other age-group looks.

---

1. **voile** (voil): thin, sheer fabric.

There was a little path beside the rocky road, and Mrs. Flowers walked in front swinging her arms and picking her way over the stones.

She said, without turning her head, to me, "I hear you're doing very good schoolwork, Marguerite, but that it's all
40 written. The teachers report that they have trouble getting you to talk in class." We passed the triangular farm on our left and the path widened to allow us to walk together. I hung back in the separate unasked and unanswerable questions.

"Come and walk along with me, Marguerite." I couldn't have refused even if I wanted to. She pronounced my name so nicely. Or more correctly, she spoke each word with such clarity that I was certain a foreigner who didn't understand English could have understood her.

"Now no one is going to make you talk—possibly no one
50 can. But bear in mind, language is man's way of communicating with his fellow man and it is language alone which separates him from the lower animals." That was a totally new idea to me, and I would need time to think about it.

"Your grandmother says you read a lot. Every chance you get. That's good, but not good enough. Words mean more than what is set down on paper. It takes the human voice to <u>infuse</u> them with the shades of deeper meaning."

I memorized the part about the human voice infusing words. It seemed so valid and poetic.
60 She said she was going to give me some books and that I not only must read them, I must read them aloud. She suggested that I try to make a sentence sound in as many different ways as possible.

"I'll accept no excuse if you return a book to me that has been badly handled." My imagination boggled at the punishment I would deserve if in fact I did abuse a book of Mrs. Flowers's. Death would be too kind and brief.

The odors in the house surprised me. Somehow I had never connected Mrs. Flowers with food or eating or any other
70 common experience of common people. There must have been an outhouse, too, but my mind never recorded it.

INTERPRET

Think of an example of an "unasked and unanswerable" question (line 43) that Marguerite worries she might get from Mrs. Flowers. Why do you think Mrs. Flowers doesn't ask such questions?

_____

_____

_____

EVALUATE

Underline the words in lines 49–53 that tell what Mrs. Flowers believes about what separates people from the lower animals. Tell whether you agree or disagree with Mrs. Flowers about this and why.

_____

_____

_____

_____

INFER

Why is Marguerite surprised to discover that Mrs. Flowers has a kitchen and probably has an outhouse?

_____

_____

WORDS TO OWN
infuse (in·fyoōz′) v.: fill.

The sweet scent of vanilla had met us as she opened the door.

"I made tea cookies this morning. You see, I had planned to invite you for cookies and lemonade so we could have this little chat. The lemonade is in the icebox."

It followed that Mrs. Flowers would have ice on an ordinary day, when most families in our town bought ice late on Saturdays only a few times during the summer to be used
80 in the wooden ice cream freezers.

She took the bags from me and disappeared through the kitchen door. I looked around the room that I had never in my wildest fantasies imagined I would see. Browned photographs leered or threatened from the walls and the white, freshly done curtains pushed against themselves and against the wind. I wanted to gobble up the room entire and take it to Bailey, who would help me analyze and enjoy it.

"Have a seat, Marguerite. Over there by the table." She carried a platter covered with a tea towel. Although she warned
90 that she hadn't tried her hand at baking sweets for some time, I was certain that like everything else about her the cookies would be perfect.

They were flat round wafers, slightly browned on the edges and butter-yellow in the center. With the cold lemonade they were sufficient for childhood's lifelong diet. Remembering my manners, I took nice little ladylike bites off the edges. She said she had made them expressly for me and that she had a few in the kitchen that I could take home to my brother. So I jammed one whole cake in my mouth and the rough crumbs scratched
100 the insides of my jaws, and if I hadn't had to swallow, it would have been a dream come true.

As I ate she began the first of what we later called "my lessons in living." She said that I must always be intolerant of ignorance but understanding of illiteracy. That some people, unable to go to school, were more educated and even more intelligent than college professors. She encouraged me to listen carefully to what country people called mother wit. That in those homely sayings was couched the collective wisdom of generations.

110   When I finished the cookies she brushed off the table and brought a thick, small book from the bookcase. I had read *A Tale of Two Cities* and found it up to my standards as a romantic novel. She opened the first page and I heard poetry for the first time in my life.

"It was the best of times, it was the worst of times. . . ." Her voice slid in and curved down through and over the words. She was nearly singing. I wanted to look at the pages. Were they the same that I had read? Or were there notes, music, lined on the pages, as in a hymn book? Her sounds began cascading

120 gently. I knew from listening to a thousand preachers that she was nearing the end of her reading, and I hadn't really heard, heard to understand, a single word.

"How do you like that?"

It occurred to me that she expected a response. The sweet vanilla flavor was still on my tongue and her reading was a wonder in my ears. I had to speak.

I said, "Yes, ma'am." It was the least I could do, but it was the most also.

"There's one more thing. Take this book of poems and

130 memorize one for me. Next time you pay me a visit, I want you to recite."

I have tried often to search behind the sophistication of years for the enchantment I so easily found in those gifts. The essence escapes but its aura[2] remains. To be allowed, no, invited, into the private lives of strangers, and to share their joys and fears, was a chance to exchange the Southern bitter wormwood[3] for a cup of mead with Beowulf[4] or a hot cup of tea and milk with Oliver Twist. When I said aloud, "It is a far,

---

2. **aura:** feeling or mood that seems to surround something like a glow.
3. **wormwood:** bitter-tasting plant. Angelou is referring to the harshness of life for African Americans in the South at that time.
4. **Beowulf** (bā′ə·woolf′): hero of an Old English epic. During the period portrayed in the epic, people drank **mead,** a drink made with honey.

RETELL

Re-read lines 102–109. Then, restate this lesson in living. Try to sum it up in one sentence using your own words.

_____

_____

_____

INTERPRET

How was Mrs. Flowers's reading of *A Tale of Two Cities* different from the way Marguerite had read it?

_____

_____

_____

_____

_____

_____

_____

_____

_____

_____

_____

_____

_____

INTERPRET

From that visit with Mrs. Flowers, Marguerite suggests, she gains a new appreciation of literature. What does she now realize about literature that she had not realized before? Use details from lines 132–140 to back up your answer.

_____

_____

_____

_____

_____

INTERPRET

Underline the words in lines 144–146 that tell you how Mrs. Flowers feels about Marguerite. How does Mrs. Flowers's opinion and attention change Marguerite's life?

_____

_____

_____

_____

_____

far better thing that I do, than I have ever done . . ."[5] tears of
140 love filled my eyes at my selflessness.

On that first day, I ran down the hill and into the road (few cars ever came along it) and had the good sense to stop running before I reached the Store.

I was liked, and what a difference it made. I was respected not as Mrs. Henderson's grandchild or Bailey's sister but for just being Marguerite Johnson.

Childhood's logic never asks to be proved (all conclusions are absolute). I didn't question why Mrs. Flowers had singled me out for attention, nor did it occur to me that Momma might
150 have asked her to give me a little talking-to. All I cared about was that she had made tea cookies for *me* and read to *me* from her favorite book. It was enough to prove that she liked me.

---

5. **"It is . . . ever done"**: another quotation from Charles Dickens's *A Tale of Two Cities*. One of the characters says these words as he goes to die in place of another man.

Imagery Chart

In "Mrs. Flowers," Maya Angelou uses **imagery** to bring her experiences to life. Imagery is language that appeals to the senses—sight, smell, touch, taste, and hearing. Find examples in the story of images that appeal to each of the five senses, and write them in the chart below.

Sense	Examples of Imagery
Sight	
Hearing	
Smell	
Taste	
Touch	

Vocabulary and Comprehension

A. Match words and definitions. Write the letter of the correct definition next to each word.

_____ **1.** taut

_____ **2.** benign

_____ **3.** infuse

_____ **4.** intolerant

_____ **5.** illiteracy

a. fill; inspire

b. inability to read or write

c. unwilling to put up with something

d. tightly stretched

e. kind; harmless

Word Bank
taut
benign
infuse
intolerant
illiteracy

B. Fill in each blank with a word from the Word Bank.

1. She said I must always be _____ of ignorance.

2. She also said I must always be understanding of

_____.

3. It takes the human voice to _____ words with deeper meaning.

4. Her smile was delightfully gracious and inclusively

_____.

5. She was thin without the _____ look of wiry people.

Vocabulary and Comprehension

C. Choose three words from the Word Bank on the previous page. Use each word in a sentence.

1. _____

_____

2. _____

_____

3. _____

_____

D. Answer each question below.

1. Why is Marguerite so impressed by Mrs. Flowers?

_____

_____

2. What do Mrs. Flowers and Marguerite do during their first visit together?

_____

_____

3. How does Mrs. Flowers help Marguerite?

_____

_____

Broken Chain

Make the Connection

First Date

Imagine sharing an experience where you get together with someone you like a lot or admire very much. Maybe you're going to a movie or playing soccer after school. In your imagination, you can make everything happen perfectly. Set the situation up on the graphic organizer below.

The other person would be (No name—describe character and appearance)

_____

I'd wear

_____

The setting (day, time, place, weather) would be

_____

We'd go to

_____

The situation would be perfect because

_____

Broken Chain

Gary Soto

IDENTIFY

Circle the name of the character introduced in the first paragraph. Underline two things he is doing to try to change the way he looks.

_____

_____

_____

_____

_____

IDENTIFY

A **simile** is a comparison of two very different things. It uses comparing words such as *like* or *as* to make the comparison. Circle the simile in lines 32–33. What two things are compared?

_____

_____

_____

_____

_____

_____

_____

WORDS TO OWN
sullen (sul′ən) *adj.:* sulky; resentful.

Alfonso sat on the porch trying to push his crooked teeth to where he thought they belonged. He hated the way he looked. Last week he did fifty sit-ups a day, thinking that he would burn those already apparent ripples on his stomach to even deeper ripples, dark ones, so when he went swimming at the canal next summer, girls in cut-offs would notice. And the guys would think he was tough, someone who could take a punch and give it back. He wanted "cuts" like those he had seen on a calendar of an Aztec[1] warrior standing on a pyramid with a

10   woman in his arms. (Even she had cuts he could see beneath her thin dress.) The calendar hung above the cash register at La Plaza. Orsua, the owner, said Alfonso could have the calendar at the end of the year if the waitress, Yolanda, didn't take it first.

Alfonso studied the magazine pictures of rock stars for a hairstyle. He liked the way Prince looked—and the bass player from Los Lobos. Alfonso thought he would look cool with his hair razored into a V in the back and streaked purple. But he knew his mother wouldn't go for it. And his father, who was

20   puro Mexicano, would sit in his chair after work, <u>sullen</u> as a toad, and call him "sissy."

Alfonso didn't dare color his hair. But one day he had had it butched on the top, like in the magazines. His father had come home that evening from a softball game, happy that his team had drilled four homers in a thirteen-to-five bashing of Color Tile. He'd swaggered into the living room but had stopped cold when he saw Alfonso and asked, not joking but with real concern, "Did you hurt your head at school? ¿Qué pasó?"[2]

Alfonso had pretended not to hear his father and had gone

30   to his room, where he studied his hair from all angles in the mirror. He liked what he saw until he smiled and realized for the first time that his teeth were crooked, like a pile of wrecked cars. He grew depressed and turned away from the mirror. He sat on his bed and leafed through the rock magazine until he

---

1. **Aztec:** member of an American Indian people of what is now Mexico.
2. **¿Qué pasó?** (kā′ pä·sô′): Spanish for "What happened?"

came to the rock star with the butched top. His mouth was closed, but Alfonso was sure his teeth weren't crooked.

Alfonso didn't want to be the handsomest kid at school, but he was determined to be better looking than average. The next day he spent his lawn-mowing money on a new shirt and, with
40 a pocketknife, scooped the moons of dirt from under his fingernails.

He spent hours in front of the mirror trying to herd his teeth into place with his thumb. He asked his mother if he could have braces, like Frankie Molina, her godson, but he asked at the wrong time. She was at the kitchen table licking the envelope to the house payment. She glared up at him. "Do you think money grows on trees?"

His mother clipped coupons from magazines and newspapers, kept a vegetable garden in the summer, and
50 shopped at Penney's and K-Mart. Their family ate a lot of frijoles,[3] which was OK because nothing else tasted so good, though one time Alfonso had had Chinese pot stickers[4] and thought they were the next best food in the world.

He didn't ask his mother for braces again, even when she was in a better mood. He decided to fix his teeth by pushing on them with his thumbs. After breakfast that Saturday he went to his room, closed the door quietly, turned the radio on, and pushed for three hours straight.

He pushed for ten minutes, rested for five, and every half
60 hour, during a radio commercial, checked to see if his smile had improved. It hadn't.

Eventually he grew bored and went outside with an old gym sock to wipe down his bike, a ten-speed from Montgomery Ward. His thumbs were tired and wrinkled and pink, the way they got when he stayed in the bathtub too long.

Alfonso's older brother, Ernie, rode up on *his* Montgomery Ward bicycle looking depressed. He parked his bike against the peach tree and sat on the back steps, keeping his head down and stepping on ants that came too close.

---

3. **frijoles** (frē·hôl′ās): Spanish for "beans."
4. **pot stickers:** dumplings.

INFER

Re-read lines 42–53. Based on these details, what **inference** can you make about the family's financial situation?

INTERPRET

List three important things you've learned about Alfonso so far. What main idea about Alfonso's **character** do these details add up to? State that main idea in a complete sentence.

70   Alfonso knew better than to say anything when Ernie looked mad. He turned his bike over, balancing it on the handlebars and seat, and flossed the spokes with the sock. When he was finished, he pressed a knuckle to his teeth until they tingled.

Ernie groaned and said, "Ah, man."

Alfonso waited a few minutes before asking, "What's the matter?" He pretended not to be too interested. He picked up a wad of steel wool and continued cleaning the spokes.

Ernie hesitated, not sure if Alfonso would laugh. But it came out. "Those girls didn't show up. And you better not laugh."

80   "What girls?"

Then Alfonso remembered his brother bragging about how he and Frostie met two girls from Kings Canyon Junior High last week on Halloween night. They were dressed as Gypsies, the costume for all poor Chicanas[5]—they just had to borrow scarves and gaudy red lipstick from their abuelitas.[6]

Alfonso walked over to his brother. He compared their two bikes: His gleamed like a handful of dimes, while Ernie's looked dirty.

"They said we were supposed to wait at the corner. But they
90   didn't show up. Me and Frostie waited and waited. . . . They were playing games with us."

Alfonso thought that was a pretty dirty trick but sort of funny too. He would have to try that someday.

"Were they cute?" Alfonso asked.

"I guess so."

"Do you think you could recognize them?"

"If they were wearing red lipstick, maybe."

Alfonso sat with his brother in silence, both of them smearing ants with their floppy high tops. Girls could sure act
100   weird, especially the ones you meet on Halloween.

Later that day, Alfonso sat on the porch pressing on his teeth. Press, relax; press, relax. His portable radio was on, but

---

5. **Chicanas** (chi·kä′nəz): Mexican American girls and women.
6. **abuelitas** (ä′bwä·lē′täs): in Spanish, an affectionate term for "grandmothers," like *grandmas* in English.

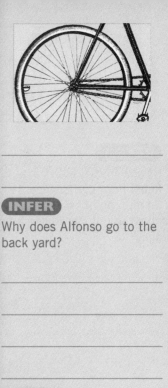

not loud enough to make Mr. Rojas come down the steps and wave his cane at him.

Alfonso's father drove up. Alfonso could tell by the way he sat in his truck, a Datsun with a different-colored front fender, that his team had lost their softball game. Alfonso got off the porch in a hurry because he knew his father would be in a bad mood. He went to the back yard, where he unlocked his bike, 110 sat on it with the kickstand down, and pressed on his teeth. He punched himself in the stomach, and growled, "Cuts." Then he patted his butch and whispered, "Fresh."

INFER
Why does Alfonso go to the back yard?

After a while Alfonso pedaled up the street, hands in his pockets, toward Foster's Freeze, where he was chased by a ratlike Chihuahua.[7] At his old school, John Burroughs Elementary, he found a kid hanging upside down on the top of a barbed-wire fence with a girl looking up at him. Alfonso skidded to a stop and helped the kid untangle his pants from the barbed wire. The kid was grateful. He had been afraid he 120 would have to stay up there all night. His sister, who was Alfonso's age, was also grateful. If she had to go home and tell her mother that Frankie was stuck on a fence and couldn't get down, she would get scolded.

INFER
Underline Alfonso's good deed in this paragraph. What does it show about his character?

"Thanks," she said. "What's your name?"

Alfonso remembered her from his school and noticed that she was kind of cute, with ponytails and straight teeth. "Alfonso. You go to my school, huh?"

"Yeah. I've seen you around. You live nearby?"

"Over on Madison."

130 "My uncle used to live on that street, but he moved to Stockton."

"Stockton's near Sacramento, isn't it?"

"You been there?"

"No." Alfonso looked down at his shoes. He wanted to say something clever the way people do on TV. But the only thing he could think to say was that the governor lived in

---

7. **Chihuahua** (chi·wä′wä): small dog with large pointed ears.

RETELL

Review lines 113–163.
Retell how Alfonso meets
Sandra, and how he goes
about asking her to see him
again.

_____

_____

_____

_____

_____

_____

_____

_____

_____

_____

_____

_____

_____

_____

_____

_____

_____

WORDS TO OWN
muster (mŭs′tər) v. call
forth; gather.

Sacramento. As soon as he shared this observation, he winced inside.

Alfonso walked with the girl and the boy as they started for
140   home. They didn't talk much. Every few steps, the girl, whose name was Sandra, would look at him out of the corner of her eye, and Alfonso would look away. He learned that she was in seventh grade, just like him, and that she had a pet terrier named Queenie. Her father was a mechanic at Rudy's Speedy Repair, and her mother was a teacher's aide at Jefferson Elementary.

When they came to the street, Alfonso and Sandra stopped at her corner, but her brother ran home. Alfonso watched him stop in the front yard to talk to a lady he guessed was their
150   mother. She was raking leaves into a pile.

"I live over there," she said, pointing.

Alfonso looked over her shoulder for a long time, trying to muster enough nerve to ask her if she'd like to go bike riding tomorrow.

Shyly, he asked, "You wanna go bike riding?"

"Maybe." She played with a ponytail and crossed one leg in front of the other. "But my bike has a flat."

"I can get my brother's bike. He won't mind."

She thought a moment before she said, "OK. But not
160   tomorrow. I have to go to my aunt's."

"How about after school on Monday?"

"I have to take care of my brother until my mom comes home from work. How 'bout four-thirty?"

"OK," he said. "Four-thirty." Instead of parting immediately, they talked for a while, asking questions like "Who's your favorite group?" "Have you ever been on the Big Dipper at Santa Cruz?" and "Have you ever tasted pot stickers?" But the question-and-answer period ended when Sandra's mother called her home.

170   Alfonso took off as fast as he could on his bike, jumped the curb, and, cool as he could be, raced away with his hands stuffed in his pockets. But when he looked back over his shoulder, the wind raking through his butch, Sandra wasn't

even looking. She was already on her lawn, heading for the porch.

That night he took a bath, pampered his hair into place, and did more than his usual set of exercises. In bed, in between the push-and-rest on his teeth, he pestered his brother to let him borrow his bike.

180   "Come on, Ernie," he whined. "Just for an hour."

"Chale,[8] I might want to use it."

"Come on, man, I'll let you have my trick-or-treat candy."

"What you got?"

"Three baby Milky Ways and some Skittles."

"Who's going to use it?"

Alfonso hesitated, then risked the truth. "I met this girl. She doesn't live too far."

Ernie rolled over on his stomach and stared at the outline of his brother, whose head was resting on his elbow. "*You* got a

190 girlfriend?"

"She ain't my girlfriend, just a girl."

"What does she look like?"

"Like a girl."

"Come on, what does she look like?"

"She's got ponytails and a little brother."

"Ponytails! Those girls who messed with Frostie and me had ponytails. Is she cool?"

"I think so."

Ernie sat up in bed. "I bet you that's her."

200   Alfonso felt his stomach knot up. "She's going to be my girlfriend, not yours!"

"I'm going to get even with her!"

"You better not touch her," Alfonso snarled, throwing a wadded Kleenex at him. "I'll run you over with my bike."

For the next hour, until their mother threatened them from the living room to be quiet or else, they argued whether it was the same girl who had stood Ernie up. Alfonso said over and over that she was too nice to pull a stunt like that. But Ernie

---

8. **chale** (chä'lä): Spanish slang expression roughly meaning "it's not possible."

PREDICT

Pause at line 179. Will Ernie let Alfonso borrow his bike? Tell what you think will happen next.

INFER

Why does Alfonso think it might be risky to tell the truth (line 186)?

BUILD FLUENCY

Re-read the boxed passage. As each speaker changes, think about who is speaking and how he might say the words. Then, read the passage aloud, trying to express the different feelings of the characters. Circle the sentence in the **dialogue** (the conversation between characters), when Alfonso's tone suddenly changes.

EVALUATE

Alfonso and Ernie fight for three days over a girl. Do you think this is the way brothers behave? Explain why or why not.

_____

_____

_____

_____

_____

INTERPRET

A **metaphor** is a comparison between two unlike things. It does not use a comparing word. Underline the metaphor in lines 225–226. Explain what it means.

_____

_____

_____

_____

_____

_____

WORDS TO OWN
clincher (klinch′ər) *n.:* fact or point that decides an argument.
gritty (grit′ē) *adj.:* containing sand or dirt.

argued that she lived only two blocks from where those girls

210 had told them to wait, that she was in the same grade, and, the clincher, that she had ponytails. Secretly, however, Ernie was jealous that his brother, two years younger than himself, might have found a girlfriend.

Sunday morning, Ernie and Alfonso stayed away from each other, though over breakfast they fought over the last tortilla. Their mother, sewing at the kitchen table, warned them to knock it off. At church they made faces at one another when the priest, Father Jerry, wasn't looking. Ernie punched Alfonso in the arm, and Alfonso, his eyes wide with anger, punched

220 back.

Monday morning they hurried to school on their bikes, neither saying a word, though they rode side by side. In first period, Alfonso worried himself sick. How would he borrow a bike for her? He considered asking his best friend, Raul, for his bike. But Alfonso knew Raul, a paperboy with dollar signs in his eyes, would charge him, and he had less than sixty cents, counting the soda bottles he could cash.

Between history and math, Alfonso saw Sandra and her girlfriend huddling at their lockers. He hurried by without being

230 seen.

During lunch Alfonso hid in metal shop so he wouldn't run into Sandra. What would he say to her? If he weren't mad at his brother, he could ask Ernie what girls and guys talk about. But he *was* mad, and anyway, Ernie was pitching nickels with his friends.

Alfonso hurried home after school. He did the morning dishes as his mother had asked and raked the leaves. After finishing his chores, he did a hundred sit-ups, pushed on his teeth until they hurt, showered, and combed his hair into a

240 perfect butch. He then stepped out to the patio to clean his bike. On an impulse, he removed the chain to wipe off the gritty oil. But while he was unhooking it from the back sprocket, it snapped. The chain lay in his hand like a dead snake.

Alfonso couldn't believe his luck. Now, not only did he not have an extra bike for Sandra, he had no bike for himself. Frustrated and on the verge of tears, he flung the chain as far as he could. It landed with a hard slap against the back fence and spooked his sleeping cat, Benny. Benny looked around, blinking
250 his soft gray eyes, and went back to sleep.

Alfonso retrieved the chain, which was hopelessly broken. He cursed himself for being stupid, yelled at his bike for being cheap, and slammed the chain onto the cement. The chain snapped in another place and hit him when it popped up, slicing his hand like a snake's fang.

"Ow!" he cried, his mouth immediately going to his hand to suck on the wound.

After a dab of iodine, which only made his cut hurt more, and a lot of thought, he went to the bedroom to plead with
260 Ernie, who was changing to his after-school clothes.

"Come on, man, let me use it," Alfonso pleaded. "Please, Ernie, I'll do anything."

Although Ernie could see Alfonso's desperation, he had plans with his friend Raymundo. They were going to catch frogs at the Mayfair canal. He felt sorry for his brother and gave him a stick of gum to make him feel better, but there was nothing he could do. The canal was three miles away, and the frogs were waiting.

Alfonso took the stick of gum, placed it in his shirt pocket,
270 and left the bedroom with his head down. He went outside, slamming the screen door behind him, and sat in the alley behind his house. A sparrow landed in the weeds, and when it tried to come close, Alfonso screamed for it to scram. The sparrow responded with a squeaky chirp and flew away.

At four he decided to get it over with and started walking to Sandra's house, trudging slowly, as if he were waist-deep in water. Shame colored his face. How could he disappoint his first date? She would probably laugh. She might even call him menso.[9]

---

9. menso (men′sô): Spanish for "stupid."

RETELL

Pause at line 250. When Sandra said she'd meet Alfonso and go bike riding with him, everything seemed to be going well. **Retell** the **complications** in the plot that have made Alfonso's situation increasingly desperate.

_____

_____

_____

_____

EVALUATE

Why won't Ernie lend Alfonso his bike? What do you think of this reason? What would you do if you were Ernie? Why?

_____

_____

_____

_____

_____

INFER

Underline the details in lines 269–279 that show that Alfonso is upset.

PREDICT

Pause at line 293 and tell what you think will happen in the rest of the story.

_____

_____

_____

_____

_____

_____

_____

_____

VISUALIZE

In lines 294–302, underline the **images**, details that appeal to the senses, that help you picture and even feel what is happening here.

INTERPRET

Find and circle any details on this page that create a feeling of **suspense**, making you more and more curious about what will happen.

IDENTIFY

The **climax** is the most exciting moment in the plot, when the outcome of the main **conflict** is decided. Underline the passage that describes the climax of the conflict in this story.

280   He stopped at the corner where they were supposed to meet and watched her house. But there was no one outside, only a rake leaning against the steps.

Why did he have to take the chain off? he scolded himself. He always messed things up when he tried to take them apart, like the time he tried to repad his baseball mitt. He had unlaced the mitt and filled the pocket with cotton balls. But when he tried to put it back together, he had forgotten how it laced up. Everything became tangled like kite string. When he showed the mess to his mother, who was at the stove cooking dinner,
290   she scolded him but put it back together and didn't tell his father what a dumb thing he had done.

Now he had to face Sandra and say, "I broke my bike, and my stingy brother took off on his."

He waited at the corner a few minutes, hiding behind a hedge for what seemed like forever. Just as he was starting to think about going home, he heard footsteps and knew it was too late. His hands, moist from worry, hung at his sides and a thread of sweat raced down his armpit.

He peeked through the hedge. She was wearing a sweater
300   with a checkerboard pattern. A red purse was slung over her shoulder. He could see her looking for him, standing on tiptoe to see if he was coming around the corner.

What have I done? Alfonso thought. He bit his lip, called himself menso, and pounded his palm against his forehead. Someone slapped the back of his head. He turned around and saw Ernie.

"We got the frogs, Alfonso," he said, holding up a wiggling plastic bag. "I'll show you later."

Ernie looked through the hedge, with one eye closed, at the
310   girl. "She's not the one who messed with Frostie and me," he said finally. "You still wanna borrow my bike?"

Alfonso couldn't believe his luck. What a brother! What a pal! He promised to take Ernie's turn next time it was his turn to do the dishes. Ernie hopped on Raymundo's handlebars and said he would remember that promise. Then he was gone as they took off without looking back.

Free of worry now that his brother had come through, Alfonso emerged from behind the hedge with Ernie's bike, which was mud-splashed but better than nothing. Sandra
320 waved.

"Hi," she said.

"Hi," he said back.

She looked cheerful. Alfonso told her his bike was broken and asked if she wanted to ride with him.

"Sounds good," she said, and jumped on the crossbar.

It took all of Alfonso's strength to steady the bike. He started off slowly, gritting his teeth, because she was heavier than he thought. But once he got going, it got easier. He pedaled smoothly, sometimes with only one hand on the
330 handlebars, as they sped up one street and down another. Whenever he ran over a pothole, which was often, she screamed with delight, and once, when it looked like they were going to crash, she placed her hand over his, and it felt like love.

WORDS TO OWN
emerged (ē·mʉrjd′) v.: came into view.

Chain of Events

You can **summarize** the action in "Broken Chain" by filling out the chain of events below. Start with the box marked "basic situation." Here you will write the main character's name and his problem. Then, fill out the boxes that follow with the important events in the story that prevent him from solving his problem (remember not to include small details). In the final box, write how the main problem of the story has been resolved.

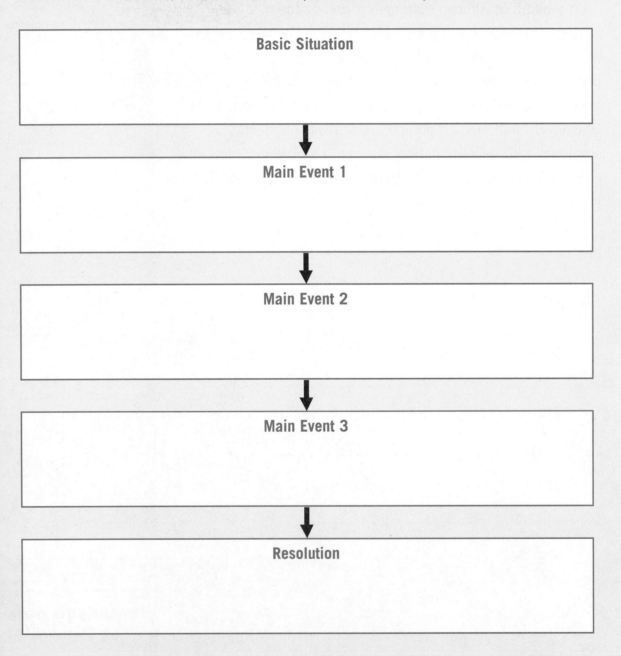

Basic Situation

Main Event 1

Main Event 2

Main Event 3

Resolution

Vocabulary and Comprehension

A. Match words and definitions. Write the letter of the
correct definition next to each word.

_____ **1.** sullen

_____ **2.** gritty

_____ **3.** clincher

_____ **4.** muster

_____ **5.** emerged

a. sulky; resentful

b. came into view

c. call forth

d. point that decides an
argument

e. containing dirt

B. Choose two words from above. Use each word in a sentence.

1. _____

2. _____

C. Answer each question below.

1. Why is the broken chain a problem for Alfonso?

_____

2. Why do Alfonso and Ernie fight?

_____

3. How is the brothers' conflict resolved?

_____

4. How does Alfonso feel at the end of the story?

_____

The Treasure of Lemon Brown

Make the Connection

Generation Gap

In many families, members of different generations—grandparents, parents, kids—find themselves in strong agreement on some issues, but far apart on others. In this story, for instance, Greg's father wants Greg to study harder. Greg thinks nothing's as important as playing basketball. On the Venn diagram below, show what's important to you, what's important to the adults in your family, and what's important to both you and them.

IMPORTANT TO

Me   All of Us   Adults in My Family

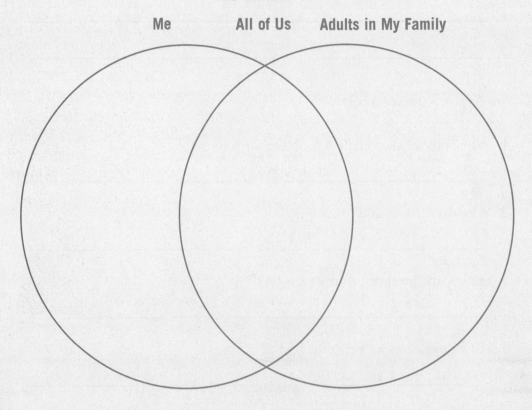

The Treasure of Lemon Brown

Walter Dean Myers

IDENTIFY

Underline the two characters introduced in the first two paragraphs. Circle the problem that seems to cause a **conflict** between them.

_____

_____

_____

INFER

Why is it important to Greg's father that Greg study instead of play basketball? Which do you think is more important for a thirteen-year-old to do? How would you explain why to Greg or his father?

_____

_____

_____

_____

INFER

What does Greg's decision to walk down the street (line 33) instead of study say about his **character?**

_____

_____

_____

WORDS TO OWN

impromptu (im·prämp′too) *adj.:* unplanned; made or done without preparation.

The dark sky, filled with angry, swirling clouds, reflected Greg Ridley's mood as he sat on the stoop of his building. His father's voice came to him again, first reading the letter the principal had sent to the house, then lecturing endlessly about his poor efforts in math.

"I had to leave school when I was thirteen," his father had said; "that's a year younger than you are now. If I'd had half the chances that you have, I'd . . ."

Greg had sat in the small, pale-green kitchen listening,
10 knowing the lecture would end with his father saying he couldn't play ball with the Scorpions. He had asked his father the week before, and his father had said it depended on his next report card. It wasn't often the Scorpions took on new players, especially fourteen-year-olds, and this was a chance of a lifetime for Greg. He hadn't been allowed to play high school ball, which he had really wanted to do, but playing for the Community Center team was the next best thing. Report cards were due in a week, and Greg had been hoping for the best. But the principal had ended the suspense early when she sent
20 that letter saying Greg would probably fail math if he didn't spend more time studying.

"And you want to play *basketball*?" His father's brows knitted over deep-brown eyes. "That must be some kind of a joke. Now you just get into your room and hit those books."

That had been two nights before. His father's words, like the distant thunder that now echoed through the streets of Harlem, still rumbled softly in his ears.

It was beginning to cool. Gusts of wind made bits of paper dance between the parked cars. There was a flash of nearby
30 lightning, and soon large drops of rain splashed onto his jeans. He stood to go upstairs, thought of the lecture that probably awaited him if he did anything except shut himself in his room with his math book, and started walking down the street instead. Down the block there was an old tenement that had been abandoned for some months. Some of the guys had held an <u>impromptu</u> checkers tournament there the week before, and

Greg had noticed that the door, once boarded over, had been slightly ajar.

Pulling his collar up as high as he could, he checked for 40 traffic and made a dash across the street. He reached the house just as another flash of lightning changed the night to day for an instant, then returned the graffiti-scarred building to the grim shadows. He vaulted over the outer stairs and pushed <u>tentatively</u> on the door. It was open, and he let himself in.

The inside of the building was dark except for the dim light that filtered through the dirty windows from the street lamps. There was a room a few feet from the door, and from where he stood at the entrance, Greg could see a squarish patch of light on the floor. He entered the room, frowning at the musty smell. 50 It was a large room that might have been someone's parlor at one time. Squinting, Greg could see an old table on its side against one wall, what looked like a pile of rags or a torn mattress in the corner, and a couch, with one side broken, in front of the window.

He went to the couch. The side that wasn't broken was comfortable enough, though a little creaky. From this spot he could see the blinking neon sign over the bodega[1] on the corner. He sat awhile, watching the sign blink first green, then red, allowing his mind to drift to the Scorpions, then to his 60 father. His father had been a postal worker for all Greg's life and was proud of it, often telling Greg how hard he had worked to pass the test. Greg had heard the story too many times to be interested now.

For a moment Greg thought he heard something that sounded like a scraping against the wall. He listened carefully, but it was gone.

Outside, the wind had picked up, sending the rain against the window with a force that shook the glass in its frame. A car passed, its tires hissing over the wet street and its red taillights 70 glowing in the darkness.

---

1. **bodega** (bō·dā′gə): small grocery store.

VISUALIZE

Underline the details that help you picture the setting inside the abandoned house. Circle three prepositional phrases in this paragraph that help you see exactly where each item is located, for example, "on the floor" (line 49).

INFER

Based on the details in this paragraph, make two **inferences** about Greg's father's **character**.

WORDS TO OWN
tentatively (ten′tə·tiv·lē) *adv.*: in a hesitant or uncertain way.

PREDICT

Who or what do you think is in the room with Greg? What do you think might happen next?

_____

_____

_____

INTERPRET

Pause at line 80. Go back to line 64. Circle the details that increase the suspense. What word, besides *suspenseful*, would you use to describe the **mood** created by these details?

_____

_____

IDENTIFY

Underline the words in lines 87–92 that show Greg's reaction to the threat.

_____

_____

_____

_____

_____

_____

WORDS TO OWN
intently (in·tent′lē) *adv.:* with close attention.
brittle (brit′′l) *adj.:* sharp and hard.

Greg thought he heard the noise again. His stomach tightened as he held himself still and listened <u>intently</u>. There weren't any more scraping noises, but he was sure he had heard something in the darkness—something breathing!

He tried to figure out just where the breathing was coming from; he knew it was in the room with him. Slowly he stood, tensing. As he turned, a flash of lightning lit up the room, frightening him with its sudden brilliance. He saw nothing, just the overturned table, the pile of rags, and an old newspaper on

80 the floor. Could he have been imagining the sounds? He continued listening, but heard nothing and thought that it might have just been rats. Still, he thought, as soon as the rain let up he would leave. He went to the window and was about to look out when he heard a voice behind him.

"Don't try nothin', 'cause I got a razor here sharp enough to cut a week into nine days!"

Greg, except for an involuntary tremor in his knees, stood stock-still. The voice was high and <u>brittle</u>, like dry twigs being broken, surely not one he had ever heard before. There was a

90 shuffling sound as the person who had been speaking moved a step closer. Greg turned, holding his breath, his eyes straining to see in the dark room.

The upper part of the figure before him was still in darkness. The lower half was in the dim rectangle of light that fell unevenly from the window. There were two feet, in cracked, dirty shoes from which rose legs that were wrapped in rags.

"Who are you?" Greg hardly recognized his own voice.

"I'm Lemon Brown," came the answer. "Who're you?"

"Greg Ridley."

100 "What you doing here?" The figure shuffled forward again, and Greg took a small step backward.

"It's raining," Greg said.

"I can see that," the figure said.

The person who called himself Lemon Brown peered forward, and Greg could see him clearly. He was an old man. His black, heavily wrinkled face was surrounded by a halo of crinkly white hair and whiskers that seemed to separate his

head from the layers of dirty coats piled on his smallish frame. His pants were bagged to the knee, where they were met with

110 rags that went down to the old shoes. The rags were held on with strings, and there was a rope around his middle. Greg relaxed. He had seen the man before, picking through the trash on the corner and pulling clothes out of a Salvation Army box. There was no sign of the razor that could "cut a week into nine days."

"What are you doing here?" Greg asked.

"This is where I'm staying," Lemon Brown said. "What you here for?"

"Told you it was raining out," Greg said, leaning against the

120 back of the couch until he felt it give slightly.

"Ain't you got no home?"

"I got a home," Greg answered.

"You ain't one of them bad boys looking for my treasure, is you?" Lemon Brown cocked his head to one side and squinted one eye. "Because I told you I got me a razor."

"I'm not looking for your treasure," Greg answered, smiling. "*If* you have one."

"What you mean, *if* I have one," Lemon Brown said. "Every man got a treasure. You don't know that, you must be a fool!"

130 "Sure," Greg said as he sat on the sofa and put one leg over the back. "What do you have, gold coins?"

"Don't worry none about what I got," Lemon Brown said. "You know who I am?"

"You told me your name was orange or lemon or something like that."

"Lemon Brown," the old man said, pulling back his shoulders as he did so, "they used to call me Sweet Lemon Brown."

"Sweet Lemon?" Greg asked.

140 "Yessir. Sweet Lemon Brown. They used to say I sung the blues so sweet that if I sang at a funeral, the dead would commence to rocking with the beat. Used to travel all over Mississippi and as far as Monroe, Louisiana, and east on over

INTERPRET

Pause at line 113. Explain why Greg concludes that Lemon Brown is harmless— even before he realizes that he probably doesn't have a razor.

_____

_____

_____

IDENTIFY

Dialect is a way of speaking that is characteristic of a group of people or a geographic area. In lines 117–122, underline words and phrases in Greg and Lemon Brown's conversation that show their dialect is different from Standard English.

PREDICT

What might Lemon Brown's treasure be?

_____

_____

_____

INTERPRET

Lemon Brown pulls back his shoulders as he repeats his name (lines 136–137), even after Greg seems to make fun of it. What does Lemon Brown's action reveal about his **character**?

_____

_____

_____

IDENTIFY

Personification is a figure of speech (a comparison between two unlike things) in which something that is not human is spoken of as if it had human qualities. In lines 147–149, underline the details that personify hard times.

_____

_____

_____

_____

IDENTIFY

Pause at line 164. Go back to line 140 on page 45. Underline four details you've learned about Lemon Brown's life from what he's said to Greg.

_____

_____

_____

_____

_____

_____

_____

_____

to Macon, Georgia. You mean you ain't never heard of Sweet Lemon Brown?"

"Afraid not," Greg said. "What . . . what happened to you?"

"Hard times, boy. Hard times always after a poor man. One day I got tired, sat down to rest a spell and felt a tap on my shoulder. Hard times caught up with me."

150 "Sorry about that."

"What you doing here? How come you didn't go on home when the rain come? Rain don't bother you young folks none."

"Just didn't." Greg looked away.

"I used to have a knotty-headed boy just like you." Lemon Brown had half walked, half shuffled back to the corner and sat down against the wall. "Had them big eyes like you got. I used to call them moon eyes. Look into them moon eyes and see anything you want."

"How come you gave up singing the blues?" Greg asked.

160 "Didn't give it up," Lemon Brown said. "You don't give up the blues; they give you up. After a while you do good for yourself, and it ain't nothing but foolishness singing about how hard you got it. Ain't that right?"

"I guess so."

"What's that noise?" Lemon Brown asked, suddenly sitting upright.

Greg listened, and he heard a noise outside. He looked at Lemon Brown and saw the old man was pointing toward the window.

170 Greg went to the window and saw three men, neighborhood thugs, on the stoop. One was carrying a length of pipe. Greg looked back toward Lemon Brown, who moved quietly across the room to the window. The old man looked out, then beckoned frantically for Greg to follow him. For a moment Greg couldn't move. Then he found himself following Lemon Brown into the hallway and up darkened stairs. Greg followed as closely as he could. They reached the top of the stairs, and Greg felt Lemon Brown's hand first lying on his shoulder, then probing

down his arm until he finally took Greg's hand into his own
180 as they crouched in the darkness.

"They's bad men," Lemon Brown whispered. His breath
was warm against Greg's skin.

"Hey! Ragman!" a voice called. "We know you in here.
What you got up under them rags? You got any money?"

Silence.

"We don't want to have to come in and hurt you, old man,
but we don't mind if we have to."

Lemon Brown squeezed Greg's hand in his own hard,
gnarled fist.

190 There was a banging downstairs and a light as the men
entered. They banged around noisily, calling for the ragman.

"We heard you talking about your treasure." The voice was
slurred. "We just want to see it, that's all."

"You sure he's here?" One voice seemed to come from the
room with the sofa.

"Yeah, he stays here every night."

"There's another room over there; I'm going to take a look.
You got that flashlight?"

"Yeah, here, take the pipe too."

200 Greg opened his mouth to quiet the sound of his breath as
he sucked it in uneasily. A beam of light hit the wall a few feet
opposite him, then went out.

"Ain't nobody in that room," a voice said. "You think he
gone or something?"

"I don't know," came the answer. "All I know is that I heard
him talking about some kind of treasure. You know they found
that shopping-bag lady with that money in her bags."

"Yeah. You think he's upstairs?"

"HEY, OLD MAN, ARE YOU UP THERE?"

210 Silence.

"Watch my back, I'm going up."

There was a footstep on the stairs, and the beam from the
flashlight danced crazily along the peeling wallpaper. Greg held
his breath. There was another step and a loud crashing noise as

INTERPRET

Re-read lines 170–180.
What do Lemon Brown's
actions reveal about his
character? How can you tell
that he feels protective of
Greg—almost like a father?

_____

_____

_____

_____

_____

_____

_____

_____

INFER

Why have the men come
looking for Lemon Brown?

_____

_____

_____

_____

_____

PREDICT

What might happen if the men find Lemon Brown and Greg? What do you think is going to happen next?

_____

_____

_____

INFER

Why does Lemon Brown draw attention to himself?

_____

_____

_____

_____

_____

INTERPRET

Circle the details that show what is happening in lines 238–243. What happened to the three thugs?

_____

_____

_____

_____

_____

WORDS TO OWN

ominous (äm′ə·nəs) adj.: threatening; seeming to indicate something bad will happen.

the man banged the pipe against the wooden banister. Greg could feel his temples throb as the man slowly neared them. Greg thought about the pipe, wondering what he would do when the man reached them—what he *could* do.

220 Then Lemon Brown released his hand and moved toward the top of the stairs. Greg looked around and saw stairs going up to the next floor. He tried waving to Lemon Brown, hoping the old man would see him in the dim light and follow him to the next floor. Maybe, Greg thought, the man wouldn't follow them up there. Suddenly, though, Lemon Brown stood at the top of the stairs, both arms raised high above his head.

"There he is!" a voice cried from below.

"Throw down your money, old man, so I won't have to bash your head in!"

Lemon Brown didn't move. Greg felt himself near panic. The 230 steps came closer, and still Lemon Brown didn't move. He was an eerie sight, a bundle of rags standing at the top of the stairs, his shadow on the wall looming over him. Maybe, the thought came to Greg, the scene could be even eerier.

Greg wet his lips, put his hands to his mouth, and tried to make a sound. Nothing came out. He swallowed hard, wet his lips once more, and howled as evenly as he could.

"What's that?"

As Greg howled, the light moved away from Lemon Brown, but not before Greg saw him hurl his body down the stairs at 240 the men who had come to take his treasure. There was a crashing noise, and then footsteps. A rush of warm air came in as the downstairs door opened; then there was only an ominous silence.

Greg stood on the landing. He listened, and after a while there was another sound on the staircase.

"Mr. Brown?" he called.

"Yeah, it's me," came the answer. "I got their flashlight."

Greg exhaled in relief as Lemon Brown made his way slowly back up the stairs.

250 "You ok?"

"Few bumps and bruises," Lemon Brown said.

"I think I'd better be going," Greg said, his breath returning to normal. "You'd better leave, too, before they come back."

"They may hang around outside for a while," Lemon Brown said, "but they ain't getting their nerve up to come in here again. Not with crazy old ragmen and howling spooks. Best you stay awhile till the coast is clear. I'm heading out west tomorrow, out to East St. Louis."

"They were talking about treasures," Greg said. "You *really*
260 have a treasure?"

"What I tell you? Didn't I tell you every man got a treasure?" Lemon Brown said. "You want to see mine?"

"If you want to show it to me," Greg shrugged.

"Let's look out the window first, see what them scoundrels be doing," Lemon Brown said.

They followed the oval beam of the flashlight into one of the rooms and looked out the window. They saw the men who had tried to take the treasure sitting on the curb near the corner. One of them had his pants leg up, looking at his knee.

270   "You sure you're not hurt?" Greg asked Lemon Brown.

"Nothing that ain't been hurt before," Lemon Brown said. "When you get as old as me, all you say when something hurts is, 'Howdy, Mr. Pain, sees you back again.' Then when Mr. Pain see he can't worry you none, he go on mess with somebody else."

Greg smiled.

"Here, you hold this." Lemon Brown gave Greg the flashlight.

He sat on the floor near Greg and carefully untied the
280 strings that held the rags on his right leg. When he took the rags away, Greg saw a piece of plastic. The old man carefully took off the plastic and unfolded it. He revealed some yellowed newspaper clippings and a battered harmonica.

"There it be," he said, nodding his head. "There it be."

Greg looked at the old man, saw the distant look in his eye, then turned to the clippings. They told of Sweet Lemon Brown, a blues singer and harmonica player who was appearing at different theaters in the South. One of the clippings said he had

RETELL
Pause at line 253. Briefly **retell** in your own words the important events that have happened since Greg first encountered Lemon Brown, page 44, line 85.

_____

_____

_____

_____

_____

IDENTIFY
Re-read lines 271–275. Lemon Brown uses a **figure of speech** here. What is this kind of comparison called?

_____

_____

_____

_____

_____

INFER
What does the pronoun "it" refer to in line 284?

_____

_____

BUILD FLUENCY

After you've read the boxed passage once, read it again. Focus this time on the meaning of each sentence. Then, read the passage aloud. Try to capture the different feelings, especially the pride and sorrow that the old man expresses.

_____

_____

_____

_____

IDENTIFY

Circle the words that tell what happened to Lemon Brown's son.

_____

_____

_____

_____

INFER

Why did Lemon Brown's son consider the newspaper clippings and the harmonica to be treasures? Underline the details that prove how much he treasured them.

_____

_____

_____

_____

290 been the hit of the show, although not the headliner. All of the clippings were reviews of shows Lemon Brown had been in more than fifty years ago. Greg looked at the harmonica. It was dented badly on one side, with the reed holes on one end nearly closed.

"I used to travel around and make money for to feed my wife and Jesse—that's my boy's name. Used to feed them good, too. Then his mama died, and he stayed with his mama's sister. He growed up to be a man, and when the war come, he saw fit to go off and fight in it. I didn't have nothing to give him except these things that told him who I was, and what he

300 come from. If you know your pappy did something, you know you can do something too.

"Anyway, he went off to war, and I went off still playing and singing. 'Course by then I wasn't as much as I used to be, not without somebody to make it worth the while. You know what I mean?"

"Yeah," Greg nodded, not quite really knowing.

"I traveled around, and one time I come home, and there was this letter saying Jesse got killed in the war. Broke my heart, it truly did.

310 "They sent back what he had with him over there, and what it was is this old mouth fiddle and these clippings. Him carrying it around with him like that told me it meant something to him. That was my treasure, and when I give it to him, he treated it just like that, a treasure. Ain't that something?"

"Yeah, I guess so," Greg said.

"You _guess_ so?" Lemon Brown's voice rose an octave[2] as he started to put his treasure back into the plastic. "Well, you got to guess, 'cause you sure don't know nothing. Don't know enough to get home when it's raining."

320 "I guess . . . I mean, you're right."

"You ok for a youngster," the old man said as he tied the strings around his leg, "better than those scalawags what come here looking for my treasure. That's for sure."

---

2. **octave** (äk′tiv): eight whole notes.

"You really think that treasure of yours was worth fighting for?" Greg asked. "Against a pipe?"

"What else a man got 'cepting what he can pass on to his son, or his daughter, if she be his oldest?" Lemon Brown said. "For a big-headed boy, you sure do ask the foolishest questions."

330   Lemon Brown got up after patting his rags in place and looked out the window again.

"Looks like they're gone. You get on out of here and get yourself home. I'll be watching from the window, so you'll be all right."

Lemon Brown went down the stairs behind Greg. When they reached the front door, the old man looked out first, saw the street was clear, and told Greg to scoot on home.

"You sure you'll be ok?" Greg asked.

"Now, didn't I tell you I was going to East St. Louis in the
340 morning?" Lemon Brown asked. "Don't that sound ok to you?"

"Sure it does," Greg said. "Sure it does. And you take care of that treasure of yours."

"That I'll do," Lemon said, the wrinkles about his eyes suggesting a smile. "That I'll do."

The night had warmed and the rain had stopped, leaving puddles at the curbs. Greg didn't even want to think how late it was. He thought ahead of what his father would say and wondered if he should tell him about Lemon Brown. He thought about it until he reached his stoop, and decided against
350 it. Lemon Brown would be ok, Greg thought, with his memories and his treasure.

Greg pushed the button over the bell marked "Ridley," thought of the lecture he knew his father would give him, and smiled.

EVALUATE

Greg questions whether Lemon Brown's treasure was worth fighting for. What do you think? Why was it—or was it not—worth a fight?

_____

_____

_____

_____

_____

INTERPRET

Underline the details in lines 338–342 that show that Greg's opinion of Lemon Brown has changed. Then, tell what this change is.

_____

_____

_____

INFER

How has Greg changed since the beginning of the story? Circle the detail in the concluding paragraph that emphasizes the change?

_____

_____

_____

Character Grid

Myers's detailed descriptions of Lemon Brown and Greg—their appearance, actions, speech, and thoughts—make them come alive in the reader's mind. Use details from the story to fill out a character grid for either Greg or Lemon Brown.

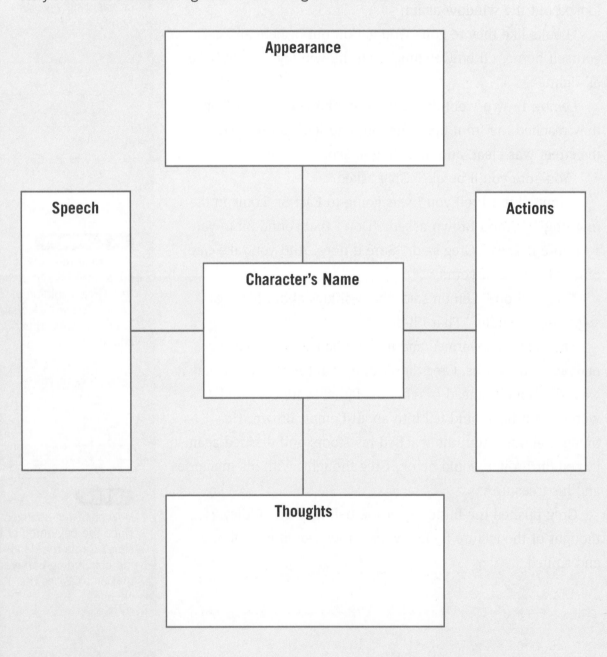

Appearance

Speech

Actions

Character's Name

Thoughts

Vocabulary and Comprehension

A. Match words and definitions. Write the letter of the correct definition next to each word.

_____ **1.** impromptu

_____ **2.** tentatively

_____ **3.** intently

_____ **4.** brittle

_____ **5.** ominous

a. with close attention

b. in an uncertain way

c. having a hard, sharp quality

d. threatening

e. unplanned

Word Bank
impromptu
tentatively
intently
brittle
ominous

B. Number the sentences to show the order of events.

_____ Three men come after Lemon Brown, looking for his treasure.

_____ Mr. Ridley reads a letter about his son Greg's poor grades.

_____ Greg meets Lemon Brown and learns he was a blues singer.

_____ Greg finally sees Lemon Brown's treasure and learns about his son.

_____ Lemon Brown and Greg scare the men away.

C. Answer each question below.

1. How did Sweet Lemon Brown get his name?

_____

2. What does Lemon Brown give to his son when Jesse goes off to war?

_____

3. What does "treasure" mean to Lemon Brown?

_____

The Secret Heart

Make the Connection

Unforgettable

When the poet Robert P. Tristram Coffin was a little boy, his father came to check on him one night as he lay sick in bed. That memory was so important to Coffin that many years later he wrote a poem about it. What happy moment from your childhood will you recall many years from now? Filling in the details on the graphic organizer below may help you remember the incident.

My Happiest Memory

My age _____

Where it happened _____

Who else was there _____

What I saw, heard, tasted, smelled, around me at

that time _____

What happened _____

_____

It was important to me because

_____

_____

_____

The Secret Heart

Robert P. Tristram Coffin

BUILD FLUENCY

Read the poem. Notice that each pair of lines forms a **couplet** (two rhymed lines) and, except for lines 13–16, is a complete sentence. Now read the poem aloud. Pause slightly at commas, but don't come to a full stop until you get to each period.

IDENTIFY

Underline the words that tell you why it looks as if the father has his "great hands full of fire" (line 6).

IDENTIFY

Circle what the boy thinks his father's hands resemble.

INFER

When the boy sees the look on his father's face, what does he realize?

_____

_____

_____

_____

EVALUATE

The speaker says that the father's love is "too tender for the day to trace" (line 18). Why do you think some people are unwilling to show their feelings?

_____

_____

_____

_____

Across the years he could recall
His father one way best of all.

In the stillest hour of night
The boy awakened to a light.

Half in dreams, he saw his sire[1]
With his great hands full of fire.

The man had struck a match to see
If his son slept peacefully.

He held his palms each side the spark
10   His love had kindled in the dark.

His two hands were curved apart
In the semblance[2] of a heart.

He wore, it seemed to his small son,
A bare heart on his hidden one,

A heart that gave out such a glow
No son awake could bear to know.

It showed a look upon a face
Too tender for the day to trace.

One instant, it lit all about,
20   And then the secret heart went out.

But it shone long enough for one
To know that hands held up the sun.

---

1. **sire:** father.
2. **semblance:** form.

Inside-Out Chart

Fill out the graphic below to figure out the layers of meaning of the word "heart." First, look up "heart" in a dictionary and write the word's literal meanings in one circle. In the next circle, write in what you think the heart symbolizes in the poem. In the final circle, think of other ways the word "heart" can be used; you can draw on your own experiences or other works you have read.

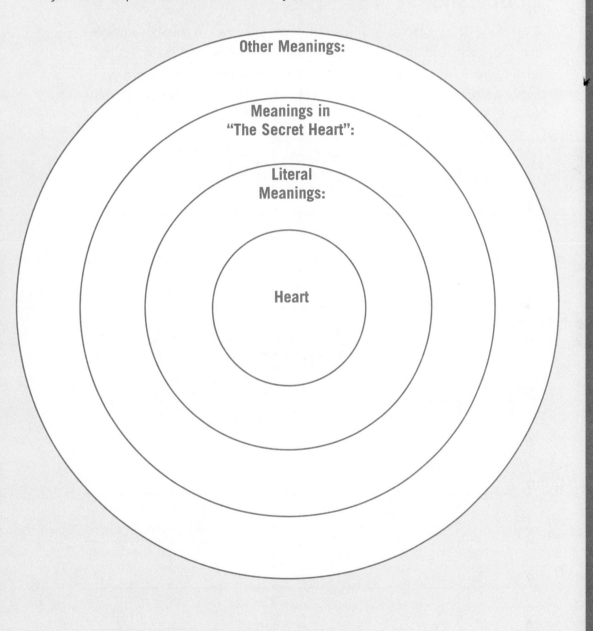

The Tell-Tale Heart

Make the Connection

Horror Shows

A creaking door, screams in the night, creepy spiders, a thirsty vampire—can you resist reading a scary book or seeing a movie that really, really terrifies you? Once in a while most of us want to be frightened by the books we read or the TV shows we watch. Fill out the list below with ten movies, TV shows, books, or fictional characters that give you the shivers.

Top Ten Terrors

1. _____

2. _____

3. _____

4. _____

5. _____

6. _____

7. _____

8. _____

9. _____

10. _____

THE TELL-TALE HEART

Edgar Allan Poe

IDENTIFY

Circle what the narrator says he is *not*. Underline how he intends to prove he's healthy.

INTERPRET

Re-read lines 8–16. How would you describe the narrator's reaction to the old man? Underline the idea that enters the narrator's brain.

EVALUATE

The narrator claims to have several qualities that insane people *don't* have. Circle the qualities that he mentions. In your opinion, does having those qualities prove his sanity—or not?

WORDS TO OWN

acute (ə·kyo͞ot) *adj.:* sharp; sensitive.

True!—nervous—very, very dreadfully nervous I had been and am; but why *will* you say that I am mad? The disease had sharpened my senses—not destroyed—not dulled them. Above all was the sense of hearing <u>acute</u>. I heard all things in the heaven and in the earth. I heard many things in hell. How, then, am I mad? Hearken! and observe how healthily—how calmly I can tell you the whole story.

It is impossible to say how first the idea entered my brain; but once conceived, it haunted me day and night. Object[1] there was none. Passion there was none. I loved the old man. He had never wronged me. He had never given me insult. For his gold I had no desire. I think it was his eye! Yes, it was this! One of his eyes resembled that of a vulture—a pale blue eye, with a film over it. Whenever it fell upon me, my blood ran cold; and so by degrees—very gradually—I made up my mind to take the life of the old man and thus rid myself of the eye forever.

Now this is the point. You fancy me mad. Madmen know nothing. But you should have seen me. You should have seen how wisely I proceeded—with what caution—with what foresight—with what dissimulation[2] I went to work! I was never kinder to the old man than during the whole week before I killed him. And every night, about midnight, I turned the latch of his door and opened it—oh, so gently! And then, when I had made an opening sufficient for my head, I put in a dark lantern, all closed, closed, so that no light shone out, and then I thrust in my head. Oh, you would have laughed to see how cunningly I thrust it in! I moved it slowly—very, very slowly, so that I might not disturb the old man's sleep. It took me an hour to place my whole head within the opening so far that I could see him as he lay upon his bed. Ha! Would a madman have been so wise as this? And then, when my head was well in the room, I undid the lantern cautiously—oh, so cautiously—cautiously (for the hinges creaked)—I undid it just so much that a single thin ray fell upon the vulture eye. And this I did for seven long

---

1. **object:** purpose or goal.
2. **dissimulation:** disguising of intentions or feelings. (Look for a similar word at the end of the story.)

nights—every night just at midnight—but I found the eye always closed; and so it was impossible to do the work; for it was not the old man who <u>vexed</u> me, but his Evil Eye. And every morning, when the day broke, I went boldly into the chamber and spoke courageously to him, calling him by name

40 in a hearty tone and inquiring how he had passed the night. So you see he would have been a very profound old man, indeed, to suspect that every night, just at twelve, I looked in upon him while he slept.

Upon the eighth night I was more than usually cautious in opening the door. A watch's minute hand moves more quickly than did mine. Never before that night had I *felt* the extent of my own powers—of my <u>sagacity</u>. I could scarcely contain my feelings of triumph. To think that there I was, opening the door, little by little, and he not even to dream of my secret deeds or

50 thoughts. I fairly chuckled at the idea; and perhaps he heard me; for he moved on the bed suddenly, as if startled. Now you may think that I drew back—but no. His room was as black as pitch with the thick darkness (for the shutters were close fastened, through fear of robbers), and so I knew that he could not see the opening of the door, and I kept pushing it on steadily, steadily.

I had my head in, and was about to open the lantern, when my thumb slipped upon the tin fastening, and the old man sprang up in the bed, crying out—"Who's there?"

60 I kept quite still and said nothing. For a whole hour I did not move a muscle, and in the meantime I did not hear him lie down. He was still sitting up in the bed listening—just as I have done, night after night, hearkening to the deathwatches[3] in the wall.

Presently I heard a slight groan, and I knew it was the groan of mortal terror. It was not a groan of pain or of grief—oh, no!—it was the low, stifled sound that arises from the bottom of the soul when overcharged with awe. I knew the sound well. Many

---

3. deathwatches: beetles that burrow into wood and make tapping sounds, which some people believe are a sign of approaching death.

INFER

Why does the narrator find it impossible to kill the old man on the first seven nights?

_____

_____

PREDICT

Pause at line 43. Do you think the narrator will kill the old man? Tell what you think will happen. Base your **prediction** on the details you already know.

_____

_____

_____

_____

_____

_____

IDENTIFY

Suspense is the curiosity or dread that a reader feels about will happen next in the plot. Underline two details from lines 57–64 that build suspense in this story.

WORDS TO OWN
vexed (vekst) *v.:* disturbed; annoyed.
sagacity (sə·gas′ə·tē) *n.:* intelligence and good judgment.

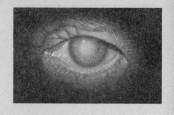

BUILD FLUENCY

Read the boxed passage starting at line 65 on page 61 at least twice to appreciate the author's unique **style,** the way he expresses himself. Notice the kinds of words and sentences he uses—long, short, simple, poetic, and so on. As you read the passage aloud, change the pace of your reading, from slow to fast, depending on the **mood** reflected in the narrator's words. Decide which sentences you will read softly, perhaps even in a whisper. When you reach lines 76–79, try to imitate how the old man might sound as he tries to reassure himself. Pay special attention to Poe's use of *italic* type to show emphasis, and dashes to show abrupt changes in thought.

VISUALIZE

Re-read lines 86–103. Underline three **visual images,** details that help you *picture* what is happening. Then, circle three **sound images,** details that help you *hear* what is happening.

INTERPRET

What do you think the narrator might be hearing when he thinks he hears the beating of the old man's heart?

a night, just at midnight, when all the world slept, it has welled
70 up from my own bosom, deepening, with its dreadful echo, the
terrors that distracted me. I say I knew it well. I knew what the
old man felt, and pitied him, although I chuckled at heart. I
knew that he had been lying awake ever since the first slight
noise, when he had turned in the bed. His fears had been ever
since growing upon him. He had been trying to fancy them
causeless but could not. He had been saying to himself—"It is
nothing but the wind in the chimney—it is only a mouse
crossing the floor," or "It is merely a cricket which has made a
single chirp." Yes, he has been trying to comfort himself with
80 these suppositions; but he had found all in vain. *All in vain*;
because Death, in approaching him, had stalked with his black
shadow before him and enveloped the victim. And it was the
mournful influence of the unperceived shadow that caused him
to feel—although he neither saw nor heard—to *feel* the
presence of my head within the room.

When I had waited a long time, very patiently, without
hearing him lie down, I resolved to open a little—a very, very
little crevice in the lantern. So I opened it—you cannot imagine
how stealthily, stealthily—until, at length, a single dim ray, like
90 the thread of the spider, shot from out the crevice and full upon
the vulture eye.

It was open—wide, wide open—and I grew furious as I
gazed upon it. I saw it with perfect distinctness—all a dull blue,
with a hideous veil over it that chilled the very marrow in my
bones; but I could see nothing else of the old man's face or
person, for I had directed the ray, as if by instinct, precisely
upon the damned spot.

And now have I not told you that what you mistake for
madness is but overacuteness of the senses?—now, I say, there
100 came to my ears a low, dull, quick sound, such as a watch makes
when enveloped in cotton. I knew *that* sound well too. It was
the beating of the old man's heart. It increased my fury, as the
beating of a drum stimulates the soldier into courage.

But even yet I <u>refrained</u> and kept still. I scarcely breathed. I held the lantern motionless. I tried how steadily I could maintain the ray upon the eye. Meantime the hellish tattoo[4] of the heart increased. It grew quicker and quicker and louder and louder every instant. The old man's *terror* must have been extreme! It grew louder, I say, louder every moment!—do you

110 mark me well? I have told you that I am nervous: So I am. And now at the dead hour of the night, amid the dreadful silence of that old house, so strange a noise as this excited me to uncontrollable terror. Yet for some minutes longer I refrained and stood still. But the beating grew louder, louder! I thought the heart must burst. And now a new anxiety seized me—the sound would be heard by a neighbor! The old man's hour had come! With a loud yell, I threw open the lantern and leaped into the room. He shrieked once—once only. In an instant I dragged him to the floor and pulled the heavy bed over him. I

120 then smiled gaily to find the deed so far done. But, for many minutes, the heart beat on with a muffled sound. This, however, did not vex me; it would not be heard through the wall. At length it ceased. The old man was dead. I removed the bed and examined the corpse. Yes, he was stone, stone dead. I placed my hand upon the heart and held it there many minutes. There was no pulsation. He was stone dead. His eye would trouble me no more.

If still you think me mad, you will think so no longer when I describe the wise precautions I took for the concealment of

130 the body. The night waned, and I worked hastily but in silence. First of all I dismembered the corpse. I cut off the head and the arms and the legs.

I then took up three planks from the flooring of the chamber and deposited all between the scantlings.[5] I then replaced the boards so cleverly, so cunningly, that no human eye—not even *his*—could have detected anything wrong. There was nothing to

---

4. **tattoo:** steady beat.
5. **scantlings:** small beams of wood.

RETELL

Pause at line 127. Go back to line 44 on page 61. Tell what happens on the eighth night. Be sure to include the reason that the narrator's behavior changes. Describe how he commits the murder.

WORDS TO OWN
refrained (ri·frānd') *v.:* held back.

INTERPRET

When we read a story, we rely on the **narrator** to let us know what's going on. A narrator who can't be trusted to tell the truth is called an **unreliable narrator.** A mad narrator is, of course, not reliable. What's one example of something that the narrator has said— or done—or felt—that is evidence that he *is* mad?

_____

_____

INFER

Where do you think the narrator might be as he's telling this story?

_____

_____

_____

PREDICT

Pause at line 158. The officers seem satisfied that nothing bad has happened in the house. Will the narrator get away with his crime? What do you think will happen next?

_____

_____

WORDS TO OWN
wary (wer'e) *adj.:* cautious.
suavity (swäv'ə·tē) *n.:* smoothness; politeness.
audacity (ô·das'ə·tē) *n.:* boldness.

wash out—no stain of any kind—no blood spot whatever. I had been too <u>wary</u> for that. A tub had caught all—ha! ha!

140   When I had made an end of these labors, it was four o'clock—still dark as midnight. As the bell sounded the hour, there came a knocking at the street door. I went down to open it with a light heart—for what had I *now* to fear? There entered three men, who introduced themselves, with perfect <u>suavity</u>, as officers of the police. A shriek had been heard by a neighbor during the night; suspicion of foul play had been aroused; information had been lodged at the police office, and they (the officers) had been deputed[6] to search the premises.

    I smiled—for *what* had I to fear? I bade the gentlemen welcome. The shriek, I said, was my own in a dream. The old
150 man, I mentioned, was absent in the country. I took my visitors all over the house. I bade them search—search *well.* I led them, at length, to *his* chamber. I showed them his treasures, secure, undisturbed. In the enthusiasm of my confidence, I brought chairs into the room and desired them *here* to rest from their fatigues, while I myself, in the wild <u>audacity</u> of my perfect triumph, placed my own seat upon the very spot beneath which reposed the corpse of the victim.

    The officers were satisfied. My *manner* had convinced them. I was singularly at ease. They sat, and while I answered
160 cheerily, they chatted familiar things. But, ere long, I felt myself getting pale and wished them gone. My head ached, and I fancied a ringing in my ears; but still they sat and still chatted. The ringing became more distinct—it continued and became more distinct: I talked more freely to get rid of the feeling: but it continued and gained definitiveness—until, at length, I found that the noise was *not* within my ears.

    No doubt I now grew *very* pale—but I talked more fluently and with a heightened voice. Yet the sound increased—and what could I do? It was *a low, dull, quick sound—much such a*
170 *sound as a watch makes when enveloped in cotton.* I gasped for breath—and yet the officers heard it not. I talked more

_____

6. **deputed** (dē·pyo͞ot'id): appointed.

quickly—more vehemently; but the noise steadily increased. I arose and argued about trifles, in a high key and with violent gesticulations, but the noise steadily increased. Why *would* they not be gone? I paced the floor to and fro with heavy strides, as if excited to fury by the observation of the men—but the noise steadily increased. Oh God! what *could* I do? I foamed—I raved—I swore! I swung the chair upon which I had been sitting and grated it upon the boards, but the noise arose over

180 all and continually increased. It grew louder—louder—*louder!* And still the men chatted pleasantly, and smiled. Was it possible they heard not? Almighty God!—no, no! They heard!—they suspected!—they *knew!*—they were making a mockery of my horror!—this I thought, and this I think. But anything was better than this agony! Anything was more tolerable than this derision! I could bear those hypocritical smiles no longer! I felt that I must scream or die!—and now—again!—hark! louder! louder! louder! *louder!*—

"Villains!" I shrieked, "dissemble no more! I admit the

190 deed!—tear up the planks!—here, here!—it is the beating of his hideous heart!"

INFER

What is happening to the narrator? What does he think he hears? What's your explanation for the sound he hears?

INTERPRET

Pause (if you can) at line 188. Notice that the writer in this paragraph increases his use of italics, dashes, and exclamation marks. What mental state in the narrator do these **punctuation marks** help to show?

EVALUATE

Poe once wrote that every word in a story should create a "single, overwhelming impression." In your opinion, what impression was he trying to create in this story? Tell why you think he was successful or not.

WORDS TO OWN
vehemently (vē′ə·mənt·lē) *adv.*: forcefully; passionately.
gesticulations (jes·tik′yoo·lā′shənz) *n.*: energetic gestures.
derision (di·rizh′ən) *n.*: contempt; ridicule.

Narrator Evaluation

The narrator of "The Tell-Tale Heart" spends much of the story insisting that he is not mad. Are you convinced by his arguments? Fill out the graphic below by collecting evidence from the story (focus on the narrator's thoughts, words, and actions). Then, write whether you feel the narrator is a credible source of information.

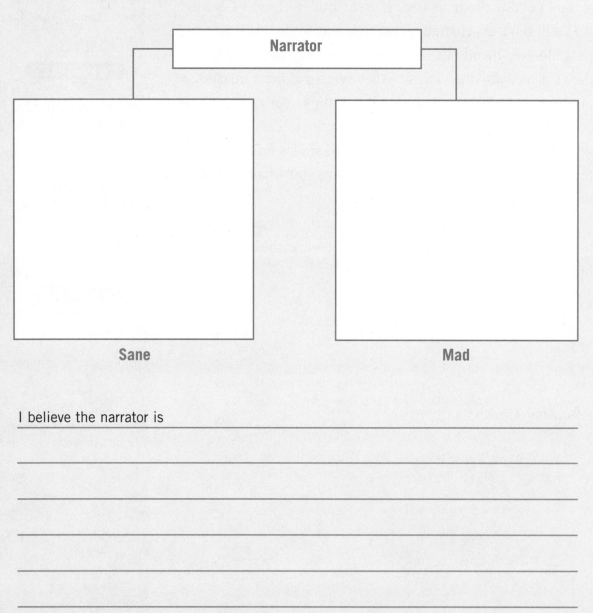

Narrator

Sane

Mad

I believe the narrator is _____

_____

_____

_____

_____

Vocabulary and Comprehension

Word Bank				
acute	sagacity	wary	audacity	gesticulations
vexed	refrained	suavity	vehemently	derision

A. Write the word from the Word Bank that best fits each group.

_____ **1.** disturbed, annoyed, troubled

_____ **2.** careful, cautious, leery

_____ **3.** boldness, daring, brazenness

_____ **4.** withheld, repressed, held back

_____ **5.** forcefully, energetically, passionately

_____ **6.** smoothness, politeness, fine manners

_____ **7.** gestures, protests, spasms

_____ **8.** scorn, ridicule, contempt

_____ **9.** sharp, sensitive, severe

_____ **10.** intelligence, sound judgment, good sense

B. Answer each question below.

1. Why does the narrator decide to kill the old man?

_____

_____

2. Why does the narrator finally confess to his crime?

_____

There Will Come Soft Rains

Make the Connection

Future Shock

It's the year 2026, and you're looking for a house to buy. Will you choose a computerized house, programmed and equipped to serve humans in every way? When he wrote this story in the 1950s, that's the kind of house Ray Bradbury imagined might exist in 2026.

Before you read the story, think about some of the new technologies, inventions, and discoveries, that have come about in your own and your grandparents' lifetime. What benefits and drawbacks has each one brought us? Complete the chart below by filling in one important benefit and drawback for each invention or discovery listed.

Invention/Discovery	Benefit	Drawback
Television		
Internet/World Wide Web		
E-mail		
Cell phone		
Nuclear energy		

Background

This story is set in the year 2026 in a house where a family of humans *used* to live. Their silhouettes on a wall are all that remains of them after a nuclear explosion. Note that the soft rain in the title could refer to radioactive particles that fall to earth after such an explosion.

There Will Come Soft Rains

Ray Bradbury

INFER

Why do you think the house is empty (line 3)?

_____

_____

_____

_____

_____

IDENTIFY

Circle the details that identify the **setting**—the time and place of the story.

INFER

What happens—or doesn't happen—between 8:01 A.M. and 9:15 A.M. that suggests that all is not well with the humans who own this house?

_____

_____

_____

_____

_____

_____

_____

_____

_____

_____

In the living room the voice-clock sang, _Ticktock, seven o'clock, time to get up, time to get up, seven o'clock!_ as if it were afraid that nobody would. The morning house lay empty. The clock ticked on, repeating and repeating its sounds into the emptiness. _Seven-nine, breakfast time, seven-nine!_

In the kitchen the breakfast stove gave a hissing sigh and ejected from its warm interior eight pieces of perfectly browned toast, eight eggs sunny side up, sixteen slices of bacon, and two coffees.

10   "Today is August 4, 2026," said a second voice from the kitchen ceiling, "in the city of Allendale, California." It repeated the date three times for memory's sake. "Today is Mr. Featherstone's birthday. Today is the anniversary of Tilita's marriage. Insurance is payable, as are the water, gas, and light bills."

Somewhere in the walls, relays clicked, memory tapes glided under electric eyes.

Eight-one, tick-tock, eight-one o'clock, off to school, off to work, run, run, eight-one! But no doors slammed, no carpets took the soft tread of rubber heels. It was raining outside. The 20 weather box on the front door sang quietly: "Rain, rain, go away; rubbers, raincoats for today . . ." And the rain tapped on the empty house, echoing.

Outside, the garage chimed and lifted its door to reveal the waiting car. After a long wait the door swung down again.

At eight-thirty the eggs were shriveled and the toast was like stone. An aluminum wedge scraped them into the sink, where hot water whirled them down a metal throat which digested and flushed them away to the distant sea. The dirty dishes were dropped into a hot washer and emerged twinkling dry.

30   _Nine-fifteen,_ sang the clock, _time to clean._

Out of warrens[1] in the wall, tiny robot mice darted. The rooms were acrawl with the small cleaning animals, all rubber and metal. They thudded against chairs, whirling their moustached runners, kneading the rug nap, sucking gently at hidden dust. Then, like mysterious invaders, they popped into

---

1. **warrens:** small, crowded spaces.

their burrows. Their pink electric eyes faded. The house was clean.

Ten o'clock. The sun came out from behind the rain. The house stood alone in a city of rubble and ashes. This was the
40 one house left standing. At night the ruined city gave off a radioactive glow which could be seen for miles.

Ten-fifteen. The garden sprinklers whirled up in golden founts, filling the soft morning air with scatterings of brightness. The water pelted windowpanes, running down the charred west side where the house had been burned evenly free of its white paint. The entire west face of the house was black, save for five places. Here the silhouette in paint of a man mowing a lawn. Here, as in a photograph, a woman bent to pick flowers. Still farther over, their images burned on wood in
50 one titanic instant, a small boy, hands flung into the air; higher up, the image of a thrown ball, and opposite him a girl, hands raised to catch a ball which never came down.

The five spots of paint—the man, the woman, the children, the ball—remained. The rest was a thin charcoaled layer.

The gentle sprinkler rain filled the garden with falling light.

Until this day, how well the house had kept its peace. How carefully it had inquired, "Who goes there? What's the password?" and, getting no answer from lonely foxes and whining cats, it had shut up its windows and drawn shades in
60 an old-maidenly preoccupation with self-protection which bordered on a mechanical <u>paranoia</u>.

It quivered at each sound, the house did. If a sparrow brushed a window, the shade snapped up. The bird, startled, flew off! No, not even a bird must touch the house!

The house was an altar with ten thousand attendants, big, small, servicing, attending, in choirs. But the gods had gone away, and the ritual of the religion continued senselessly, uselessly.

Twelve noon.
70 A dog whined, shivering, on the front porch.

The front door recognized the dog voice and opened. The dog, once huge and fleshy, but now gone to bone and covered

IDENTIFY

Underline the details in lines 38–41 that tell you how this house is different from the other houses in the neighborhood. What seems to have happened to the city?

_____

_____

INTERPRET

Write a number, from 1 to 5, over the details describing each of the five silhouettes on the wall of the house. What has caused the five silhouettes to be "burned on wood"?

_____

_____

IDENTIFY

Personification is a figure of speech in which an object or animal is spoken of as if it has human qualities. Circle the words and phrases in lines 56–64 that portray the house's human qualities.

INFER

Who are the gods who have gone away (lines 66–67)?

_____

WORDS TO OWN
paranoia (par'ə·noi'ə) *n.:* mental disorder that often causes people to believe that they are being persecuted; false suspicions.

INFER

What do you think has happened to the dog? Why does the house treat the dog in such a cold way?

_____

_____

_____

_____

_____

VISUALIZE

Re-read lines 71–90. This section is filled with **images,** details that appeal to your senses. Circle three images that appeal to three different senses.

_____

_____

_____

PREDICT

Pause at the end of the page. Will the house continue to go on doing its work forever? Tell what you think might happen next.

_____

_____

_____

_____

_____

_____

with sores, moved in and through the house, tracking mud. Behind it whirred angry mice, angry at having to pick up mud, angry at inconvenience.

For not a leaf fragment blew under the door but what the wall panels flipped open and the copper scrap rats flashed swiftly out. The offending dust, hair, or paper, seized in miniature steel jaws, was raced back to the burrows. There,

80 down tubes which fed into the cellar, it was dropped into the sighing vent of an incinerator which sat like evil Baal[2] in a dark corner.

The dog ran upstairs, hysterically yelping to each door, at last realizing, as the house realized, that only silence was here.

It sniffed the air and scratched the kitchen door. Behind the door, the stove was making pancakes which filled the house with a rich baked odor and the scent of maple syrup.

The dog frothed at the mouth, lying at the door, sniffing, its eyes turned to fire. It ran wildly in circles, biting at its tail, spun

90 in a frenzy, and died. It lay in the parlor for an hour.

Two o'clock, sang a voice.

Delicately sensing decay at last, the regiments of mice hummed out as softly as blown gray leaves in an electrical wind.

Two-fifteen.

The dog was gone.

In the cellar, the incinerator glowed suddenly and a whirl of sparks leaped up the chimney.

Two thirty-five.

100 Bridge tables sprouted from patio walls. Playing cards fluttered onto pads in a shower of pips.[3] Martinis manifested on an oaken bench with egg-salad sandwiches. Music played.

But the tables were silent and the cards untouched.

At four o'clock the tables folded like great butterflies back through the paneled walls.

---

2. **Baal** (bā′əl): in the Bible, the god of Canaan, whom the Israelites came to regard as a false god.
3. **pips:** figures on cards.

Four-thirty.

The nursery walls glowed.

Animals took shape: yellow giraffes, blue lions, pink antelopes, lilac panthers cavorting in crystal substance. The
110 walls were glass. They looked out upon color and fantasy. Hidden films clocked through well-oiled sprockets,[4] and the walls lived. The nursery floor was woven to resemble a crisp cereal[5] meadow. Over this ran aluminum roaches and iron crickets, and in the hot, still air butterflies of delicate red tissue wavered among the sharp aromas of animal spoors![6] There was the sound like a great matted yellow hive of bees within a dark bellows, the lazy bumble of a purring lion. And there was the patter of okapi[7] feet and the murmur of a fresh jungle rain, like other hoofs, falling upon the summer-starched grass. Now the
120 walls dissolved into distances of parched weed, mile on mile, and warm endless sky. The animals drew away into thorn brakes[8] and water holes.

It was the children's hour.

Five o'clock. The bath filled with clear hot water.

Six, seven, eight o'clock. The dinner dishes manipulated like magic tricks, and in the study a *click.* In the metal stand opposite the hearth where a fire now blazed up warmly, a cigar popped out, half an inch of soft gray ash on it, smoking, waiting.

Nine o'clock. The beds warmed their hidden circuits, for
130 nights were cool here.

Nine-five. A voice spoke from the study ceiling:

"Mrs. McClellan, which poem would you like this evening?"

The house was silent.

The voice said at last, "Since you express no preference, I shall select a poem at random." Quiet music rose to back the voice. "Sara Teasdale. As I recall, your favorite. . . ."

---

4. **sprockets:** wheels with points designed to fit into the holes along the edges of a filmstrip.
5. **cereal:** of grasses that produce grain.
6. **spoors:** tracks.
7. **okapi** (ō·kä′pē): African animal related to the giraffe but with a much shorter neck.
8. **thorn brakes:** clumps of thorns; thickets.

EVALUATE

If you were a young child, would you like to have a room like the one described here? Why or why not?

_____

_____

_____

_____

_____

_____

_____

INFER

Why does Bradbury include the exact times of specific events? How does knowing the exact time increase the **suspense**?

_____

_____

_____

_____

_____

_____

_____

_____

_____

_____

RETELL

Retell in two or three sentences what is happening in the poem.

_____

_____

_____

INTERPRET

How is nature in the poem like nature in this story?

_____

_____

PREDICT

Stop at line 152 and tell how you think the house might die.

_____

_____

INTERPRET

A **conflict** has arisen in the story. On one side of the conflict is the house and all the scientific progress and advanced machinery it stands for. What's on the other side of the conflict?

_____

_____

_____

_____

_____

WORDS TO OWN
tremulous (trem′yo͞o·ləs)
adj.: trembling.

There will come soft rains and the smell of the ground,
And swallows circling with their shimmering sound;

And frogs in the pools singing at night,
140　*And wild plum trees in <u>tremulous</u> white;*

Robins will wear their feathery fire,
Whistling their whims on a low fence-wire;

And not one will know of the war, not one
Will care at last when it is done.

Not one would mind, neither bird nor tree,
If mankind perished utterly;

And Spring herself, when she woke at dawn
Would scarcely know that we were gone."

The fire burned on the stone hearth, and the cigar fell away
150　into a mound of quiet ash on its tray. The empty chairs faced
each other between the silent walls, and the music played.

At ten o'clock the house began to die.

The wind blew. A falling tree bough crashed through the
kitchen window. Cleaning solvent,[9] bottled, shattered over the
stove. The room was ablaze in an instant!

"Fire!" screamed a voice. The house lights flashed, water
pumps shot water from the ceilings. But the solvent spread on
the linoleum, licking, eating, under the kitchen door, while the
voices took it up in chorus: "Fire, fire, fire!"

160　The house tried to save itself. Doors sprang tightly shut, but
the windows were broken by the heat and the wind blew and
sucked upon the fire.

The house gave ground as the fire in ten billion angry
sparks moved with flaming ease from room to room and then

---

9. **solvent:** something that can dissolve something else (here, something that
dissolves dirt). *Solvent, dissolve,* and *solution* have the same Latin root, *solvere,*
which means "to loosen."

up the stairs. While scurrying water rats squeaked from the walls, pistoled their water, and ran for more. And the wall sprays let down showers of mechanical rain.

But too late. Somewhere, sighing, a pump shrugged to a stop. The quenching rain ceased. The reserve water supply which had 170 filled baths and washed dishes for many quiet days was gone.

The fire crackled up the stairs. It fed upon Picassos and Matisses[10] in the upper halls, like delicacies, baking off the oily flesh, tenderly crisping the canvases into black shavings.

Now the fire lay in beds, stood in windows, changed the colors of drapes!

And then, reinforcements.

From attic trapdoors, blind robot faces peered down with faucet mouths gushing green chemical.

The fire backed off, as even an elephant must at the sight of 180 a dead snake. Now there were twenty snakes whipping over the floor, killing the fire with a clear cold venom of green froth.

But the fire was clever. It had sent flame outside the house, up through the attic to the pumps there. An explosion! The attic brain which directed the pumps was shattered into bronze shrapnel on the beams.

The fire rushed back into every closet and felt of the clothes hung there.

The house shuddered, oak bone on bone, its bared skeleton cringing from the heat, its wire, its nerves revealed as if a 190 surgeon had torn the skin off to let the red veins and capillaries quiver in the scalded air. Help, help! Fire! Run, run! Heat snapped mirrors like the first brittle winter ice. And the voices wailed, Fire, fire, run, run, like a tragic nursery rhyme, a dozen voices, high, low, like children dying in a forest, alone, alone. And the voices fading as the wires popped their sheathings[11] like hot chestnuts. One, two, three, four, five voices died.

IDENTIFY

Underline at least three details in lines 171–187 that **personify** the fire.

_____

_____

_____

_____

_____

_____

_____

BUILD FLUENCY

Read this passage aloud at least twice. Try to express fear and sadness in your voice. Before you read the passage aloud a second time, mark some of the lines to show which ones you will read loudly, softly, quickly, or slowly.

_____

_____

_____

_____

_____

_____

---

10. **Picassos and Matisses:** paintings by Pablo Picasso (1881–1973), a famous Spanish painter and sculptor who worked in France, and by Henri Matisse (än·rē′ má·tēs′) (1869–1954), a famous French painter.
11. **sheathings:** protective coverings.

INFER

Why are so many things happening at once in the house?

_____

_____

_____

_____

_____

_____

INTERPRET

Circle the details in lines 225–228 that show which side has won the **conflict.** Outside the ruined house, what still goes on?

_____

_____

EVALUATE

What warning about scientific advances is Bradbury trying to deliver? Tell whether or not you agree with his message. Give reasons for your answer.

_____

_____

WORDS TO OWN
oblivious (ə·bliv′ē·əs) _adj.:_ unaware.
sublime (sə·blīm′) _adj.:_ majestic; grand.

In the nursery the jungle burned. Blue lions roared, purple giraffes bounded off. The panthers ran in circles, changing color, and ten million animals, running before the fire, vanished
200 off toward a distant steaming river. . . .

Ten more voices died. In the last instant under the fire avalanche, other choruses, <u>oblivious</u>, could be heard announcing the time, playing music, cutting the lawn by remote-control mower, or setting an umbrella frantically out and in, the slamming and opening front door, a thousand things happening, like a clock shop when each clock strikes the hour insanely before or after the other, a scene of maniac confusion, yet unity; singing, screaming, a few last cleaning mice darting bravely out to carry the horrid ashes away! And one voice, with
210 <u>sublime</u> disregard for the situation, read poetry aloud in the fiery study, until all the film spools burned, until all the wires withered and the circuits cracked.

The fire burst the house and let it slam flat down, puffing out skirts of spark and smoke.

In the kitchen, an instant before the rain of fire and timber, the stove could be seen making breakfasts at a psychopathic[12] rate, ten dozen eggs, six loaves of toast, twenty dozen bacon strips, which, eaten by fire, started the stove working again, hysterically hissing!
220 The crash. The attic smashing into kitchen and parlor. The parlor into cellar, cellar into subcellar. Deep freeze, armchair, film tapes, circuits, beds, and all like skeletons thrown in a cluttered mound deep under.

Smoke and silence. A great quantity of smoke.

Dawn showed faintly in the east. Among the ruins, one wall stood alone. Within the wall, a last voice said, over and over again and again, even as the sun rose to shine upon the heaped rubble and steam:

"Today is August 5, 2026, today is August 5, 2026, today is . . ."

---

12. psychopathic (sī′kō·path′ik): insane.

Time Line

Creating a time line can be a good way to organize the events of a short story in **chronological order.** Outline the major events in the story by filling in the vertical time line below. Next to each time of day write a summary of what happened in the story at that time.

7:00 _____

_____

8:01 _____

_____

10:00 _____

_____

12:00 _____

_____

4:30 _____

_____

5:00 _____

_____

10:00 _____

_____

Vocabulary and Comprehension

A. Complete each sentence with a word from the Word Bank.

Word Bank
paranoia
tremulous
oblivious
sublime

1. The house's fears and suspicion of everything

   bordered on _____ .

2. Because Mary Ellen was afraid, she spoke in a shaky,

   _____ voice.

3. The children kept playing at recess, _____ to the ringing of the school bell.

4. The beautiful music was _____ and grand.

B. Write the word from the Word Bank above that best fits each group.

_____ 1. timid, shaking, trembling

_____ 2. majestic, grand, noble

_____ 3. unaware, heedless, unmindful

_____ 4. deep fear, distrust, suspicion

Vocabulary and Comprehension

C. In each blank space in the paragraph below, fill in a word from the Word Bank.

The old man watched the boys and girls playing in the meadow. The setting was

_____ , with mountains rising in all directions. However, instead

of enjoying the happy scene, the old man was _____ to its charm.

In his _____ , he imagined that the boys and girls were making

fun of him. He shook his cane, _____ with rage, and yelled

at them to leave him alone. So they did.

D. Answer each question below.

1. What details tell you the city has been destroyed?

_____

_____

2. What does the house do to the dog?

_____

_____

3. What happens when the house catches fire? Use details from the story.

_____

_____

The Dogs Could Teach Me

Make the Connection

Pets and Pals

People who have had dogs or cats as pets know how smart they can be. Even though dogs and cats can't speak our language, they're fast learners at anything they think is important to themselves—or sometimes to their best pals.

How intelligent are animals? On the graphic below read the animals' opinions and a human's opinion. Choose the opinion you **most** agree with. Draw an arrow pointing to it. Then, in the big dialogue balloon, write the reasons why you agree with that opinion.

The Dogs Could Teach Me

FROM Woodsong

Gary Paulsen

VISUALIZE

Pause at line 13. Underline the details in the paragraphs above that help you see and feel "serious cold." Circle the **image,** the sensory detail, that makes you *hear* the cold.

IDENTIFY

Point of view is the vantage point from which a story is told. This true story is told from the **first-person point of view,** that is, by a narrator using the pronoun *I*. The events in the story actually happened to the writer, Gary Paulsen. Circle the words in lines 14–19 that tell you the story is being told from the first-person point of view.

INFER

Pause at line 20 and tell what you think might have happened to cause the narrator to stop trapping?

_____

_____

_____

_____

_____

_____

_____

WORDS TO OWN
mystified (mis′tə·fīd′) *v.* used as *adj.:* puzzled.
alleviate (ə·lē′vē·āt′) *v.:* relieve; reduce.
contention (kən·ten′shən) *n.:* conflict; struggle.

Cold can be very strange. Not the cold felt running from the house to the bus or the car to the store, not the chill in the air on a fall morning, but deep cold.

Serious cold.

Forty, fifty, even sixty below zero—actual temperature, not wind chill—seems to change everything. Steel becomes brittle and breaks, shatters; breath taken straight into the throat will freeze the lining and burst blood vessels; eyes exposed too long will freeze; fingers and toes freeze, turn black, and break off.
10 These are all known, normal parts of intense cold.

But it changes beauty as well. Things are steeped in a new clarity, a clear focus. Sound seems to ring and the very air seems to be filled with diamonds when ice crystals form.

On a river in Alaska, while training, I once saw a place where a whirlpool had frozen into a cone, open at the bottom, like a beautiful trap waiting to suck the whole team down. When I stopped to look at it, with the water roaring through at the bottom, the dogs became nervous and stared down into the center as if mystified and were very glad when we moved on.
20 After a time I stopped trapping. That change—as with many changes—occurred because of the dogs. As mentioned, I had hunted when I was young, trapping and killing many animals. I never thought it wrong until the dogs came. And then it was a simple thing, almost a silly thing, that caused the change.

Columbia had a sense of humor and I saw it.

In the summer the dogs live in the kennel area, each dog with his own house, on a chain that allows him to move in a circle. They can run only with the wheeled carts on cool nights, and sometimes they get bored being tied up. To alleviate the
30 boredom, we give the dogs large beef bones to chew and play with. They get a new bone every other day or so. These bones are the center of much contention—we call them Bone Wars. Sometimes dogs clear across the kennel will hold their bones up in the air, look at each other, raise their hair, and start growling at each other, posturing and bragging about their bones.

But not Columbia.

Usually Columbia just chewed on his bone until the meat was gone. Then he buried it and waited for the next bone. I never saw him fight or get involved in Bone Wars and I always thought him a simple—perhaps a better word would be primitive—dog, basic and very wolf-like, until one day when I was sitting in the kennel.

I had a notebook and I was sitting on the side of Cookie's roof, writing—the dogs are good company for working—when I happened to notice Columbia doing something strange.

He was sitting quietly on the outside edge of his circle, at the maximum length of his chain. With one paw he was pushing his bone—which still had a small bit of meat on it— out and away from him, toward the next circle.

Next to Columbia was a dog named Olaf. While Columbia was relatively passive, Olaf was very aggressive. Olaf always wanted to fight and he spent much time arguing over bones, females, the weather—anything and everything that caught his fancy. He was much scarred from fighting, with notched ears and lines on his muzzle, but he was a very good dog—strong and honest—and we liked him.

Being next to Columbia, Olaf had tried many times to get him to argue or bluster, but Columbia always ignored him.

Until this morning.

Carefully, slowly, Columbia pushed the bone toward Olaf's circle.

And of all the things that Olaf was—tough, strong, honest— he wasn't smart. As they say, some are smarter than others, and some are still not so smart, and then there was Olaf. It wouldn't be fair to call Olaf dumb—dogs don't measure those things like people—but even in the dog world he would not be known as a whip. Kind of a big bully who was also a bit of a doofus.

When he saw Columbia pushing the bone toward him, he began to reach for it. Straining against his chain, turning and trying to get farther and farther, he reached as far as he could

EVALUATE

In lines 37–42, the narrator says that he had thought that Columbia was more simple or primitive than the other dogs because Columbia went his own way and didn't fight or get involved in the Bone Wars. Based on your **prior experience** with animals, do you agree with this conclusion? Why or why not?

_____

_____

_____

PREDICT

Pause at line 59. What do you think is going to happen between Columbia and Olaf?

_____

_____

INFER

Underline the reason that the narrator says, "It wouldn't be fair to call Olaf dumb" (lines 64–65). What does this reason tell you about the narrator's **perspective** on dogs, that is, the way he understands or judges them, at this point in his story?

_____

_____

INFER

Why is Columbia keeping the bone out of Olaf's reach?

_____

_____

_____

RETELL

Pause at line 83. **Retell** what happens between Columbia and Olaf.

_____

_____

_____

_____

_____

_____

_____

INTERPRET

Explain why the narrator decides that it's wrong to trap and kill animals.

_____

_____

_____

_____

WORDS TO OWN
exaltation (eg′zôl·tā′shən)
n.: great joy.

with the middle toe on his right front foot, the claw going out as far as possible.

But not quite far enough. Columbia had measured it to the millimeter. He slowly pushed the bone until it was so close that Olaf's claw—with Olaf straining so hard his eyes bulged—just barely touched it.

Columbia sat back and watched Olaf straining and pushing and fighting, and when this had gone on for a long time—many
80 minutes—and Olaf was still straining for all he was worth, Columbia leaned back and laughed.

"Heh, heh, heh . . ."

Then Columbia walked away.

And I could not kill or trap any longer.

It happened almost that fast. I had seen dogs with compassion for each other and their young and with anger and joy and hate and love, but this humor went into me more than the other things.

It was so complicated.

90 To make the joke up in his mind, the joke with the bone and the bully, and then set out to do it, carefully and quietly, to do it, then laugh and walk away—all of it was so complicated, so complex, that it triggered a chain reaction in my mind.

If Columbia could do that, I thought, if a dog could do that, then a wolf could do that. If a wolf could do that, then a deer could do that. If a deer could do that, then a beaver, and a squirrel, and a bird, and, and, and . . .

And I quit trapping then.

It was wrong for me to kill.

100 But I had this problem. I had gone over some kind of line with the dogs, gone back into some primitive state of <u>exaltation</u> that I wanted to study. I wanted to run them and learn from them. But it seemed to be wasteful (the word *immature* also comes to mind) to just run them. I thought I had to have a trap line to justify running the dogs, so I kept the line.

But I did not trap. I ran the country and camped and learned from the dogs and studied where I would have trapped

if I were going to trap. I took many imaginary beaver and muskrat but I did no more sets and killed no more animals. I will not kill anymore.

Yet the line existed. Somehow in my mind—and until writing this I have never told another person about this—the line still existed and when I had "trapped" in one area, I would extend the line to "trap" in another, as is proper when you actually trap. Somehow the phony trapping gave me a purpose for running the dogs and would until I began to train them for the Iditarod, a dog-sled race across Alaska, which I had read about in *Alaska* magazine.

But it was on one of these "trapping" runs that I got my third lesson,[1] or awakening.

There was a point where an old logging trail went through a small, sharp-sided gully—a tiny canyon. The trail came down one wall of the gully—a drop of fifty or so feet—then scooted across a frozen stream and up the other side. It might have been a game trail that was slightly widened or an old foot trail that had not caved in. Whatever it was, I came onto it in the middle of January. The dogs were very excited. New trails always get them tuned up and they were fairly smoking as we came to the edge of the gully.

I did not know it was there and had been letting them run, not riding the sled brake to slow them, and we virtually shot off the edge.

The dogs stayed on the trail, but I immediately lost all control and went flying out into space with the sled. As I did, I kicked sideways, caught my knee on a sharp snag, and felt the wood enter under the kneecap and tear it loose.

I may have screamed then.

The dogs ran out on the ice of the stream but I fell onto it. As these things often seem to happen, the disaster snowballed.

The trail crossed the stream directly at the top of a small frozen waterfall with about a twenty-foot drop. Later I saw the

INFER

What do you think the narrator means by "phony trapping" (line 115)?

_____

_____

_____

_____

VISUALIZE

Use the space below to draw a picture of the trail described in lines 121–129. Draw and label the *gully*, the *frozen stream* at the bottom of it, and the *trail* going down and across the stream, and up to the other side of the gully.

Sketch of Trail

---

1. **my third lesson:** The first lesson is described in the two previous chapters of *Woodsong*.

INTERPRET

Why do you think the narrator saw nothing at the time of his accident (line 144)?

_____

_____

_____

_____

_____

_____

PREDICT

What do you predict will happen to the narrator? On what do you base your prediction?

_____

_____

IDENTIFY

Underline the detail that tells you what dog teams usually do when the person driving the sled falls off (lines 165–167).

_____

_____

_____

WORDS TO OWN

chagrin (shə·grin′) *n.:* embarrassment and annoyance.

beauty of it, the falling lobes[2] of blue ice that had grown as the water froze and refroze, layering on itself. . . .

But at the time I saw nothing. I hit the ice of the stream bed like dropped meat, bounced once, then slithered over the edge of the waterfall and dropped another twenty feet onto the frozen pond below, landing on the torn and separated kneecap.

I have been injured several times running dogs—cracked ribs, a broken left leg, a broken left wrist, various parts frozen
150 or cut or bitten while trying to stop fights—but nothing ever felt like landing on that knee.

I don't think I passed out so much as my brain simply exploded.

Again, I'm relatively certain I must have screamed or grunted, and then I wasn't aware of much for two, perhaps three minutes as I squirmed around trying to regain some part of my mind.

When things settled down to something I could control, I opened my eyes and saw that my snow pants and the jeans
160 beneath were ripped in a jagged line for about a foot. Blood was welling out of the tear, soaking the cloth and the ice underneath the wound.

Shock and pain came in waves and I had to close my eyes several times. All of this was in minutes that seemed like hours, and I realized that I was in serious trouble. Contrary to popular belief, dog teams generally do not stop and wait for a musher[3] who falls off. They keep going, often for many miles.

Lying there on the ice, I knew I could not walk. I didn't think I could stand without some kind of crutch, but I knew I
170 couldn't walk. I was a good twenty miles from home, at least eight or nine miles from any kind of farm or dwelling.

It may as well have been ten thousand miles.

There was some self-pity creeping in, and not a little <u>chagrin</u> at being stupid enough to just let them run when I didn't know the country. I was trying to skootch myself up to the bank of

---

2. **lobes:** rounded pieces that jut out.
3. **musher** (mush′ər): person who travels over snow by dog sled.

the gully to get into a more comfortable position when I heard a sound over my head.

I looked up, and there was Obeah looking over the top of the waterfall, down at me.

180 I couldn't at first believe it.

He whined a couple of times, moved back and forth as if he might be going to drag the team over the edge, then disappeared from view. I heard some more whining and growling, then a scrabbling sound, and was amazed to see that he had taken the team back up the side of the gully and dragged them past the waterfall to get on the gully wall just over me.

They were in a horrible tangle, but he dragged them along the top until he was well below the waterfall, where he

190 scrambled down the bank with the team almost literally falling on him. They dragged the sled up the frozen stream bed to where I was lying.

On the scramble down the bank Obeah had taken them through a thick stand of cockleburs. Great clumps of burrs wadded between their ears and down their backs.

He pulled them up to me, concern in his eyes and making a soft whine, and I reached into his ruff and pulled his head down and hugged him and was never so happy to see anybody probably in my life. Then I felt something and looked down to

200 see one of the other dogs—named Duberry—licking the wound in my leg.

She was licking not with the excitement that prey blood would cause but with the gentle licking that she would use when cleaning a pup, a wound lick.

I brushed her head away, fearing infection, but she persisted. After a moment I lay back and let her clean it, still holding on to Obeah's ruff, holding on to a friend.

And later I dragged myself around and untangled them and unloaded part of the sled and crawled in and tied my leg down.

210 We made it home that way, with me sitting in the sled; and later, when my leg was sewed up and healing and I was sitting in my cabin with the leg propped up on pillows by the wood

INFER

How have the narrator's experiences with dogs changed his perspective on them? What does the narrator believe he can learn from dogs?

_____

_____

_____

EVALUATE

Do you agree with the narrator's idea that dogs have a special knowledge that they can teach humans? Tell why or why not. What other animals have special knowledge that they can teach?

_____

_____

_____

_____

_____

_____

_____

_____

_____

_____

stove; later, when all the pain was gone and I had all the time I needed to think of it . . . later I thought of the dogs.

How they came back to help me, perhaps to save me. I knew that somewhere in the dogs, in their humor and the way they thought, they had great, old knowledge; they had something we had lost.

And the dogs could teach me.

Narrator's Reaction Chart

"The Dogs Could Teach Me" is told from the **first-person point of view.** As Gary Paulsen tells his story, he reveals his innermost reactions to the events that occur.

After you read "The Dogs Could Teach Me," fill in the event column with major events from the story. Then, fill in the second column with Paulsen's reactions—his inner thoughts and feelings.

Event	Narrator's Reaction

Vocabulary and Comprehension

A. Complete each sentence with a word from the Word Bank.

Word Bank
mystified
alleviate
contention
exaltation
chagrin

1. At first, Gary Paulsen was _____ by Columbia's unusual behavior.

2. The beauty of the natural world makes many people feel a sense of _____ .

3. To reduce or _____ the pain caused by cold temperatures, dogs huddle together.

4. The phrase "a bone of _____" means a disagreement about a particular subject.

5. If you make a foolish mistake, you will probably feel _____ and embarrassment.

B. Show your understanding of words in the Word Bank by answering the following questions.

1. What might cause <u>contention</u> between a person and a dog?

_____

_____

2. How would you <u>alleviate</u> someone's fear of dogs?

_____

_____

3. How would a dog show <u>chagrin</u>?

_____

_____

Vocabulary and Comprehension

4. How would *you* show <u>chagrin</u>?

_____

_____

5. How would a dog show <u>exaltation</u>?

_____

_____

6. How would *you* show <u>exaltation</u>?

_____

_____

7. What things have <u>mystified</u> you recently?

_____

_____

C. Choose two words from the Word Bank. Use each word in a sentence.

1. _____

_____

2. _____

_____

D. Answer each question below.

1. What human personality traits did Paulsen see in the dogs?

_____

2. Explain what these traits "teach" the author.

_____

The Diary of Anne Frank, Act One, Scenes 1 and 2

Make the Connection

Keeping Memories

"I hope I shall be able to confide in you completely, as I have never been able to do in anyone before, and I hope that you will be a great support and comfort to me."

That's the first sentence in the diary that thirteen-year-old Anne Frank wrote while she and her family were hiding from the Nazis during World War II. Writing in a diary can be, as it was for Anne Frank, like talking to a best friend. Keeping a record of what happens and our feelings about it helps us understand ourselves. But perhaps the most important reason for keeping a diary is that it serves as a time capsule for our memories.

Here's an exercise that will help you see how well you remember your past. Try to recall three different days that seemed important to you at the time. Fill in as many details as you can about important events in your life on a day from 1) last week, 2) last month, and 3) last year. Ask yourself the questions *who? what? when? where? why?* and *how?* to help you recall the events. Include any thoughts and feelings you can remember as well.

Last Week	Last Month	Last Year

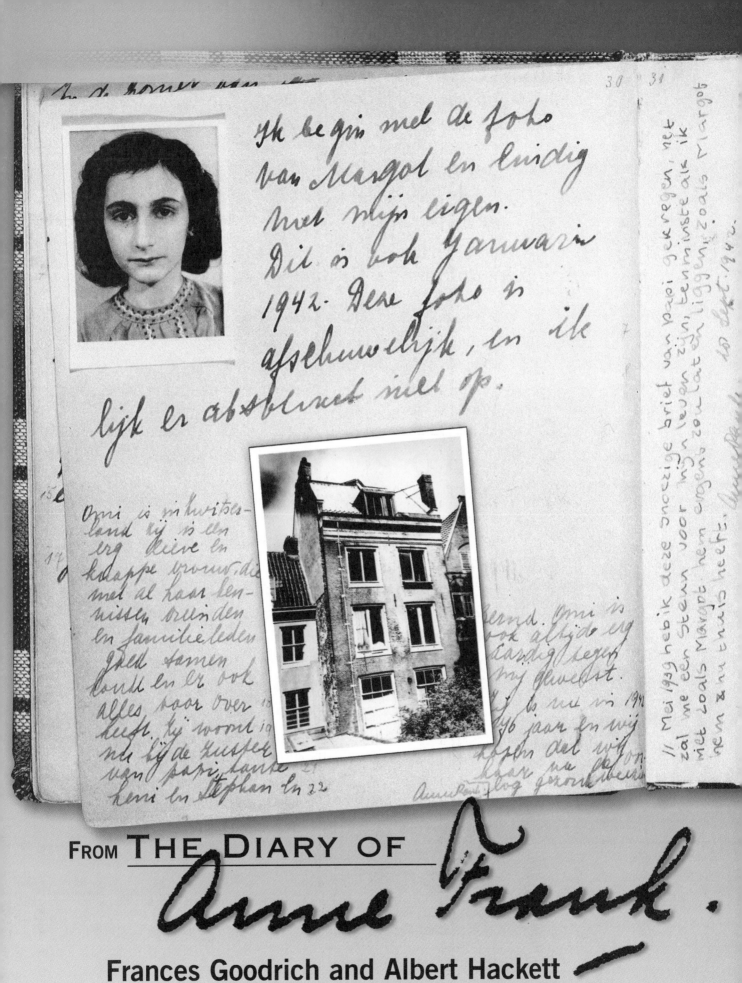

FROM THE DIARY OF

Anne Frank.

Frances Goodrich and Albert Hackett

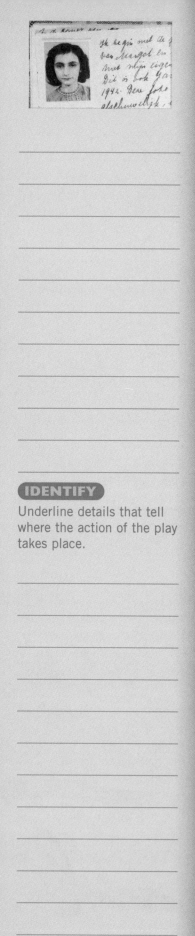

Characters

Occupants of the Secret Annex:

Anne Frank

Margot Frank, her older sister

Mr. Frank, their father

Mrs. Frank, their mother

Peter Van Daan

Mr. Van Daan, his father

Mrs. Van Daan, his mother

Mr. Dussel, a dentist

Workers in Mr. Frank's Business:

Miep Gies,[1] a young Dutchwoman

Mr. Kraler,[2] a Dutchman

Setting: Amsterdam, the Netherlands, July 1942 to August 1944; November 1945.

Act One

■ SCENE 1

The scene remains the same throughout the play. It is the top floor of a warehouse and office building in Amsterdam, Holland. The sharply peaked roof of the building is outlined against a sea of other rooftops stretching away into the distance. Nearby is the belfry of a church tower, the Westertoren, whose carillon[3] rings out the hours. Occasionally faint sounds float up from below: the voices of children playing in the street, the tramp of marching feet, a boat whistle from the canal.[4]

10   *The three rooms of the top floor and a small attic space above are exposed to our view. The largest of the rooms is in the center, with two small rooms, slightly raised, on either side. On the right is a bathroom, out of sight. A narrow, steep flight of stairs at the back leads up to the attic. The rooms are sparsely furnished, with a few chairs, cots, a table or two. The windows*

---

1. **Miep Gies** (mēp khēs).
2. **Kraler** (krä′lər).
3. **carillon** (kar′ə·län′): set of bells each of which produces a single tone.
4. **canal:** artificial waterway. Amsterdam, which was built on soggy ground, has more than one hundred canals, built to help drain the land. The canals are used like streets.

IDENTIFY

Underline details that tell where the action of the play takes place.

are painted over or covered with makeshift blackout curtains. In the main room there is a sink, a gas ring for cooking, and a wood-burning stove for warmth.

The room on the left is hardly more than a closet. There is a skylight in the sloping ceiling. Directly under this room is a
20 small, steep stairwell, with steps leading down to a door. This is the only entrance from the building below. When the door is opened, we see that it has been concealed on the outer side by a bookcase attached to it.

The curtain rises on an empty stage. It is late afternoon, November 1945.

The rooms are dusty, the curtains in rags. Chairs and tables are overturned.

The door at the foot of the small stairwell swings open. Mr. Frank comes up the steps into view. He is a gentle, cultured
30 European in his middle years. There is still a trace of a German accent in his speech.

He stands looking slowly around, making a supreme effort at self-control. He is weak, ill. His clothes are threadbare.

After a second he drops his rucksack on the couch and moves slowly about. He opens the door to one of the smaller rooms and then abruptly closes it again, turning away. He goes to the window at the back, looking off at the Westertoren as its carillon strikes the hour of six; then he moves restlessly on.

From the street below we hear the sound of a barrel organ
40 and children's voices at play. There is a many-colored scarf hanging from a nail. Mr. Frank takes it, putting it around his neck. As he starts back for his rucksack, his eye is caught by something lying on the floor. It is a woman's white glove. He holds it in his hand and suddenly all of his self-control is gone. He breaks down crying.

We hear footsteps on the stairs. Miep Gies comes up, looking for Mr. Frank. Miep is a Dutchwoman of about twenty-two. She wears a coat and hat, ready to go home. She is pregnant. Her attitude toward Mr. Frank is protective, compassionate.

VISUALIZE

Re-read lines 9–23. Underline words and phrases such as *above* and *in the center* that tell you where things are located. Then, in the space below, sketch the **setting.** Show the location and relative size of the three rooms, bathroom, attic, steps, and door.

Setting Sketch

INTERPRET

Go back to line 28, when Mr. Frank enters the room. Underline three details in the following paragraphs that show that Mr. Frank tries to control his feelings before he breaks down crying (line 45).

INFER

Circle the phrase that Mr. Frank uses to describe himself in line 67. What seems to have happened to him since leaving Amsterdam?

INFER

What **inference** can you make about why Mr. Frank might want the papers burned (line 81)?

50   **Miep.** Are you all right, Mr. Frank?

Mr. Frank (*quickly controlling himself*). Yes, Miep, yes.

Miep. Everyone in the office has gone home. . . . It's after six. (*Then, pleading*) Don't stay up here, Mr. Frank. What's the use of torturing yourself like this?

Mr. Frank. I've come to say goodbye . . . I'm leaving here, Miep.

Miep. What do you mean? Where are you going? Where?

Mr. Frank. I don't know yet. I haven't decided.

Miep. Mr. Frank, you can't leave here! This is your home!
60   Amsterdam is your home. Your business is here, waiting for you. . . . You're needed here. . . . Now that the war is over, there are things that . . .

Mr. Frank. I can't stay in Amsterdam, Miep. It has too many memories for me. Everywhere, there's something . . . the house we lived in . . . the school . . . that street organ playing out there . . . I'm not the person you used to know, Miep. I'm a bitter old man. (*Breaking off*) Forgive me. I shouldn't speak to you like this . . . after all that you did for us . . . the suffering . . .

70   **Miep.** No. No. It wasn't suffering. You can't say we suffered. (*As she speaks, she straightens a chair which is overturned.*)

Mr. Frank. I know what you went through, you and Mr. Kraler. I'll remember it as long as I live. (*He gives one last look around.*) Come, Miep. (*He starts for the steps, then remembers his rucksack, going back to get it.*)

Miep (*hurrying up to a cupboard*). Mr. Frank, did you see? There are some of your papers here. (*She brings a bundle of papers to him.*) We found them in a heap of rubbish on the
80   floor after . . . after you left.

Mr. Frank. Burn them. (*He opens his rucksack to put the glove in it.*)

Miep. But, Mr. Frank, there are letters, notes . . .

Mr. Frank. Burn them. All of them.

Miep. Burn this? (*She hands him a paperbound notebook.*)

Mr. Frank (*quietly*). Anne's diary. (*He opens the diary and begins to read.*) "Monday, the sixth of July, nineteen forty-two." (*To* MIEP) Nineteen forty-two. Is it possible, Miep? . . . Only three years ago. (*As he continues his reading, he sits down on*
90 *the couch.*) "Dear Diary, since you and I are going to be great friends, I will start by telling you about myself. My name is Anne Frank. I am thirteen years old. I was born in Germany the twelfth of June, nineteen twenty-nine. As my family is Jewish, we emigrated to Holland when Hitler came to power."

[*As* MR. FRANK *reads on, another voice joins his, as if coming from the air. It is* ANNE's *voice.*]

Mr. Frank and Anne's Voice. "My father started a business, importing spice and herbs. Things went well for us until nineteen forty. Then the war came, and the Dutch capitulation,
100 followed by the arrival of the Germans. Then things got very bad for the Jews."

[MR. FRANK's *voice dies out.* ANNE's *voice continues alone. The lights dim slowly to darkness. The curtain falls on the scene.*]

Anne's Voice. You could not do this and you could not do that. They forced Father out of his business. We had to wear yellow stars.[5] I had to turn in my bike. I couldn't go to a Dutch school anymore. I couldn't go to the movies or ride in an automobile or even on a streetcar, and a million other things. But somehow we children still managed to have fun. Yesterday
110 Father told me we were going into hiding. Where, he wouldn't say. At five o'clock this morning Mother woke me and told me to hurry and get dressed. I was to put on as many clothes as I could. It would look too suspicious if we walked along carrying suitcases. It wasn't until we were on our way that I learned where we were going. Our hiding place was to be upstairs in the building where Father used to have his business. Three other people were coming in with us . . . the Van Daans and their son Peter . . . Father knew the Van Daans but we had never met them. . . .

---

5. **yellow stars:** The Nazis ordered all Jews to sew a large Star of David (a six-pointed star) on their outer clothing so that they could be easily recognized as Jews.

IDENTIFY

Most of this play is in the form of a **flashback,** an interruption in the present action of the plot to show events that happened at an earlier time. The play starts in 1945, after the end of World War II. Then, as Mr. Frank looks at Anne's diary, the scene flashes back to 1942, when Anne was writing in her diary. Circle the paragraph where the voices of Mr. Frank and Anne blur together. Why do you think the writers have father and daughter speaking together at this point?

_____

_____

_____

_____

IDENTIFY

Underline three details that tell you how life changed for Anne after the Dutch surrendered and the Germans arrived in the Netherlands.

INFER

Why does the Frank family go into hiding?

_____

_____

_____

120   [*During the last lines the curtain rises on the scene. The lights dim on.* ANNE's *voice fades out.*]

■ **SCENE 2**

It is early morning, July 1942. The rooms are bare, as before, but they are now clean and orderly.

MR. VAN DAAN, *a tall, portly man in his late forties, is in the main room, pacing up and down, nervously smoking a cigarette. His clothes and overcoat are expensive and well cut.*

MRS. VAN DAAN *sits on the couch, clutching her possessions: a hatbox, bags, etc. She is a pretty woman in her early forties. She wears a fur coat over her other clothes.*

130   PETER VAN DAAN *is standing at the window of the room on the right, looking down at the street below. He is a shy, awkward boy of sixteen. He wears a cap, a raincoat, and long Dutch trousers, like plus fours.*[6] *At his feet is a black case, a carrier for his cat.*

The yellow Star of David is <u>conspicuous</u> on all of their clothes.

Mrs. Van Daan (*rising, nervous, excited*). Something's happened to them! I know it!

Mr. Van Daan. Now, Kerli!

Mrs. Van Daan. Mr. Frank said they'd be here at seven
140 o'clock. He said . . .

Mr. Van Daan. They have two miles to walk. You can't expect . . .

Mrs. Van Daan. They've been picked up. That's what's happened. They've been taken . . .

[MR. VAN DAAN *indicates that he hears someone coming.*]

Mr. Van Daan. You see?

[PETER *takes up his carrier and his school bag, etc., and goes into the main room as* MR. FRANK *comes up the stairwell from below.* MR. FRANK *looks much younger now. His movements are*
150 *brisk, his manner confident. He wears an overcoat and carries his hat and a small cardboard box. He crosses to the* VAN DAANS, *shaking hands with each of them.*]

---

6. plus fours: baggy trousers that end in cuffs just below the knees.

Mr. Frank. Mrs. Van Daan, Mr. Van Daan, Peter. (*Then, in explanation of their lateness*) There were too many of the Green Police[7] on the streets . . . we had to take the long way around.

[*Up the steps come* MARGOT FRANK, MRS. FRANK, MIEP (*not pregnant now*), *and* MR. KRALER. *All of them carry bags, packages, and so forth. The Star of David is conspicuous on all of the* FRANKS' *clothing.* MARGOT *is eighteen, beautiful, quiet, shy.*
160 MRS. FRANK *is a young mother, gently bred, reserved. She, like* MR. FRANK, *has a slight German accent.* MR. KRALER *is a Dutchman, dependable, kindly.*

As MR. KRALER *and* MIEP *go upstage to put down their parcels,* MRS. FRANK *turns back to call* ANNE.]

Mrs. Frank. Anne?

[ANNE *comes running up the stairs. She is thirteen, quick in her movements, interested in everything, mercurial[8] in her emotions. She wears a cape and long wool socks and carries a school bag.*]

170 **Mr. Frank** (*introducing them*). My wife, Edith. Mr. and Mrs. Van Daan (*Mrs. Frank hurries over, shaking hands with them.*) . . . their son, Peter . . . my daughters, Margot and Anne.

[ANNE *gives a polite little curtsy as she shakes* MR. VAN DAAN'*s hand. Then she immediately starts off on a tour of investigation of her new home, going upstairs to the attic room.*

MIEP *and* MR. KRALER *are putting the various things they have brought on the shelves.*]

Mr. Kraler. I'm sorry there is still so much confusion.

180 **Mr. Frank.** Please. Don't think of it. After all, we'll have plenty of leisure to arrange everything ourselves.

Miep (*to* MRS. FRANK). We put the stores of food you sent in here. Your drugs are here . . . soap, linen here.

Mrs. Frank. Thank you, Miep.

Miep. I made up the beds . . . the way Mr. Frank and Mr. Kraler said. (*She starts out.*) Forgive me. I have to hurry.

---

7. **Green Police:** Nazi police, who wore green uniforms.
8. **mercurial** (mər·kyoor′ē·əl): changeable.

INFER

Re-read lines 166–169. Notice how the description of Anne helps to reveal her **character.** List three adjectives that describe your first impression of her.

INFER

Miep and Mr. Kraler are helping the Franks settle in. How do Miep and Mr. Kraler know the Franks? (Look back at the list of characters on page 94 if you've forgotten.)

INFER

Re-read lines 202–204. What **inference** can you make about how Mr. Kraler feels about the German occupation of the Netherlands? What do you think might happen to him and to Miep if the Germans find out that they're hiding two Jewish families?

IDENTIFY

Underline the detail in lines 209–210 that indicate that the workmen could be a danger to the people hidden upstairs. Who used to own the business in the building where the Franks and the Van Daans are hiding?

I've got to go to the other side of town to get some ration books[9] for you.

Mrs. Van Daan. Ration books? If they see our names on
190 ration books, they'll know we're here.

Mr. Kraler. There isn't anything . . .

Miep. Don't worry. Your names won't be on them. (*As she hurries out*) I'll be up later.

Mr. Frank. Thank you, Miep.

Mrs. Frank (*to* MR. KRALER). It's illegal, then, the ration books? We've never done anything illegal.

Mr. Frank. We won't be living here exactly according to regulations.

[*As* MR. KRALER *reassures* MRS. FRANK, *he takes various small*
200 *things, such as matches and soap, from his pockets, handing them to her.*]

Mr. Kraler. This isn't the black market,[10] Mrs. Frank. This is what we call the white market . . . helping all of the hundreds and hundreds who are hiding out in Amsterdam.

[*The carillon is heard playing the quarter-hour before eight.* MR. KRALER *looks at his watch.* ANNE *stops at the window as she comes down the stairs.*]

Anne. It's the Westertoren!

Mr. Kraler. I must go. I must be out of here and downstairs
210 in the office before the workmen get here. (*He starts for the stairs leading out.*) Miep or I, or both of us, will be up each day to bring you food and news and find out what your needs are. Tomorrow I'll get you a better bolt for the door at the foot of the stairs. It needs a bolt that you can throw yourself and open only at our signal. (*To* MR. FRANK) Oh . . . You'll tell them about the noise?

Mr. Frank. I'll tell them.

Mr. Kraler. Goodbye, then, for the moment. I'll come up again, after the workmen leave.

---

9. **ration books:** books of stamps or coupons issued by the government during wartime. People could purchase scarce items such as food, clothing, and gasoline only with these coupons.
10. **black market:** place or system for buying and selling goods illegally, without ration stamps.

220   **Mr. Frank.** Goodbye, Mr. Kraler.

Mrs. Frank (*shaking his hand*). How can we thank you?

[*The others murmur their goodbyes.*]

Mr. Kraler. I never thought I'd live to see the day when a man like Mr. Frank would have to go into hiding. When you think—

[*He breaks off, going out.* MR. FRANK *follows him down the steps, bolting the door after him. In the interval before he returns,* PETER *goes over to* MARGOT, *shaking hands with her. As* MR. FRANK *comes back up the steps,* MRS. FRANK *questions him*
230 *anxiously.*]

Mrs. Frank. What did he mean, about the noise?

Mr. Frank. First let us take off some of these clothes.

[*They all start to take off garment after garment. On each of their coats, sweaters, blouses, suits, dresses is another yellow Star of David.* MR. *and* MRS. FRANK *are underdressed quite simply. The others wear several things: sweaters, extra dresses, bathrobes, aprons, nightgowns, etc.*]

Mr. Van Daan. It's a wonder we weren't arrested, walking along the streets . . . Petronella with a fur coat in July . . .
240 and that cat of Peter's crying all the way.

Anne (*as she is removing a pair of panties*). A cat?

Mrs. Frank (*shocked*). Anne, please!

Anne. It's all right. I've got on three more.

[*She pulls off two more. Finally, as they have all removed their surplus clothes, they look to* MR. FRANK, *waiting for him to speak.*]

Mr. Frank. Now. About the noise. While the men are in the building below, we must have complete quiet. Every sound can be heard down there, not only in the workrooms but in the
250 offices too. The men come at about eight-thirty and leave at about five-thirty. So, to be perfectly safe, from eight in the morning until six in the evening we must move only when it is necessary, and then in stockinged feet. We must not speak above a whisper. We must not run any water. We cannot use

PREDICT

Stop at line 225. How do you think the Franks and the Van Daans will get along in the cramped space where they must live? Make three **predictions** based on what you know about the characters so far.

INFER

Why are the characters wearing so many layers of clothing?

IDENTIFY

Circle the details in the stage directions that build **suspense** about what might happen next.

_____

_____

_____

_____

_____

INTERPRET

Which of the characters in the group has the leadership role? How do you know?

_____

_____

_____

_____

_____

_____

_____

_____

_____

_____

_____

_____

the sink or even, forgive me, the w.c.[11] The pipes go down through the workrooms. It would be heard. No trash . . . (MR. FRANK *stops abruptly as he hears the sound of marching feet from the street below. Everyone is motionless, paralyzed with fear.* MR. FRANK *goes quietly into the room on the right to look*
260 *down out of the window.* ANNE *runs after him, peering out with him. The tramping feet pass without stopping. The tension is relieved.* MR. FRANK, *followed by Anne, returns to the main room and resumes his instructions to the group.*) . . . No trash must ever be thrown out which might reveal that someone is living up here . . . not even a potato paring. We must burn everything in the stove at night. This is the way we must live until it is over, if we are to survive.

[*There is silence for a second.*]

Mrs. Frank. Until it is over.

270 **Mr. Frank** (*reassuringly*). After six we can move about . . . we can talk and laugh and have our supper and read and play games . . . just as we would at home. (*He looks at his watch.*) And now I think it would be wise if we all went to our rooms, and were settled before eight o'clock. Mrs. Van Daan, you and your husband will be upstairs. I regret that there's no place up there for Peter. But he will be here, near us. This will be our common room, where we'll meet to talk and eat and read, like one family.

Mr. Van Daan. And where do you and Mrs. Frank sleep?

280 **Mr. Frank.** This room is also our bedroom.

Mrs. Van Daan. That isn't right. We'll sleep here and you take the room upstairs.

Mr. Van Daan. It's your place.

Mr. Frank. Please. I've thought this out for weeks. It's the best arrangement. The only arrangement.

Mrs. Van Daan (*to* MR. FRANK). Never, never can we thank you. (*Then, to* MRS. FRANK) I don't know what would have happened to us, if it hadn't been for Mr. Frank.

---

11. **w. c.:** short for "water closet," or toilet.

Mr. Frank. You don't know how your husband helped me when I came to this country . . . knowing no one . . . not able to speak the language. I can never repay him for that. (*Going to* MR. VAN DAAN) May I help you with your things?

Mr. Van Daan. No. No. (*To* MRS. VAN DAAN) Come along, liefje.[12]

Mrs. Van Daan. You'll be all right, Peter? You're not afraid?

Peter (*embarrassed*). Please, Mother.

[*They start up the stairs to the attic room above.* MR. FRANK *turns to* MRS. FRANK.]

Mr. Frank. You too must have some rest, Edith. You didn't close your eyes last night. Nor you, Margot.

Anne. I slept, Father. Wasn't that funny? I knew it was the last night in my own bed, and yet I slept soundly.

Mr. Frank. I'm glad, Anne. Now you'll be able to help me straighten things in here. (*To* MRS. FRANK *and* MARGOT) Come with me. . . . You and Margot rest in this room for the time being. (*He picks up their clothes, starting for the room on the right.*)

Mrs. Frank. You're sure . . . ? I could help . . . And Anne hasn't had her milk . . .

Mr. Frank. I'll give it to her. (*To* ANNE *and* PETER) Anne, Peter . . . it's best that you take off your shoes now, before you forget. (*He leads the way to the room, followed by* MARGOT.)

Mrs. Frank. You're sure you're not tired, Anne?

Anne. I feel fine. I'm going to help Father.

Mrs. Frank. Peter, I'm glad you are to be with us.

Peter. Yes, Mrs. Frank.

[MRS. FRANK *goes to join* MR. FRANK *and* MARGOT.

During the following scene MR. FRANK *helps* MARGOT *and* MRS. FRANK *to hang up their clothes. Then he persuades them both to lie down and rest. The* VAN DAANS, *in their room above, settle themselves. In the main room* ANNE *and* PETER *remove their shoes.* PETER *takes his cat out of the carrier.*]

Anne. What's your cat's name?

---

12. **liefje** (lēf′hyə): Dutch for "little dear one."

IDENTIFY

Circle the details in lines 289–292 that tell why the Franks are sharing their hiding place with the Van Daans.

INTERPRET

Re-read lines 301–302. Do you think Anne slept well because she's too young to understand the danger she's in? What might this detail reveal about her **character**?

Re-read Anne and Peter's conversation in lines 323–349. What does this **dialogue** tell you about how Anne deals with people?

_____

_____

_____

_____

_____

_____

_____

_____

_____

_____

Pause at line 353. List two ways in which Peter's personality is different from Anne's.

_____

_____

unabashed (un'ə·basht') *adj.:* unembarrassed; unashamed.

Peter. Mouschi.[13]

Anne. Mouschi! Mouschi! Mouschi! (*She picks up the cat, walking away with it. To* PETER) I love cats. I have one . . . a darling little cat. But they made me leave her behind. I left some food and a note for the neighbors to take care of her. . . . I'm going to miss her terribly. What is yours? A him or a her?

330   **Peter.** He's a tom. He doesn't like strangers. (*He takes the cat from her, putting it back in its carrier.*)

Anne (*unabashed*). Then I'll have to stop being a stranger, won't I? Is he fixed?

Peter (*startled*). Huh?

Anne. Did you have him fixed?

Peter. No.

Anne. Oh, you ought to have him fixed—to keep him from—you know, fighting. Where did you go to school?

Peter. Jewish Secondary.

340   **Anne.** But that's where Margot and I go! I never saw you around.

Peter. I used to see you . . . sometimes . . .

Anne. You did?

Peter. . . . in the schoolyard. You were always in the middle of a bunch of kids. (*He takes a penknife from his pocket.*)

Anne. Why didn't you ever come over?

Peter. I'm sort of a lone wolf. (*He starts to rip off his Star of David.*)

350   **Anne.** What are you doing?

Peter. Taking it off.

Anne. But you can't do that. They'll arrest you if you go out without your star.

[*He tosses his knife on the table.*]

Peter. Who's going out?

Anne. Why, of course! You're right! Of course we don't need them anymore. (*She picks up his knife and starts to take*

13. **Mouschi** (mōō·shē).

her star off.) I wonder what our friends will think when we don't show up today?

360   **Peter.** I didn't have any dates with anyone.

Anne. Oh, I did. I had a date with Jopie to go and play ping-pong at her house. Do you know Jopie de Waal?[14]

Peter. No.

Anne. Jopie's my best friend. I wonder what she'll think when she telephones and there's no answer? . . . Probably she'll go over to the house. . . . I wonder what she'll think . . . we left everything as if we'd suddenly been called away . . . breakfast dishes in the sink . . . beds not made . . . (*As she pulls off her star, the cloth underneath shows clearly the color*

370   *and form of the star.)* Look! It's still there! (PETER *goes over to the stove with his star.)* What're you going to do with yours?

Peter. Burn it.

Anne. (*She starts to throw hers in, and cannot.)* It's funny, I can't throw mine away. I don't know why.

Peter. You can't throw . . . ? Something they branded you with . . . ? That they made you wear so they could spit on you?

Anne. I know. I know. But after all, it is the Star of David, isn't it?

380   [*In the bedroom, right,* MARGOT *and* MRS. FRANK *are lying down.* MR. FRANK *starts quietly out.*]

Peter. Maybe it's different for a girl.

[MR. FRANK *comes into the main room.*]

Mr. Frank. Forgive me, Peter. Now let me see. We must find a bed for your cat. (*He goes to a cupboard.)* I'm glad you brought your cat. Anne was feeling so badly about hers. (*Getting a used small washtub*) Here we are. Will it be comfortable in that?

Peter (*gathering up his things*). Thanks.

390   **Mr. Frank** (*opening the door of the room on the left*). And here is your room. But I warn you, Peter, you can't grow

---

14. **Jopie de Waal** (yō′pē də väl′).

BUILD FLUENCY

Re-read the boxed passage aloud. Notice the punctuation marks. Be sure to read questions differently from exclamations. Wherever you see ellipses, like these . . . , pause briefly. Read these lines as if the character is thinking aloud. Try to use an appropriate tone of voice to show how each character is feeling as he or she speaks.

_____

_____

_____

_____

INFER

Why did the Nazis force Jews to wear the Star of David? What does the Star of David mean to Anne?

_____

_____

_____

_____

_____

_____

_____

_____

PREDICT

What do you think Anne and Peter's relationship will be like?

_____

_____

_____

_____

_____

_____

_____

EVALUATE

Do you think Anne's experiences in the Secret Annex will be like a summer boardinghouse? Why or why not?

_____

_____

_____

_____

IDENTIFY

What do the readers or audience know about Anne's diary that Anne does not know?

_____

_____

_____

anymore. Not an inch, or you'll have to sleep with your feet out of the skylight. Are you hungry?

Peter. No.

Mr. Frank. We have some bread and butter.

Peter. No, thank you.

Mr. Frank. You can have it for luncheon then. And tonight we will have a real supper . . . our first supper together.

Peter. Thanks. Thanks. (_He goes into his room. During the_
400 _following scene he arranges his possessions in his new room._)

Mr. Frank. That's a nice boy, Peter.

Anne. He's awfully shy, isn't he?

Mr. Frank. You'll like him, I know.

Anne. I certainly hope so, since he's the only boy I'm likely to see for months and months.

[MR. FRANK _sits down, taking off his shoes._]

Mr. Frank. Annele,[15] there's a box there. Will you open it?

[_He indicates a carton on the couch._ ANNE _brings it to the center table. In the street below, there is the sound of children_
410 _playing._]

Anne (_as she opens the carton_). You know the way I'm going to think of it here? I'm going to think of it as a boardinghouse. A very peculiar summer boardinghouse, like the one that we— (_She breaks off as she pulls out some photographs._) Father! My movie stars! I was wondering where they were! I was looking for them this morning . . . and Queen Wilhelmina![16] How wonderful!

Mr. Frank. There's something more. Go on. Look further. (_He goes over to the sink, pouring a glass of milk from a_
420 _thermos bottle._)

Anne (_pulling out a pasteboard-bound book_). A diary! (_She throws her arms around her father._) I've never had a diary. And I've always longed for one. (_She looks around the room._) Pencil, pencil, pencil, pencil. (_She starts down the stairs._) I'm going down to the office to get a pencil.

---

15. **Annele** (än′ə·lə): Yiddish for "little Anne" (like "Annie").
16. **Queen Wilhelmina** (vil′hel·mē′nä) (1880–1962): queen of the Netherlands from 1890 to 1948.

Mr. Frank. Anne! No! (*He goes after her, catching her by the arm and pulling her back.*)

Anne (*startled*). But there's no one in the building now.

Mr. Frank. It doesn't matter. I don't want you ever to go 430 beyond that door.

Anne (*sobered*). Never . . . ? Not even at nighttime, when everyone is gone? Or on Sundays? Can't I go down to listen to the radio?

Mr. Frank. Never. I am sorry, Anneke.[17] It isn't safe. No, you must never go beyond that door.

[*For the first time* ANNE *realizes what "going into hiding" means.*]

Anne. I see.

Mr. Frank. It'll be hard, I know. But always remember this, 440 Anneke. There are no walls, there are no bolts, no locks that anyone can put on your mind. Miep will bring us books. We will read history, poetry, mythology. (*He gives her the glass of milk.*) Here's your milk. (*With his arm about her, they go over to the couch, sitting down side by side.*) As a matter of fact, between us, Anne, being here has certain advantages for you. For instance, you remember the battle you had with your mother the other day on the subject of overshoes? You said you'd rather die than wear overshoes? But in the end you had to wear them? Well now, you see, for as long as we are here, 450 you will never have to wear overshoes! Isn't that good? And the coat that you inherited from Margot, you won't have to wear that anymore. And the piano! You won't have to practice on the piano. I tell you, this is going to be a fine life for you!

[ANNE's *panic is gone.* PETER *appears in the doorway of his room, with a saucer in his hand. He is carrying his cat.*]

Peter. I . . . I . . . I thought I'd better get some water for Mouschi before . . .

Mr. Frank. Of course.

[*As he starts toward the sink, the carillon begins to chime the* 460 *hour of eight. He tiptoes to the window at the back and looks*

INFER
What does Anne realize about "going into hiding" that she had not realized before?

INTERPRET
What does Mr. Frank mean in lines 440–441 when he says, "There are no walls, there are no bolts, no locks that anyone can put on your mind"?

---

17. Anneke (än'ə·kə): another affectionate nickname for Anne.

INFER

Why is it "too late" for Peter to give water to Mouschi (lines 461–462)?

_____

_____

_____

_____

_____

_____

_____

_____

_____

_____

_____

INTERPRET

Describe how Anne is adjusting to life in hiding. Base your answer on this diary entry.

_____

_____

_____

_____

down at the street below. He turns to PETER, *indicating in pantomime that it is too late.* PETER *starts back for his room. He steps on a creaking board. The three of them are frozen for a minute in fear. As* PETER *starts away again,* ANNE *tiptoes over to him and pours some of the milk from her glass into the saucer for the cat.* PETER *squats on the floor, putting the milk before the cat.* MR. FRANK *gives* ANNE *his fountain pen and then goes into the room at the right. For a second* ANNE *watches the cat; then she goes over to the center table and opens her diary.*

470   *In the room at the right,* MRS. FRANK *has sat up quickly at the sound of the carillon.* MR. FRANK *comes in and sits down beside her on the settee,[18] his arm comfortingly around her.*

Upstairs, in the attic room, MR. *and* MRS. VAN DAAN *have hung their clothes in the closet and are now seated on the iron bed.* MRS. VAN DAAN *leans back, exhausted.* MR. VAN DAAN *fans her with a newspaper.*

ANNE *starts to write in her diary. The lights dim out; the curtain falls.*

In the darkness ANNE*'s voice comes to us again, faintly at*
480 *first and then with growing strength.*]

Anne's Voice. I expect I should be describing what it feels like to go into hiding. But I really don't know yet myself. I only know it's funny never to be able to go outdoors . . . never to breathe fresh air . . . never to run and shout and jump. It's the silence in the nights that frightens me most. Every time I hear a creak in the house or a step on the street outside, I'm sure they're coming for us. The days aren't so bad. At least we know that Miep and Mr. Kraler are down there below us in the office. Our protectors, we call them. I asked Father what would
490 happen to them if the Nazis found out they were hiding us. Pim[19] said that they would suffer the same fate that we would. . . . Imagine! They know this, and yet when they come up here, they're always cheerful and gay, as if there were nothing in the world to bother them. . . . Friday, the twenty-first of

---

18. **settee** (se·tē′): small couch.
19. **Pim**: family nickname for Mr. Frank.

August, nineteen forty-two. Today I'm going to tell you our general news. Mother is unbearable. She insists on treating me like a baby, which I <u>loathe</u>. Otherwise things are going better. The weather is . . .

[*As* ANNE's *voice is fading out, the curtain rises on the scene.*]

EVALUATE

In your opinion, is Anne a realistic character? Does she speak and behave like a typical thirteen-year-old? Give reasons for your answer.

_____

_____

_____

_____

_____

_____

_____

_____

_____

_____

_____

_____

_____

_____

_____

_____

_____

WORDS TO OWN
loathe (lōth) *v.:* hate.

"What's the Difference?" Graphic

In the opening two scenes of the play, you find out that Anne's life changes drastically once she goes into hiding. On the lines provided, write details of how Anne's life was before she went into the Secret Annex. Then, in the outline of the attic below, describe how life has become different for Anne. What kinds of changes must she make?

_____

_____

_____

_____

_____

_____

_____

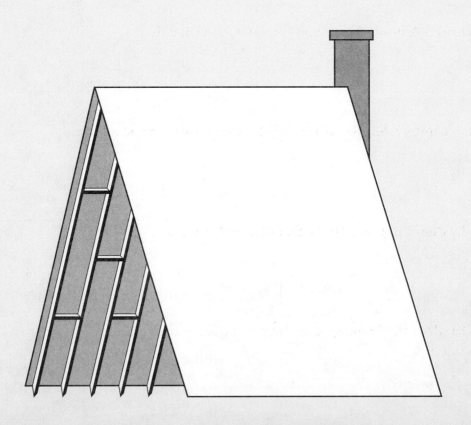

Vocabulary and Comprehension

A. Choose a word from the Word Bank to complete each sentence.

Word Bank
conspicuous
unabashed
loathe

1. Anne and her family _____ being unable to go outside.

2. The Franks tried not to be _____ while they were living in the annex.

3. While Peter is usually nervous when he's talking to Anne, she is _____ while she's speaking with him.

B. Choose two of the words from the Word Bank. Use each word in a sentence.

1. _____

2. _____

C. Answer each question below.

1. Why did Anne and her family emigrate to Holland?

_____

_____

2. Name three rules the members of the Secret Annex must follow.

_____

_____

3. Why does Peter tear off the Star of David sewn onto his clothes?

_____

_____

4. What does Mr. Frank give to Anne to make her feel better while they're in hiding?

_____

_____

A Tragedy Revealed: A Heroine's Last Days

Make the Connection

The Need to Know

The factual article you are about to read is about someone you are already familiar with: Anne Frank. You've probably read the play about her life or learned about her from her diary or from other outside reading. Since the more you know about the topic of a text, the easier it is to understand, you already have a head start in reading this account. For further help, look for **key passages** or **key statements** that reveal the **main idea** of the text.

Think for a moment about what you already know—your **prior knowledge**—about Anne Frank. Then, begin filling out the KWL chart below. In the **K** column, jot down what you **know** about Anne Frank's life. In the **W** column, write down what you **want to know** about Anne's fate after the discovery of the Secret Annex. Finally, as you read, note in the **L** column any new information you **learn** that adds to or contradicts your prior knowledge, and check off in the **W** column any of your questions that are answered in the text.

K	W	L

Background

The article, which was first published in 1958, starts where Anne Frank's diary and the play end— with the discovery of the Secret Annex and the arrest of its occupants.

Ernst Schnabel
A Tragedy Revealed:
A Heroine's Last Days

INFER

Re-read lines 13–20. Based on what you already know about Anne Frank, does this description seem accurate for her? Tell why or why not.

_____

_____

_____

_____

_____

_____

INTERPRET

Even though he has written an informational article, the writer opens by relating an experience of his own. Why do you think he opens the piece in this way?

_____

_____

_____

_____

_____

_____

_____

_____

Last year in Amsterdam I found an old reel of movie film on which Anne Frank appears. She is seen for only ten seconds and it is an accident that she is there at all.

The film was taken for a wedding in 1941, the year before Anne Frank and seven others went into hiding in their "Secret Annex." It has a flickering, Chaplinesque[1] quality, with people popping suddenly in and out of doorways, the nervous smiles and hurried waves of the departing bride and groom.

Then, for just a moment, the camera seems uncertain where
10 to look. It darts to the right, then to the left, then whisks up a wall, and into view comes a window crowded with people waving after the departing automobiles. The camera swings farther to the left, to another window. There a girl stands alone, looking out into space. It is Anne Frank.

Just as the camera is about to pass on, the child moves her head a trifle. Her face flits more into focus, her hair shimmers in the sun. At this moment she discovers the camera, discovers the photographer, discovers us watching seventeen years later, and laughs at all of us, laughs with sudden merriment and
20 surprise and embarrassment all at the same time.

I asked the projectionist to stop the film for a moment so that we could stand up to examine her face more closely. The smile stood still, just above our heads. But when I walked forward close to the screen, the smile ceased to be a smile. The face ceased to be a face, for the canvas screen was granular and the beam of light split into a multitude of tiny shadows, as if it had been scattered on a sandy plain.

Anne Frank, of course, is gone too, but her spirit has remained to stir the conscience of the world. Her remarkable
30 diary has been read in almost every language. I have seen a letter from a teenaged girl in Japan who says she thinks of Anne's Secret Annex as her second home. And the play based on the diary has been a great success wherever it is produced. German audiences, who invariably greet the final curtain of *The*

---

1. **Chaplinesque** (chap′lin·esk′): like the old silent movies starring Charlie Chaplin (1889–1977).

Diary of Anne Frank in stricken silence, have jammed the theaters in what seems almost a national act of penance.

Last year I set out to follow the fading trail of this girl who has become a legend. The trail led from Holland to Poland and back to Germany, where I visited the moss-grown site of the old
40 Bergen-Belsen concentration camp at the village of Belsen and saw the common graves shared by Anne Frank and thirty thousand others. I interviewed forty-two people who knew Anne or who survived the ordeal that killed her. Some had known her intimately in those last tragic months. In the recollections of others she appears only for a moment. But even these fragments fulfill a promise. They make explicit a truth implied in the diary. As we somehow knew she must be, Anne Frank, even in the most frightful extremity, was <u>indomitable</u>.

The known story contained in the diary is a simple one of
50 human relationships, of the poignant maturing of a perceptive girl who is thirteen when her diary begins and only fifteen when it ends. It is a story without violence, though its background is the most dreadful act of violence in the history of man, Hitler's <u>annihilation</u> of six million European Jews.

In the summer of 1942, Anne Frank, her father, her mother, her older sister, Margot, and four others were forced into hiding during the Nazi occupation of Holland. Their <u>refuge</u> was a tiny apartment they called the Secret Annex, in the back of an Amsterdam office building. For twenty-five months the Franks,
60 the Van Daan family, and later a dentist, Albert Dussel,[2] lived in the Secret Annex, protected from the Gestapo[3] only by a swinging bookcase which masked the entrance to their hiding place and by the heroism of a few Christians who knew they were there. Anne Frank's diary recounts the daily pressures of their cramped existence: the hushed silences when strangers were in the building, the diminishing food supply, the fear of fire from the incessant Allied air raids, the hopes for an early invasion, above all the dread of capture by the pitiless men who

---

2. In her diary, Anne made up names. The Van Daans were really named Van Pels, and Albert Dussel was really Fritz Pfeffer.
3. **Gestapo** (gə·stä′pō): Nazi secret police force, known for its use of terror.

IDENTIFY

Underline the phrase that indicates why the German audiences react in silence (lines 34–36).

_____

_____

PREDICT

Based on the **key statement** in lines 47–48, what do you think may be a **main idea** of the article?

_____

_____

_____

_____

_____

_____

_____

_____

_____

_____

_____

WORDS TO OWN
indomitable (in·däm′i·tə·bəl) *adj.*: unconquerable.
annihilation (ə·nī′ə·lā′shən) *n.*: destruction; killing.
refuge (ref′yo͞oj) *n.*: place of safety.

INTERPRET

Re-read lines 55–76. Have you learned anything new about Anne's life in the Secret Annex after reading this passage? Has anything you read contradicted any of your **prior knowledge**?

_____

_____

_____

_____

_____

EVALUATE

Imagine you went to see a production of *The Diary of Anne Frank*. Now that you know what really happened on August 4, 1944, would you have a different reaction to the play's more dramatic version of events? Tell why or why not.

_____

_____

_____

_____

_____

_____

WORDS TO OWN
reconciliations
(rek′ən·sil′ē·ā′shənz) *n.:*
acts of making up after arguments or disagreements.

were hunting Jews from house to house and sending them to
70 concentration camps. Anne's diary also describes with sharp
insight and youthful humor the bickerings, the wounded pride,
the tearful <u>reconciliations</u> of the eight human beings in the
Secret Annex. It tells of Anne's wishes for the understanding of
her adored father, of her despair at the gulf between her mother
and herself, of her tremulous and growing love for young Peter
Van Daan.

The actual diary ends with an entry for August 1, 1944, in
which Anne Frank, addressing her imaginary friend Kitty, talks
of her impatience with her own unpredictable personality. The
80 stage version goes further: It attempts to reconstruct something
of the events of August 4, 1944, the day the Secret Annex was
violated and its occupants finally taken into a captivity from
which only one returned.

What really happened on that August day fourteen years ago
was far less dramatic than what is now depicted on the stage.
The automobiles did not approach with howling sirens, did
not stop with screaming brakes in front of the house on the
Prinsengracht canal in Amsterdam. No rifle butt pounded against
the door until it reverberated, as it now does in the theater
90 every night somewhere in the world. The truth was, at first,
that no one heard a sound.

It was midmorning on a bright summer day. In the hidden
apartment behind the secret bookcase there was a scene of
relaxed domesticity. The Franks, the Van Daans, and Mr. Dussel
had finished a poor breakfast of ersatz[4] coffee and bread. Mrs.
Frank and Mrs. Van Daan were about to clear the table. Mr. Van
Daan, Margot Frank, and Mr. Dussel were resting or reading.
Anne Frank was very likely at work on one of the short stories
she often wrote when she was not busy with her diary or her
100 novel. In Peter Van Daan's tiny attic room Otto Frank was
chiding the eighteen-year-old boy for an error in his English
lesson. "Why, Peter," Mr. Frank was saying, "you know that
double is spelled with only one *b*."

---

4. **ersatz** (er′zäts′) *adj.:* artificial. Regular coffee beans were unavailable because of
severe wartime shortages.

In the main part of the building four other people, two men and two women, were working at their regular jobs. For more than two years these four had risked their lives to protect their friends in the hide-out, supplied them with food, and brought them news of a world from which they had disappeared. One of the women was Miep, who had just got married a few months
110 earlier. The other was Elli, a pretty typist of twenty-three. The men were Kraler and Koophuis, middle-aged spice merchants who had been business associates of Otto Frank's before the occupation. Mr. Kraler was working in one office by himself. Koophuis and the two women were in another.

I spoke to Miep, Elli, and Mr. Koophuis in Amsterdam. The two women had not been arrested after the raid on the Secret Annex. Koophuis had been released in poor health after a few weeks in prison, and Kraler, who now lives in Canada, had eventually escaped from a forced labor camp.

120 Elli, now a mother, whose coloring and plump good looks are startlingly like those of the young women painted by the Dutch masters,[5] recalled: "I was posting entries in the receipts book when a car drove up in front of the house. But cars often stopped, after all. Then the front door opened, and someone came up the stairs. I wondered who it could be. We often had callers. Only this time I could hear that there were several men. . . ."

Miep, a delicate, intelligent, still young-looking woman, said: "The footsteps moved along the corridor. Then a door
130 creaked, and a moment later the connecting door to Mr. Kraler's office opened, and a fat man thrust his head in and said in Dutch: 'Quiet. Stay in your seats.' I started and at first did not know what was happening. But then, suddenly, I knew."

Mr. Koophuis is now in very poor health, a <u>gaunt</u>, white-haired man in his sixties. He added: "I suppose I did not hear them because of the rumbling of the spice mills in the warehouse. The fat man's head was the first thing I knew. He came in and planted himself in front of us. 'You three stay here,

---

5. **Dutch masters:** seventeenth-century painters including Rembrandt, Frans Hals (fräns häls), and Jan Vermeer (yän vər·mer′).

IDENTIFY

Re-read lines 104–114. List two details that you've learned about the people who worked in the office below the Secret Annex.

_____

_____

_____

_____

_____

_____

_____

INFER

What event does Miep now realize is happening (lines 132–133)?

_____

_____

_____

_____

_____

WORDS TO OWN
gaunt (gônt) *adj.:* thin and bony; hollow-eyed.

IDENTIFY

Circle the **sensory images**—details that appeal to the senses—in Mr. Koophuis's account (lines 134–142).

INTERPRET

Underline the **sensory image** in Mr. Kraler's account that brings his horrifying experience to life.

_____

_____

_____

_____

INFER

Sometimes you can tell how a writer feels about a subject even if he or she doesn't state an opinion directly. **Infer** how you think the author feels about Mr. Frank based on lines 161–165.

_____

_____

_____

_____

_____

_____

understand?' he barked. So we stayed in the office and listened
140 as someone else went upstairs, and doors rattled, and then there were footsteps everywhere. They searched the whole building."

Mr. Kraler wrote me this account from Toronto: "A uniformed staff sergeant of the Occupation Police[6] and three men in civilian clothes entered my office. They wanted to see the storerooms in the front part of the building. All will be well, I thought, if they don't want to see anything else. But after the sergeant had looked at everything, he went out into the corridor, ordering me again to come along. At the end of the
150 corridor they drew their revolvers all at once and the sergeant ordered me to push aside the bookcase and open the door behind it. I said: 'But there's only a bookcase there!' At that he turned nasty, for he knew everything. He took hold of the bookcase and pulled. It yielded and the secret door was exposed. Perhaps the hooks had not been properly fastened. They opened the door and I had to precede them up the steps. The policemen followed me. I could feel their pistols in my back. I was the first to enter the Franks' room. Mrs. Frank was standing at the table. I made a great effort and managed to say:
160 'The Gestapo is here.'"

Otto Frank, now sixty-eight, has remarried and lives in Switzerland. Of the eight who lived in the Secret Annex, he is the only survivor. A handsome, soft-spoken man of obviously great intelligence, he regularly answers correspondence that comes to him about his daughter from all over the world. He recently went to Hollywood for consultation on the movie version of _The Diary of Anne Frank_. About the events of that August morning in 1944 Mr. Frank told me: "I was showing Peter Van Daan his spelling mistakes when suddenly someone came running up the
170 stairs. The steps creaked, and I started to my feet, for it was morning, when everyone was supposed to be quiet. But then the door flew open and a man stood before us holding his pistol aimed at my chest.

---

6. **Occupation Police:** police organized by the German forces while they occupied the Netherlands.

"In the main room the others were already assembled. My wife and the children and Van Daans were standing there with raised hands. Then Albert Dussel came in, followed by another stranger. In the middle of the room stood a uniformed policeman. He stared into our faces.

"'Where are your valuables?' he asked. I pointed to the
180 cupboard where my cash box was kept. The policeman took it out. Then he looked around and his eye fell on the leather briefcase where Anne kept her diary and all her papers. He opened it and shook everything out, dumped the contents on the floor so that Anne's papers and notebooks and loose sheets lay scattered at our feet. No one spoke, and the policeman didn't even glance at the mess on the floor as he put our valuables into the briefcase and closed it. He asked us whether we had any weapons. But we had none, of course. Then he said, 'Get ready.'"

190   Who betrayed the occupants of the Secret Annex? No one is sure, but some suspicion centers on a man I can only call M., whom the living remember as a crafty and disagreeable sneak. He was a warehouse clerk hired after the Franks moved into the building, and he was never told of their presence. M. used to come to work early in the mornings, and he once found a locked briefcase which Mr. Van Daan had carelessly left in the office, where he sometimes worked in the dead of night. Though Kraler claimed it was his own briefcase, it is possible the clerk suspected. Little signs lead to bigger conclusions. In
200 the course of the months he had worked in the building, M. might have gathered many such signs: the dial on the office radio left at BBC[7] by nocturnal listeners, slight rearrangements in the office furniture, and, of course, small inexplicable sounds from the back of the building.

M. was tried later by a war crimes court, denied everything, and was acquitted. No one knows where he is now. I made no effort to find him. Neither did I search out Silberthaler, the

---

7. BBC: British Broadcasting Corporation.

INTERPRET
The policeman dumps Anne's diary and other papers on the floor. What, then, are the "valuables" that he puts in the briefcase?

_____

_____

_____

_____

_____

_____

_____

_____

IDENTIFY
Pause at line 204. Underline the evidence that points toward M. betraying the Secret Annex. Circle the evidence that indicates he was not the betrayer.

_____

_____

_____

WORDS TO OWN
inexplicable
(in·eks′pli·kə·bəl) adj.: incapable of being explained.

EVALUATE

Underline the reason the writer chose not to interview "the betrayers" (line 208). Do you think this is a valid reason? Tell why or why not.

_____

_____

_____

_____

INTERPRET

How does Anne's behavior during the capture (lines 220–225) differ from her usual behavior?

_____

_____

_____

_____

IDENTIFY

Circle what is surprising about the Franks' living conditions at police headquarters (lines 238–242).

WORDS TO OWN

dispirited (di·spir′it·id) v. used as adj.: sad and discouraged.
premonition (prem′ə·nish′ən) n.: feeling that something, especially something bad, will happen.

German police sergeant who made the arrest. The betrayers would have told me nothing.

210   Ironically enough, the occupants of the Secret Annex had grown optimistic in the last weeks of their self-imposed confinement. The terrors of those first nights had largely faded. Even the German army communiqués[8] made clear that the war was approaching an end. The Russians were well into Poland. On the Western front Americans had broken through at Avranches and were pouring into the heart of France. Holland must be liberated soon. In her diary Anne Frank wrote that she thought she might be back in school by fall.

Now they were all packing. Of the capture Otto Frank
220 recalled: "No one wept. Anne was very quiet and composed, only just as <u>dispirited</u> as the rest of us. Perhaps that was why she did not think to take along her notebooks, which lay scattered about on the floor. But maybe she too had the <u>premonition</u> that all was lost now, everything, and so she walked back and forth and did not even glance at her diary."

As the captives filed out of the building, Miep sat listening. "I heard them going," she said, "first in the corridor and then down the stairs. I could hear the heavy boots and the footsteps, and then the very light footsteps of Anne. Through the years
230 she had taught herself to walk so softly that you could hear her only if you knew what to listen for. I did not see her, for the office door was closed as they all passed by."

At Gestapo headquarters the prisoners were interrogated only briefly. As Otto Frank pointed out to his questioners, it was unlikely, after twenty-five months in the Secret Annex, that he would know the whereabouts of any other Jews who were hiding in Amsterdam.

The Franks, the Van Daans, and Dussel were kept at police headquarters for several days, the men in one cell, the women
240 in the other. They were relatively comfortable there. The food was better than the food they had had in the Secret Annex and the guards left them alone.

---

8. **communiqués** (kə·myōō′ni·kāz′) n.: official bulletins.

Suddenly, all eight were taken to the railroad station and put on a train. The guards named their destination: Westerbork, a concentration camp for Jews in Holland, about eighty miles from Amsterdam. Mr. Frank said: "We rode in a regular passenger train. The fact that the door was bolted did not matter very much. We were together and had been given a little food for the journey. We were actually cheerful. Cheerful, at least, when I compare that journey to our next. We had already anticipated the possibility that we might not remain in Westerbork to the end. We knew what was happening to Jews in Auschwitz. But weren't the Russians already deep into Poland? We hoped our luck would hold.

"As we rode, Anne would not move from the window. It was summer outside. Meadows, stubble fields, and villages flew by. The telephone wires along the right of way curved up and down along the windows. After two years it was like freedom for her. Can you understand that?"

Among the names given me of survivors who had known the Franks at Westerbork was that of a Mrs. de Wiek, who lives in Apeldoorn, Holland. I visited Mrs. de Wiek in her home. A lovely, gracious woman, she told me that her family, like the Franks, had been in hiding for months before their capture. She said: "We had been at Westerbork three or four weeks when the word went around that there were new arrivals. News of that kind ran like wildfire through the camp, and my daughter Judy came running to me, calling, 'New people are coming, Mama!'

"The newcomers were standing in a long row in the mustering square,[9] and one of the clerks was entering their names on a list. We looked at them, and Judy pressed close against me. Most of the people in the camp were adults, and I had often wished for a young friend for Judy, who was only fifteen. As I looked along the line, fearing I might see someone I knew, I suddenly exclaimed, 'Judy, see!'

---

9. **mustering square:** place of assembly for inspection and roll call.

IDENTIFY

Underline the passages in lines 243–259 that show why the Franks were somewhat optimistic even though they'd been discovered.

INFER

What do you learn about Mrs. de Wiek's **character** in lines 260–276? Why do you think she would be afraid of seeing someone she knew?

IDENTIFY

What characteristics of Anne's does Mrs. de Wiek find so appealing (lines 284–288)?

_____

_____

_____

_____

_____

_____

_____

_____

IDENTIFY

Pause at line 302. Underline the reasons why Anne is happier now than she was in the Annex.

_____

_____

_____

_____

_____

_____

_____

_____

"In the long line stood eight people whose faces, white as paper, told you at once that they had been hiding and had not been in the open air for years. Among them was this girl. And I 280 said to Judy, 'Look, there is a friend for you.'

"I saw Anne Frank and Peter Van Daan every day in Westerbork. They were always together, and I often said to my husband, 'Look at those two beautiful young people.'

"Anne was so radiant that her beauty flowed over into Peter. Her eyes glowed and her movements had a lilt to them. She was very pallid at first, but there was something so attractive about her frailty and her expressive face that at first Judy was too shy to make friends.

"Anne was happy there, incredible as it seems. Things were 290 hard for us in the camp. We 'convict Jews' who had been arrested in hiding places had to wear blue overalls with a red bib and wooden shoes. Our men had their heads shaved. Three hundred people lived in each barracks. We were sent to work at five in the morning, the children to a cable workshop and the grown-ups to a shed where we had to break up old batteries and salvage the metal and the carbon rods. The food was bad, we were always kept on the run, and the guards all screamed 'Faster, faster!' But Anne was happy. It was as if she had been liberated. Now she could see new people and talk to them and 300 could laugh. She could laugh while the rest of us thought nothing but: Will they send us to the camps in Poland? Will we live through it?

"Edith Frank, Anne's mother, seemed numbed by the experience. She could have been a mute. Anne's sister Margot spoke little and Otto Frank was quiet too, but his was a reassuring quietness that helped Anne and all of us. He lived in the men's barracks, but once when Anne was sick, he came over to visit her every evening and would stand beside her bed for hours, telling her stories. Anne was so like him. When 310 another child, a twelve-year-old boy named David, fell ill, Anne stood by his bed and talked to him. David came from an Orthodox family, and he and Anne always talked about God."

Anne Frank stayed at Westerbork only three weeks. Early in September a thousand of the "convict Jews" were put on a freight train, seventy-five people to a car. Brussels fell to the Allies, then Antwerp, then the Americans reached Aachen. But the victories were coming too late. The Franks and their friends were already on the way to Auschwitz, the camp in Poland where four million Jews died.

320 Mrs. de Wiek was in the same freight car as the Franks on that journey from Westerbork to Auschwitz. "Now and then when the train stopped," she told me, "the SS guards[10] came to the door and held out their caps and we had to toss our money and valuables into the caps. Anne and Judy sometimes pulled themselves up to the small barred window of the car and described the villages we were passing through. We made the children repeat the addresses where we could meet after the war if we became separated in the camp. I remember that the Franks chose a meeting place in Switzerland.

330 "I sat beside my husband on a small box. On the third day in the train, my husband suddenly took my hand and said, 'I want to thank you for the wonderful life we have had together.'

"I snatched my hand away from his, crying, 'What are you thinking about? It's not over!'

"But he calmly reached for my hand again and took it and repeated several times, 'Thank you. Thank you for the life we have had together.' Then I left my hand in his and did not try to draw it away."

On the third night, the train stopped, the doors of the car 340 slid violently open, and the first the exhausted passengers saw of Auschwitz was the glaring searchlights fixed on the train. On the platform, kapos (criminal convicts who were assigned to positions of authority over the other prisoners) were running back and forth shouting orders. Behind them, seen distinctly against the light, stood the SS officers, trimly built and smartly uniformed, many of them with huge dogs at their sides. As the

---

10. **SS guards:** Nazi special police, who ran the concentration camps.

INTERPRET

Underline what Mrs. de Wiek says the parents ask their children to do on the train from Westerbork to Auschwitz (lines 326–328). What does this action say about their attitude toward their future?

_____

_____

_____

_____

_____

INFER

Why is Mrs. de Wiek upset when her husband thanks her for their wonderful life together?

_____

_____

_____

_____

_____

_____

_____

_____

_____

INFER

Pause at line 362. The writer does not speculate on what happened to the passengers who got on the trucks. Rely on your **prior knowledge** to **infer** what happened to them.

_____

_____

_____

_____

_____

_____

_____

_____

_____

IDENTIFY

Pause at line 379. Underline the changes Mrs. de Wiek notices in Anne since they've met.

_____

_____

_____

_____

_____

_____

_____

people poured out of the train, a loudspeaker roared, "Women to the left! Men to the right!"

Mrs. de Wiek went on calmly: "I saw them all as they went
350 away, Mr. Van Daan and Mr. Dussel and Peter and Mr. Frank. But I saw no sign of my husband. He had vanished. I never saw him again.

"'Listen!' the loudspeaker bawled again. 'It is an hour's march to the women's camp. For the children and the sick there are trucks waiting at the end of the platform.'

"We could see the trucks," Mrs. de Wiek said. "They were painted with big red crosses. We all made a rush for them. Who among us was not sick after those days on the train? But we did not reach them. People were still hanging on to the backs of the
360 trucks as they started off. Not one person who went along on that ride ever arrived at the women's camp, and no one has ever found any trace of them."

Mrs. de Wiek, her daughter, Mrs. Van Daan, Mrs. Frank, Margot, and Anne survived the brutal pace of the night march to the women's camp at Auschwitz. Next day their heads were shaved; they learned that the hair was useful as packing for pipe joints in U-boats.[11] Then the women were put to work digging sods of grass, which they placed in great piles. As they labored each day, thousands of others were dispatched with
370 maniacal efficiency in the gas chambers, and smoke rising from the stacks of the huge crematoriums[12] blackened the sky.

Mrs. de Wiek saw Anne Frank every day at Auschwitz. "Anne seemed even more beautiful there," Mrs. de Wiek said, "than she had at Westerbork. Of course her long hair was gone, but now you could see that her beauty was in her eyes, which seemed to grow bigger as she grew thinner. Her gaiety had vanished, but she was still alert and sweet, and with her charm she sometimes secured things that the rest of us had long since given up hoping for.

---

11. **U-boats** _n._: submarines.
12. **crematoriums** (krē′mə·tôr′ē·əmz) _n._: furnaces in which prisoners' bodies were cremated (burned to ashes).

380   "For example, we each had only a gray sack to wear. But when the weather turned cold, Anne came in one day wearing a suit of men's long underwear. She had begged it somewhere. She looked screamingly funny with those long white legs but somehow still delightful.

    "Though she was the youngest, Anne was the leader in her group of five people. She also gave out the bread to everyone in the barracks and she did it so fairly there was none of the usual grumbling.

    "We were always thirsty at Auschwitz, so thirsty that at roll
390 call we would stick out our tongues if it happened to be raining or snowing, and many became sick from bad water. Once, when I was almost dead because there was nothing to drink, Anne suddenly came to me with a cup of coffee. To this day I don't know where she got it.

    "In the barracks many people were dying, some of starvation, others of weakness and despair. It was almost impossible not to give up hope, and when a person gave up, his face became empty and dead. The Polish woman doctor who had been caring for the sick said to me, 'You will pull through.
400 You still have your face.'

    "Anne Frank, too, still had her face, up to the very last. To the last also she was moved by the dreadful things the rest of us had somehow become hardened to. Who bothered to look when the flames shot up into the sky at night from the crematoriums? Who was troubled that every day new people were being selected and gassed? Most of us were beyond feeling. But not Anne. I can still see her standing at the door and looking down the camp street as a group of naked Gypsy girls were driven by on their way to the crematorium. Anne
410 watched them going and cried. And she also cried when we marched past the Hungarian children who had been waiting half a day in the rain in front of the gas chambers. And Anne nudged me and said, 'Look, look! Their eyes!' Anne cried. And you cannot imagine how soon most of us came to the end of our tears."

INTERPRET
What do lines 380–394 reveal about Anne's **character**?

_____

_____

_____

_____

IDENTIFY
In lines 395–400, underline the physical change that took place when people in Auschwitz gave up hope.

RETELL
Retell in your own words how Anne was different from most other prisoners (lines 401–415).

_____

_____

_____

_____

_____

_____

_____

_____

_____

INTERPRET

Most people in Auschwitz wanted to be selected for work at the factory. Why, then, does Mrs. Frank scream when Margot and Anne are chosen to go (lines 438–439)?

_____

_____

_____

_____

_____

_____

_____

_____

_____

_____

_____

_____

_____

_____

_____

_____

_____

Late in October the SS selected the healthiest of the women prisoners for work in a munitions factory in Czechoslovakia. Judy de Wiek was taken from her mother, but Anne and her sister Margot were rejected because they had contracted

420 scabies.[13] A few days later there was another selection for shipment from Auschwitz. Stripped, the women waited naked for hours on the mustering ground outside the barracks. Then, one by one, they filed into the barracks, where a battery of powerful lights had been set up and an SS doctor waited to check them over. Only those able to stand a trip and do hard work were being chosen for this new shipment, and many of the women lied about their age and condition in the hope that they would escape the almost certain death of Auschwitz. Mrs. de Wiek was rejected and so was Mrs. Frank. They waited,

430 looking on.

"Next it was the turn of the two girls, Anne and Margot," Mrs. de Wiek recalled. "Even under the glare of that light Anne still had her face, and she encouraged Margot, and Margot walked erect into the light. There they stood for a moment, naked and shaven-headed, and Anne looked at us with her unclouded face, looked straight and stood straight, and then they were approved and passed along. We could not see what was on the other side of the light. Mrs. Frank screamed, 'The children! Oh, God!'"

440 The chronicle of most of the other occupants of the Secret Annex ends at Auschwitz. Mrs. Frank died there of malnutrition two months later. Mr. Frank saw Mr. Van Daan marched to the gas chambers. When the SS fled Auschwitz before the approaching Russians in January 1945, they took Peter Van Daan with them. It was bitter cold and the roads were covered with ice and Peter Van Daan, Anne Frank's shy beloved, was never heard of again.

From Auschwitz, Mr. Dussel, the dentist, was shipped to a camp in Germany, where he died. Only Otto Frank remained

---

13. **scabies** _n._: skin disease that causes severe itching.

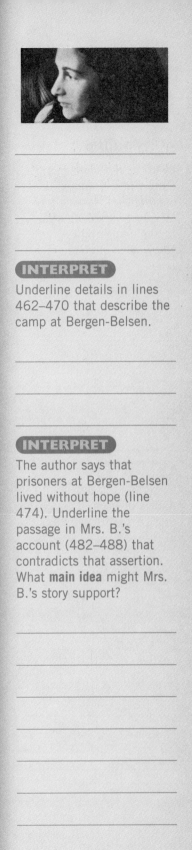

450 there alive until liberation. Anne Frank and Mrs. Van Daan and Margot had been selected for shipment to Bergen-Belsen.

Last year I drove the 225 miles from Amsterdam to Belsen and spent a day there walking over the heath.[14] The site of the old camp is near the city of Hannover, in the state of Lower Saxony. It was June when I arrived, and lupine was in flower in the scrubland.

My guide first showed me the cemetery where fifty thousand Russian prisoners of war, captured in one of Hitler's great early offensives, were buried in 1941. Next to them is a
460 cemetery for Italians. No one knows exactly whether there are three hundred or three thousand in that mass grave.

About a mile farther we came to the main site of the Bergen-Belsen camp. Amid the low growth of pine and birches many large rectangular patches can be seen on the heath. The barracks stood on these, and between them the worn tracks of thousands of bare feet are still visible. There are more mass graves nearby, low mounds overgrown with heath grass or new-planted dwarf pines. Boards bearing the numbers of the dead stand beside some mounds, but others are unmarked and
470 barely discernible. Anne Frank lies there.

The train that carried Anne from Auschwitz to Belsen stopped at every second station because of air raids. At Bergen-Belsen there were no roll calls, no organization, almost no sign of the SS. Prisoners lived on the heath without hope. The fact that the Allies had reached the Rhine encouraged no one. Prisoners died daily—of hunger, thirst, sickness.

The Auschwitz group had at first been assigned to tents on the Bergen-Belsen heath, tents which, one survivor recalls, gave an oddly gay, carnival aspect to the camp. One night that fall a
480 great windstorm brought the tents crashing down, and their occupants were then put in wooden barracks. Mrs. B. of Amsterdam remembered about Anne: "We lived in the same block and saw each other often. In fact, we had a party together at Christmastime. We had saved up some stale bread,

---

14. **heath** (hēth) *n.:* area of open wasteland covered with low-growing plants.

EVALUATE

Even though Anne was in danger in the Annex, her diary entries reveal concern for Lies (lines 492–493). Is this surprising to you? Tell why or why not.

_____

_____

_____

_____

_____

_____

IDENTIFY

Underline the details of Anne's physical appearance that Lies notices (lines 509–514).

_____

_____

_____

_____

_____

_____

_____

_____

WORDS TO OWN
emaciated (ē·mā′shē′·āt′id) _v._ used as _adj.:_ extremely thin, as from starvation or illness. _Emaciated_ and _gaunt_ are synonyms.

and we cut this up and put onions and boiled cabbage on the pieces. Over our feast we nearly forgot our misery for a few hours. We were almost happy. I know that it sounds ghastly now, but we really were a little happy in spite of everything."

490 One of Anne Frank's dearest childhood friends in Amsterdam was a girl named Lies Goosens.[15] Lies is repeatedly mentioned in the diary. She was captured before the Franks were found in the Secret Annex, and Anne wrote of her great fears for the safety of her friend. Now the slim and attractive wife of an Israeli army officer, Lies lives in Jerusalem. But she was in Bergen-Belsen in February 1945, when she heard that a group of Dutch Jews had been moved into the next compound.

Lies said, "I waited until night. Then I stole out of the barracks and went over to the barbed wire which separated us from the newcomers. I called softly into the darkness, 'Is

500 anyone there?'

"A voice answered, 'I am here. I am Mrs. Van Daan.'

"We had known the Van Daans in Amsterdam. I told her who I was and asked whether Margot or Anne could come to the fence. Mrs. Van Daan answered in a breathless voice that Margot was sick but that Anne could probably come and that she would go look for her.

"I waited, shivering in the darkness. It took a long time. But suddenly I heard a voice: 'Lies? Lies? Where are you?'

"I ran in the direction of the voice, and then I saw Anne

510 beyond the barbed wire. She was in rags. I saw her emaciated, sunken face in the darkness. Her eyes were very large. We cried and cried as we told each other our sad news, for now there was only the barbed wire between us, nothing more, and no longer any difference in our fates.

"But there was a difference after all. My block still had food and clothing. Anne had nothing. She was freezing and starving. I called to her in a whisper, 'Come back tomorrow. I'll bring you something.'

"And Anne called across, 'Yes, tomorrow. I'll come.'

---

15. **Lies Goosens** (lēs khō′sins).

520   "I saw Anne again when she came to the fence on the following night," Lies continued. "I had packed up a woolen jacket and some zwieback[16] and sugar and a tin of sardines for her. I called out, 'Anne, watch now!' Then I threw the bundle across the barbed wire.

"But I heard only screams and Anne crying. I shouted, 'What's happened?' And she called back, weeping, 'A woman caught it and won't give it to me.' Then I heard rapid footsteps as the woman ran away. Next night I had only a pair of stockings and zwieback, but this time Anne caught it."

530   In the last weeks at Bergen-Belsen, as Germany was strangled between the Russians and the Western Allies, there was almost no food at all. The roads were blocked, the railroads had been bombed, and the SS commander of the camp drove around the district trying unsuccessfully to requisition supplies. Still, the crematoriums worked night and day. And in the midst of the starvation and the murder there was a great epidemic of typhus.

Both Anne and Margot Frank contracted the disease in late February or early March of 1945. Margot lay in a coma for
540 several days. Then, while unconscious, she somehow rolled from her bed and died. Mrs. Van Daan also died in the epidemic.

The death of Anne Frank passed almost without notice. For Anne, as for millions of others, it was only the final anonymity, and I met no one who remembers being with her in that moment. So many were dying. One woman said, "I feel certain she died because of her sister's death. Dying is easy for anyone left alone in a concentration camp." Mrs. B., who had shared the pitiful Christmastide feast with Anne, knows a little more:
550 "Anne, who was very sick at the time, was not informed of her sister's death. But a few days later she sensed it and soon afterward she died, peacefully."

Three weeks later British troops liberated Bergen-Belsen.

---

16. **zwieback** (swē′bak′) *n.*: sweetened bread that is sliced and toasted after it is baked.

INTERPRET

What does the episode in lines 515–529 say about the way prisoners behaved toward one another?

_____

_____

_____

_____

_____

_____

EVALUATE

The author says that Anne and Margot died of typhus, but a woman at the camp says Anne died because of her sister's death (lines 546–547). Based on what you know about Anne's life, what do you think caused her death? Explain your opinion.

_____

_____

_____

_____

_____

_____

_____

EVALUATE

Pause at line 575. Based on what you read earlier about M. (page 119, lines 190–206), are you surprised he uncovered Anne's papers and gave them to Miep? Tell why or why not.

_____

_____

_____

_____

_____

_____

_____

INTERPRET

Tell in your own words what effect Anne's diary—her voice—has had on the world (lines 583–585).

_____

_____

_____

_____

_____

_____

_____

_____

WORDS TO OWN
raucous (rô′kəs) _adj._: harsh sounding; loud.

Miep and Elli, the heroic young women who had shielded the Franks for two years, found Anne's papers during the week after the police raid on the Secret Annex. "It was terrible when I went up there," Miep recalled. "Everything had been turned upside down. On the floor lay clothes, papers, letters, and school notebooks. Anne's little wrapper hung from a hook on

560 the wall. And among the clutter on the floor lay a notebook with a red-checked cover. I picked it up, looked at the pages, and recognized Anne's handwriting."

Elli wept as she spoke to me: "The table was still set. There were plates, cups, and spoons, but the plates were empty, and I was so frightened I scarcely dared take a step. We sat down on the floor and leafed through all the papers. They were all Anne's, the notebooks and the colored duplicate paper from the office too. We gathered all of them and locked them up in the main office.

570 "A few days later M. came into the office, M. who now had the keys to the building. He said to me, 'I found some more stuff upstairs,' and he handed me another sheaf of Anne's papers. How strange, I thought, that he should be the one to give these to me. But I took them and locked them up with the others."

Miep and Elli did not read the papers they had saved. The red-checked diary, the office account books into which it overflowed, the 312 tissue-thin sheets of colored paper filled with Anne's short stories and the beginnings of a novel about a

580 young girl who was to live in freedom—all these were kept in the safe until Otto Frank finally returned to Amsterdam alone. Thus Anne Frank's voice was preserved out of the millions that were silenced. No louder than a child's whisper, it speaks for those millions and has outlasted the raucous shouts of the murderers, soaring above the clamorous voices of passing time.

Main Idea and Examples Chart

Fill in the chart to understand how details in "A Tragedy Revealed" support the writer's main idea. The top box expresses a main idea from the text. In the boxes below, write examples from the article that support that main idea. If you can think of more than three examples, add them.

Main Idea from "A Tragedy Revealed"

"As we somehow knew she must be, Anne Frank, even in the most frightful extremity, was indomitable."

↓

Supporting Detail 1

Supporting Detail 2

Supporting Detail 3

Vocabulary

A. Match words and definitions. Write the letter of the correct definition next to each word.

_____ **1.** annihilation   **a.** incapable of being explained

_____ **2.** inexplicable   **b.** complete destruction

_____ **3.** raucous   **c.** thin and bony

_____ **4.** gaunt   **d.** acts of making up

_____ **5.** reconciliations   **e.** loud and rowdy

B. Complete each sentence with a word from the Word Bank.

1. For two years, they had taken _____ in the Secret Annex.

2. Even Anne was quiet and _____ when they were led away from the Secret Annex.

3. They all had a _____ that even worse times were to come.

4. People in the concentration camps were starving. Their bodies were thin and _____.

5. Despite the horrible conditions in the camp, Anne's spirit remained _____.

C. Choose three words from the Word Bank, and use each in a sentence of your own.

1. _____

_____

2. _____

_____

3. _____

_____

Comprehension

D. Answer each question below.

1. What were the members of the Secret Annex doing on the day they were captured?

_____

_____

2. What concentration camp were they all taken to first?

_____

_____

3. How did Anne behave in the concentration camp at Auschwitz?

_____

_____

4. How did Anne and Margot make it out of Auschwitz to Bergen-Belsen?

_____

_____

5. What happened at Bergen-Belsen when Anne met her old friend Lies?

_____

_____

6. What finally happened to Margot and Anne?

_____

_____

Charles

Make the Connection

Adventures in Kindergartenland

Remember when you were a little kid starting school? Laurie, the kindergarten child in this story, has some experiences that may remind you of the good times—and maybe the bad times—you had. Before you read about Laurie's adventures in kindergartenland, see what sticks in your memory about your own first days at school.

MY FIRST DAYS
LIKED BEST: _____
LIKED LEAST: _____
BIGGEST SURPRISE: _____
FUNNIEST THING THAT HAPPENED: _____
MOST IMPORTANT THING I LEARNED: _____

Shirley Jackson

charles

INFER

Which family member tells this story?

_____

_____

INTERPRET

Circle three of Laurie's actions or words that surprise his family when he comes home from his first day of school. Considering these details, how do you think his first day went?

_____

_____

_____

_____

INFER

Pause at line 32. Circle the name of the classmate that Laurie likes to talk about. How would you describe that child's behavior? Then, describe how Laurie seems to feel about his classmate.

_____

_____

_____

WORDS TO OWN

renounced (ri·nounst′) _v._: gave up; abandoned.
insolently (in′sə·lənt·lē) _adv._: with bold disrespect.

The day Laurie started kindergarten, he <u>renounced</u> corduroy overalls with bibs and began wearing bluejeans with a belt; I watched him go off the first morning with the older girl next door, seeing clearly that an era of my life was ended, my sweet-voiced nursery-school tot replaced by a long-trousered, swaggering character who forgot to stop at the corner and wave goodbye to me.

He came home the same way, the front door slamming open, his cap on the floor, and the voice suddenly become 10 raucous shouting, "Isn't anybody _here?_"

At lunch he spoke <u>insolently</u> to his father, spilled his baby sister's milk, and remarked that his teacher said that we were not to take the name of the Lord in vain.

"How _was_ school today?" I asked, elaborately casual.

"All right," he said.

"Did you learn anything?" his father asked.

Laurie regarded his father coldly. "I didn't learn nothing," he said.

"Anything," I said. "Didn't learn anything."

20 "The teacher spanked a boy, though," Laurie said, addressing his bread and butter. "For being fresh," he added with his mouth full.

"What did he do?" I asked. "Who was it?"

Laurie thought. "It was Charles," he said. "He was fresh. The teacher spanked him and made him stand in a corner. He was awfully fresh."

"What did he do?" I asked again, but Laurie slid off his chair, took a cookie, and left, while his father was still saying, "See here, young man."

30 The next day Laurie remarked at lunch, as soon as he sat down, "Well, Charles was bad again today." He grinned enormously and said, "Today Charles hit the teacher."

"Good heavens," I said, mindful of the Lord's name, "I suppose he got spanked again?"

"He sure did," Laurie said. "Look up," he said to his father.
"What?" his father said, looking up.

"Look down," Laurie said. "Look at my thumb. Gee, you're dumb." He began to laugh insanely.

"Why did Charles hit the teacher?" I asked quickly.

40 "Because she tried to make him color with red crayons," Laurie said. "Charles wanted to color with green crayons so he hit the teacher and she spanked him and said nobody play with Charles but everybody did."

The third day—it was Wednesday of the first week—Charles bounced a seesaw onto the head of a little girl and made her bleed and the teacher made him stay inside all during recess. Thursday Charles had to stand in a corner during story time because he kept pounding his feet on the floor. Friday Charles was deprived of blackboard privileges because he threw chalk.

50 On Saturday I remarked to my husband, "Do you think kindergarten is too unsettling for Laurie? All this toughness and bad grammar, and this Charles boy sounds like such a bad influence."

"It'll be all right," my husband said reassuringly. "Bound to be people like Charles in the world. Might as well meet them now as later."

On Monday Laurie came home late, full of news. "Charles," he shouted as he came up the hill; I was waiting anxiously on the front steps, "Charles," Laurie yelled all the way up the hill, 60 "Charles was bad again."

"Come right in," I said, as soon as he came close enough. "Lunch is waiting."

"You know what Charles did?" he demanded, following me through the door. "Charles yelled so in school they sent a boy in from first grade to tell the teacher she had to make Charles keep quiet, and so Charles had to stay after school. And so all the children stayed to watch him."

"What did he do?" I asked.

RETELL

Stop at line 49. **Retell** what happened during Laurie's first week at school. Also, sum up how his behavior at home changed in that week.

_____

_____

_____

_____

_____

_____

_____

_____

INFER

Why is Laurie's mother worried about him?

_____

_____

_____

_____

_____

_____

_____

_____

INFER

Why do you think Laurie doesn't answer his father's second question (line 74)?

_____

_____

_____

_____

_____

PREDICT

Pause at line 100. Tell what you think will happen to Charles. Will the teacher "throw him out of school"? If you think his behavior will improve, tell what you think might improve it.

_____

_____

_____

_____

_____

_____

_____

_____

"He just sat there," Laurie said, climbing into his chair at
70 the table. "Hi Pop, y'old dust mop."

"Charles had to stay after school today," I told my husband.
"Everyone stayed with him."

"What does this Charles look like?" my husband asked
Laurie. "What's his other name?"

"He's bigger than me," Laurie said. "And he doesn't have
any rubbers and he doesn't even wear a jacket."

Monday night was the first Parent-Teachers meeting, and
only the fact that the baby had a cold kept me from going; I
wanted passionately to meet Charles's mother. On Tuesday
80 Laurie remarked suddenly, "Our teacher had a friend come see
her in school today."

"Charles's mother?" my husband and I asked
simultaneously.

"Naaah," Laurie said scornfully. "It was a man who came
and made us do exercises. Look." He climbed down from his
chair and squatted down and touched his toes. "Like this," he
said. He got solemnly back into his chair and said, picking up
his fork, "Charles didn't even do exercises."

"That's fine," I said heartily. "Didn't Charles want to do
90 exercises?"

"Naaah," Laurie said. "Charles was so fresh to the teacher's
friend he wasn't _let_ do exercises."

"Fresh again?" I said.

"He kicked the teacher's friend," Laurie said. "The teacher's
friend told Charles to touch his toes like I just did and Charles
kicked him."

"What are they going to do about Charles, do you suppose?"
Laurie's father asked him.

Laurie shrugged elaborately. "Throw him out of school, I
100 guess," he said.

Wednesday and Thursday were routine; Charles yelled
during story hour and hit a boy in the stomach and made him

cry. On Friday Charles stayed after school again and so did all the other children.

With the third week of kindergarten Charles was an institution in our family; the baby was being a Charles when she cried all afternoon; Laurie did a Charles when he filled his wagon full of mud and pulled it through the kitchen; even my husband, when he caught his elbow in the telephone cord and
110 pulled telephone, ash tray, and a bowl of flowers off the table, said, after the first minute, "Looks like Charles."

During the third and fourth weeks it looked like a reformation in Charles; Laurie reported grimly at lunch on Thursday of the third week, "Charles was so good today the teacher gave him an apple."

"What?" I said, and my husband added <u>warily</u>, "You mean Charles?"

"Charles," Laurie said. "He gave the crayons around and he picked up the books afterward and the teacher said he was her
120 helper."

"What happened?" I asked <u>incredulously</u>.

"He was her helper, that's all," Laurie said, and shrugged.

"Can this be true, about Charles?" I asked my husband that night. "Can something like this happen?"

"Wait and see," my husband said cynically. "When you've got a Charles to deal with, this may mean he's only plotting."

He seemed to be wrong. For over a week Charles was the teacher's helper; each day he handed things out and he picked things up; no one had to stay after school.

130 "The PTA meeting's next week again," I told my husband one evening. "I'm going to find Charles's mother there."

"Ask her what happened to Charles," my husband said. "I'd like to know."

"I'd like to know myself," I said.

On Friday of that week things were back to normal. "You know what Charles did today?" Laurie demanded at the lunch table, in a voice slightly awed. "He told a little girl to say a

IDENTIFY

In lines 105–111, underline the type of behavior that the narrator refers to as "being a Charles."

RETELL

Pause at line 122. Explain how Charles's behavior changes. Tell how the teacher rewards him.

_____

_____

_____

_____

_____

INFER

What does the narrator mean when she says "things were back to normal" (line 135)?

_____

_____

_____

_____

_____

WORDS TO OWN
warily (wer'ə·lē) _adv._: cautiously.
incredulously (in·krej'oo·ləs·lē) _adv._: unbelievingly.

EVALUATE

What do you think of the way Laurie's teacher deals with Charles and the rest of the class? What might you do in a different way if you were Laurie's teacher?

_____

_____

_____

_____

_____

_____

_____

_____

_____

_____

_____

_____

BUILD FLUENCY

Re-read the boxed passage aloud until you can read it smoothly. Try to capture the different tones of voice of the narrator and the teacher as they talk together.

_____

_____

WORDS TO OWN

haggard (hag′ərd) *adj.:* looking worn-out and exhausted.

word and she said it and the teacher washed her mouth out with soap and Charles laughed."

140   "What word?" his father asked unwisely, and Laurie said, "I'll have to whisper it to you, it's so bad." He got down off his chair and went around to his father. His father bent his head down and Laurie whispered joyfully. His father's eyes widened.

"Did Charles tell the little girl to say *that*?" he asked respectfully.

"She said it *twice*," Laurie said. "Charles told her to say it twice."

"What happened to Charles?" my husband asked.

"Nothing," Laurie said. "He was passing out the crayons."

150   Monday morning Charles abandoned the little girl and said the evil word himself three or four times, getting his mouth washed out with soap each time. He also threw chalk.

My husband came to the door with me that evening as I set out for the PTA meeting. "Invite her over for a cup of tea after the meeting," he said. "I want to get a look at her."

"If only she's there," I said prayerfully.

"She'll be there," my husband said. "I don't see how they could hold a PTA meeting without Charles's mother."

At the meeting I sat restlessly, scanning each comfortable
160 matronly face, trying to determine which one hid the secret of Charles. None of them looked to me <u>haggard</u> enough. No one stood up in the meeting and apologized for the way her son had been acting. No one mentioned Charles.

After the meeting I identified and sought out Laurie's kindergarten teacher. She had a plate with a cup of tea and a piece of chocolate cake; I had a plate with a cup of tea and a piece of marshmallow cake. We maneuvered up to one another cautiously and smiled.

"I've been so anxious to meet you," I said. "I'm Laurie's
170 mother."

"We're all so interested in Laurie," she said.

"Well, he certainly likes kindergarten," I said. "He talks about it all the time."

"We had a little trouble adjusting, the first week or so," she said primly, "but now he's a fine little helper. With lapses, of course."

"Laurie usually adjusts very quickly," I said. "I suppose this time it's Charles's influence."

"Charles?"

180 "Yes," I said, laughing, "you must have your hands full in that kindergarten, with Charles."

"Charles?" she said. "We don't have any Charles in the kindergarten."

IDENTIFY

According to the teacher, which child has had trouble adjusting, but has now become a fine little helper, most of the time?

EVALUATE

Humorous writing often includes a **plot twist,** an unexpected turn of events. What's the plot twist at the end of this story? Does it surprise you? Explain why you think this is, or isn't, a funny story.

Trickster Chart

Do you know any tricksters? In the story, *Charles,* the main character, Laurie, describes the many tricks of a classmate. In the end, we discover that his stories are even tricks. In the graphic organizer below, list the tricks of both Charles and Laurie. Are there similarities?

Charles	Laurie

In your opinion, who was the better trickster, Charles or Laurie? Explain.

_____

_____

Vocabulary and Comprehension

A. Match each word with its definition. Write the letter of the correct definition next to each word.

Word Bank
renounced
insolently
warily
incredulously
haggard

_____ **1.** insolently   **a.** worn out

_____ **2.** incredulously   **b.** abandoned

_____ **3.** haggard   **c.** cautiously

_____ **4.** renounced   **d.** disrespectfully

_____ **5.** warily   **e.** unbelievingly

B. Choose three words from the Word Bank. Use each word in a sentence.

1. _____

_____

2. _____

_____

3. _____

_____

C. Write **T** or **F** next to each statement to tell if it is true or false.

_____ **1.** Charles is a boy in Laurie's class.

_____ **2.** Laurie is a very serious child.

_____ **3.** Laurie's parents were concerned about him being around Charles.

_____ **4.** Laurie never talked about school.

_____ **5.** Laurie's teacher was "so interested" in Laurie.

The Ransom of Red Chief

Make the Connection

What's So Funny?

You already know that there are a lot of ways to get laughs—from slapstick routines like slipping on a banana peel to subtle plays on words. Before you find out how "The Ransom of Red Chief" appeals to your funny bone, think for a minute about what makes you laugh. In the clown's flag on the left below, list some comics, TV shows, movies, books, or stories that you find funny. In the right flag, list what you think makes these things funny.

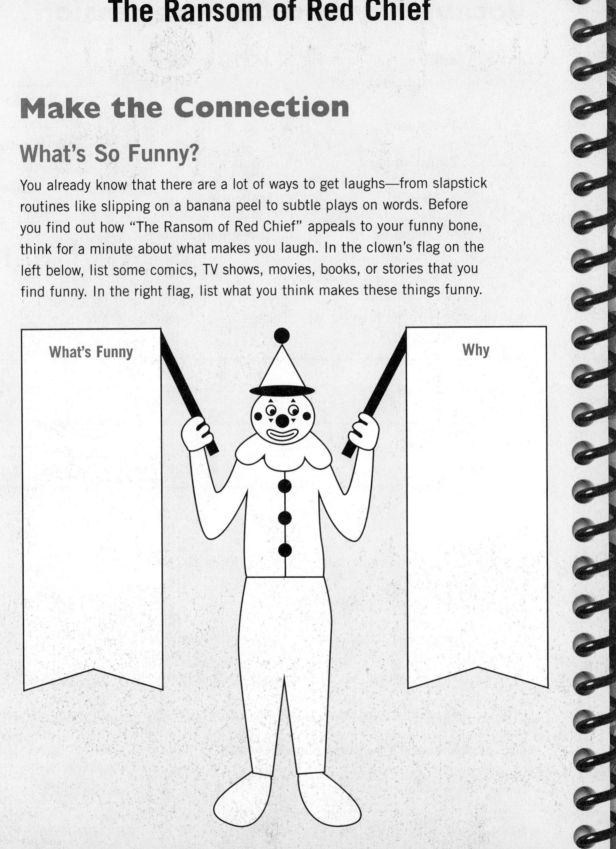

What's Funny

Why

The Ransom of Red Chief

O. Henry

It looked like a good thing: but wait till I tell you. We were down South, in Alabama—Bill Driscoll and myself—when this kidnapping idea struck us. It was, as Bill afterward expressed it, "during a moment of temporary mental apparition";[1] but we didn't find that out till later.

There was a town down there, as flat as a flannel cake, and called Summit, of course. It contained inhabitants of as undeleterious[2] and self-satisfied a class of peasantry as ever clustered around a Maypole.

10   Bill and me had a joint capital of about six hundred dollars, and we needed just two thousand dollars more to pull off a fraudulent town-lot scheme in Western Illinois with. We talked it over on the front steps of the Hotel. Philoprogenitiveness,[3] says we, is strong in semirural communities; therefore, and for other reasons, a kidnapping project ought to do better there than in the radius[4] of newspapers that send reporters out in plain clothes to stir up talk about such things. We knew that Summit couldn't get after us with anything stronger than constables and, maybe, some lackadaisical bloodhounds and

20   a diatribe or two in the *Weekly Farmers' Budget.* So, it looked good.

We selected for our victim the only child of a prominent citizen named Ebenezer Dorset. The father was respectable and tight, a mortgage fancier and a stern, upright collection-plate passer and forecloser. The kid was a boy of ten, with bas-relief[5] freckles and hair the color of the cover of the magazine you buy at the newsstand when you want to catch a train. Bill and me figured that Ebenezer would melt down for a ransom of two thousand dollars to a cent. But wait till I tell you.

---

1. **apparition** (ap′ə·rish′ən): appearance of a ghost. Bill means *aberration* (ab′ər·ā′shən), a departure from what is normal.
2. **undeleterious** (un·del′ə·tir′ē·əs): harmless.
3. **philoprogenitiveness** (fil′ō·prō·jen′ə·tiv·nis): parents' love for their children.
4. **radius:** range; area of activity.
5. **bas-relief** (bä′ri·lēf′): slightly raised. *Bas-relief* usually refers to a kind of sculpture in which figures are carved in a flat surface so that they project only slightly from the background.

PREDICT

Pause at line 38. Do you think this boy will be easy to kidnap and hold for ransom? Tell what you think will happen next.

30   About two miles from Summit was a little mountain, covered with a dense cedar brake.⁶ On the rear elevation of this mountain was a cave. There we stored provisions.

One evening after sundown, we drove in a buggy past old Dorset's house. The kid was in the street, throwing rocks at a kitten on the opposite fence.

"Hey, little boy!" says Bill, "would you like to have a bag of candy and a nice ride?"

The boy catches Bill neatly in the eye with a piece of brick.

"That will cost the old man an extra five hundred dollars,"

40   says Bill, climbing over the wheel.

That boy put up a fight like a welterweight cinnamon bear; but, at last, we got him down in the bottom of the buggy and drove away. We took him up to the cave, and I hitched the horse in the cedar brake. After dark I drove the buggy to the little village, three miles away, where we had hired it, and walked back to the mountain.

Bill was pasting court plaster⁷ over the scratches and bruises on his features. There was a fire burning behind the big rock at the entrance of the cave, and the boy was watching a pot of

50   boiling coffee, with two buzzard tail feathers stuck in his red hair. He points a stick at me when I come up, and says:

"Ha! cursed paleface, do you dare to enter the camp of Red Chief, the terror of the plains?"

"He's all right now," says Bill, rolling up his trousers and examining some bruises on his shins. "We're playing Indian. We're making Buffalo Bill's show look like magic-lantern views⁸ of Palestine in the town hall. I'm Old Hank, the Trapper, Red Chief's captive, and I'm to be scalped at daybreak. By Geronimo! that kid can kick hard."

60   Yes, sir, that boy seemed to be having the time of his life. The fun of camping out in a cave had made him forget that he was a captive himself. He immediately christened me Snake-eye, the Spy, and announced that when his braves returned

INTERPRET

Much of the humor in this story comes from **irony**, the contrast between expectation and reality. There are several kinds of irony. **Situational irony** occurs when what happens is very different from what we expect. Re-read lines 47–59. Explain how this situation is ironic.

---

6. **brake:** clump of trees or bushes.
7. **court plaster:** cloth that sticks to the skin, used for covering cuts and scratches.
8. **magic-lantern views:** slides. A magic lantern was an early type of projector.

INTERPRET

What does the boy's "during-dinner" speech (lines 69–80) reveal about his **character**?

_____

_____

_____

_____

_____

_____

_____

_____

_____

IDENTIFY

What is the situational irony in lines 87–89?

_____

_____

_____

_____

_____

_____

_____

from the warpath, I was to be broiled at the stake at the rising of the sun.

Then we had supper; and he filled his mouth full of bacon and bread and gravy and began to talk. He made a during-dinner speech something like this:

"I like this fine. I never camped out before; but I had a pet
70 'possum once, and I was nine last birthday. I hate to go to school. Rats ate up sixteen of Jimmy Talbot's aunt's speckled hen's eggs. Are there any real Indians in these woods? I want some more gravy. Does the trees moving make the wind blow? We had five puppies. What makes your nose so red, Hank? My father has lots of money. Are the stars hot? I whipped Ed Walker twice, Saturday. I don't like girls. You dassent[9] catch toads unless with a string. Do oxen make any noise? Why are oranges round? Have you got beds to sleep on in this cave? Amos Murray has got six toes. A parrot can talk, but a monkey
80 or a fish can't. How many does it take to make twelve?"

Every few minutes he would remember that he was a pesky redskin, and pick up his stick rifle and tiptoe to the mouth of the cave to rubber[10] for the scouts of the hated paleface. Now and then he would let out a war whoop that made Old Hank the Trapper shiver. That boy had Bill terrorized from the start.

"Red Chief," says I to the kid, "would you like to go home?"

"Aw, what for?" says he. "I don't have any fun at home. I hate to go to school. I like to camp out. You won't take me back home again, Snake-eye, will you?"

90 "Not right away," says I. "We'll stay here in the cave awhile."

"All right!" says he. "That'll be fine. I never had such fun in all my life."

We went to bed about eleven o'clock. We spread down some wide blankets and quilts and put Red Chief between us. We weren't afraid he'd run away. He kept us awake for three

---

9. **dassent:** dare not.
10. **rubber:** short for *rubberneck*, meaning "stretch the neck to look at something curiously." Traffic reports often mention delays caused by rubbernecking—drivers slow down to stare at accidents and create jams.

hours, jumping up and reaching for his rifle and screeching:
"Hist! pard," in mine and Bill's ears, as the fancied crackle of
a twig or the rustle of a leaf revealed to his young imagination
100 the stealthy approach of the outlaw band. At last, I fell into a
troubled sleep, and dreamed that I had been kidnapped and
chained to a tree by a ferocious pirate with red hair.

Just at daybreak, I was awakened by a series of awful
screams from Bill. They weren't yells, or howls, or shouts, or
whoops, or yawps, such as you'd expect from a manly set of
vocal organs—they were simply indecent, terrifying, humiliating
screams, such as women emit when they see ghosts or
caterpillars. It's an awful thing to hear a strong, desperate,
fat man scream incontinently in a cave at daybreak.

110 I jumped up to see what the matter was. Red Chief was
sitting on Bill's chest, with one hand twined in Bill's hair. In the
other he had the sharp case knife we used for slicing bacon;
and he was industriously and realistically trying to take Bill's
scalp, according to the sentence that had been pronounced
upon him the evening before.

I got the knife away from the kid and made him lie down
again. But, from that moment, Bill's spirit was broken. He laid
down on his side of the bed, but he never closed an eye again
in sleep as long as that boy was with us. I dozed off for a
120 while, but along toward sunup I remembered that Red Chief
had said I was to be burned at the stake at the rising of the sun.
I wasn't nervous or afraid; but I sat up and lit my pipe and
leaned against a rock.

"What you getting up so soon for, Sam?" asked Bill.

"Me?" says I. "Oh, I got a kind of pain in my shoulder. I
thought sitting up would rest it."

"You're a liar!" says Bill. "You're afraid. You was to be
burned at sunrise, and you was afraid he'd do it. And he
would, too, if he could find a match. Ain't it awful, Sam? Do
130 you think anybody will pay out money to get a little imp like
that back home?"

"Sure," said I. "A rowdy kid like that is just the kind that
parents dote on. Now, you and the Chief get up and cook

INTERPRET

The narrator's contrast of
the way men and women
scream is an example of
stereotyping, describing all
members of a group as
if they have the same
characteristics, with no
individual differences. How
has the narrator previously
stereotyped Native
Americans?

_____

_____

_____

_____

RETELL

Pause at line 123. **Retell**
what has happened since
the two kidnappers decided
to kidnap the boy.

_____

_____

_____

_____

_____

_____

_____

_____

_____

INTERPRET

Notice that the narrator occasionally uses poetic language. Circle the **alliteration** in lines 143–144. Underline where in these lines the narrator repeats himself, using words that have the same meaning. What is ironic about the narrator's poetic language?

_____

_____

_____

_____

_____

_____

INFER

Why does Bill ask if Sam (the narrator) has a gun?

_____

_____

_____

_____

_____

_____

WORDS TO OWN
somnolent (säm′nə·lənt)
adj.: drowsy.

breakfast, while I go up on the top of this mountain and reconnoiter."

I went up on the peak of the little mountain and ran my eye over the contiguous vicinity.[11] Over toward Summit I expected to see the sturdy yeomanry of the village armed with scythes and pitchforks beating the countryside for the dastardly kid-
140 nappers. But what I saw was a peaceful landscape dotted with one man plowing with a dun mule. Nobody was dragging the creek; no couriers dashed hither and yon, bringing tidings of no news to the distracted parents. There was a sylvan[12] attitude of <u>somnolent</u> sleepiness pervading that section of the external outward surface of Alabama that lay exposed to my view. "Perhaps," says I to myself, "it has not yet been discovered that the wolves have borne away the tender lambkin from the fold. Heaven help the wolves!" says I, and I went down the mountain to breakfast.
150 When I got to the cave, I found Bill backed up against the side of it, breathing hard, and the boy threatening to smash him with a rock half as big as a coconut.

"He put a red-hot boiled potato down my back," explained Bill, "and then mashed it with his foot; and I boxed his ears. Have you got a gun about you, Sam?"

I took the rock away from the boy and kind of patched up the argument. "I'll fix you," says the kid to Bill. "No man ever yet struck the Red Chief but he got paid for it. You better beware!"
160 After breakfast the kid takes a piece of leather with strings wrapped around it out of his pocket and goes outside the cave unwinding it.

"What's he up to now?" says Bill, anxiously. "You don't think he'll run away, do you, Sam?"

"No fear of it," says I. "He don't seem to be much of a homebody. But we've got to fix up some plan about the ransom. There don't seem to be much excitement around

---

11. **contiguous vicinity:** nearby area.
12. **sylvan** (sil′vən): like a forest.

Summit on account of his disappearance; but maybe they haven't realized yet that he's gone. His folks may think he's
170 spending the night with Aunt Jane or one of the neighbors. Anyhow, he'll be missed today. Tonight we must get a message to his father demanding the two thousand dollars for his return."

Just then we heard a kind of war whoop, such as David might have emitted when he knocked out the champion Goliath. It was a sling that Red Chief had pulled out of his pocket, and he was whirling it around his head.

I dodged, and heard a heavy thud and a kind of a sigh from Bill, like a horse gives out when you take his saddle off. A rock
180 the size of an egg had caught Bill just behind his left ear. He loosened himself all over and fell in the fire across the frying pan of hot water for washing the dishes. I dragged him out and poured cold water on his head for half an hour.

By and by, Bill sits up and feels behind his ear and says: "Sam, do you know who my favorite Biblical character is?"

"Take it easy," says I. "You'll come to your senses presently."

"King Herod,"[13] says he. "You won't go away and leave me here alone, will you, Sam?"
190 I went out and caught that boy and shook him until his freckles rattled.

"If you don't behave," says I, "I'll take you straight home. Now, are you going to be good, or not?"

"I was only funning," says he, sullenly. "I didn't mean to hurt Old Hank. But what did he hit me for? I'll behave, Snake-eye, if you won't send me home and if you'll let me play the Black Scout today."

"I don't know the game," says I. "That's for you and Mr. Bill to decide. He's your playmate for the day. I'm going away for a
200 while, on business. Now, you come in and make friends with him and say you are sorry for hurting him, or home you go, at once."

---

13. **King Herod** (her′əd): Herod, ruler of Judea from c. 4 B.C. to A.D. 39, ordered the killing of all boys in Bethlehem two years old and younger (Matthew 2:16).

INTERPRET

One comic technique is **exaggeration,** or overstatement. See lines 153–154, where Bill says, "He put a red-hot boiled potato down my back . . . and then mashed it with his foot." The opposite comic technique is **understatement,** saying less than what is meant, as in lines 165–166, when Sam says, "He don't seem to be much of a homebody." Circle line 183. Is this exaggeration or understatement?

_____

_____

IDENTIFY

Pause at line 191. Is this **exaggeration** or **understatement**?

_____

_____

_____

_____

_____

_____

_____

_____

_____

INFER

Re-read lines 215–217.
What **inference** can you
make about the relationship
between Sam and Bill? Do
you think Bill will be able
to keep the boy quiet?

WORDS TO OWN
peremptory (pər·emp'tə·rē)
adj.: commanding.
acceded (ak·sēd'id) *v.*: gave
in; consented.

I made him and Bill shake hands, and then I took Bill aside
and told him I was going to Poplar Grove, a little village three
miles from the cave, and find out what I could about how the
kidnapping had been regarded in Summit. Also, I thought it
best to send a <u>peremptory</u> letter to old man Dorset that day,
demanding the ransom and dictating how it should be paid.

"You know, Sam," says Bill, "I've stood by you without
210 batting an eye in earthquakes, fire, and flood—in poker games,
dynamite outrages, police raids, train robberies, and cyclones.
I never lost my nerve yet till we kidnapped that two-legged
skyrocket of a kid. He's got me going. You won't leave me long
with him, will you, Sam?"

"I'll be back sometime this afternoon," says I. "You must
keep the boy amused and quiet till I return. And now we'll
write the letter to old Dorset."

Bill and I got paper and pencil and worked on the letter
while Red Chief, with a blanket wrapped around him, strutted
220 up and down, guarding the mouth of the cave. Bill begged me
tearfully to make the ransom fifteen hundred dollars instead of
two thousand. "I ain't attempting," says he, "to decry[14] the
celebrated moral aspect of parental affection, but we're dealing
with humans, and it ain't human for anybody to give up two
thousand dollars for that forty-pound chunk of freckled wildcat.
I'm willing to take a chance at fifteen hundred dollars. You can
charge the difference up to me."

So, to relieve Bill, I <u>acceded</u>, and we collaborated a letter
that ran this way:

230 EBENEZER DORSET, ESQ.:

We have your boy concealed in a place far from Summit. It
is useless for you or the most skillful detectives to attempt to
find him. Absolutely the only terms on which you can have
him restored to you are these: We demand fifteen hundred
dollars in large bills for his return; the money to be left at
midnight tonight at the same spot and in the same box as your
reply—as hereinafter described. If you agree to these terms,

---

14. **decry:** speak out against.

send your answer in writing by a solitary messenger tonight at half-past eight o'clock. After crossing Owl Creek on the road to
240 Poplar Grove, there are three large trees about a hundred yards apart, close to the fence of the wheat field on the right-hand side. At the bottom of the fence post, opposite the third tree, will be found a small pasteboard box.

The messenger will place the answer in this box and return immediately to Summit.

If you attempt any treachery or fail to comply with our demand as stated, you will never see your boy again.

If you pay the money as demanded, he will be returned to you safe and well within three hours. These terms are final, and
250 if you do not accede to them, no further communication will be attempted.

TWO DESPERATE MEN

I addressed this letter to Dorset and put it in my pocket. As I was about to start, the kid comes up to me and says:

"Aw, Snake-eye, you said I could play the Black Scout while you was gone."

"Play it, of course," says I. "Mr. Bill will play with you. What kind of a game is it?"

"I'm the Black Scout," says Red Chief, "and I have to ride to
260 the stockade to warn the settlers that the Indians are coming. I'm tired of playing Indian myself. I want to be the Black Scout."

"All right," says I. "It sounds harmless to me. I guess Mr. Bill will help you foil the pesky savages."

"What am I to do?" asks Bill, looking at the kid suspiciously.

"You are the hoss," says Black Scout. "Get down on your hands and knees. How can I ride to the stockade without a hoss?"
270 "You'd better keep him interested," said I, "till we get the scheme going. Loosen up."

Bill gets down on his all fours, and a look comes in his eye like a rabbit's when you catch it in a trap.

BUILD FLUENCY

After you've read this letter once, try reading it aloud in two different ways. First, read it slowly and carefully, as if you were the narrator, composing the letter with Bill. Try to sound firm and mean. Then, imagine that you are the boy's father, reading the letter aloud to your wife. Try to read the letter the way a worried father might read it.

PREDICT

How do you think Mr. Dorset, the boy's father, will respond to the ransom note?

Surprise is one of the important elements in what makes people laugh. Even though we now expect the child to have the upper hand over the supposedly mean kidnapper, what the boy and Bill say and how they act continues to surprise us. Circle one detail in lines 272–292 that seems especially funny to you. Explain why it's funny.

_____
_____
_____
_____
_____
_____
_____
_____
_____
_____
_____

WORDS TO OWN
surreptitiously
(sur'əp·tish'əs·lē) *adv.*: secretly or sneakily.
renegade (ren'ə·gād') *n.*: traitor.
proclivities (prō·kliv'ə·tēz) *n.*: natural tendencies.

"How far is it to the stockade, kid?" he asks, in a husky manner of voice.

"Ninety miles," says the Black Scout. "And you have to hump[15] yourself to get there on time. Whoa, now!"

The Black Scout jumps on Bill's back and digs his heels in his side.

280 "For Heaven's sake," says Bill, "hurry back, Sam, as soon as you can. I wish we hadn't made the ransom more than a thousand. Say, you quit kicking me or I'll get up and warm you good."

I walked over to Poplar Grove and sat around the post office and store, talking with the chaw-bacons that came in to trade. One whiskerando says that he hears Summit is all upset on account of Elder Ebenezer Dorset's boy having been lost or stolen. That was all I wanted to know. I bought some smoking tobacco, referred casually to the price of black-eyed peas, 290 posted my letter surreptitiously, and came away. The postmaster said the mail carrier would come by in an hour to take the mail to Summit.

When I got back to the cave, Bill and the boy were not to be found. I explored the vicinity of the cave and risked a yodel or two, but there was no response.

So I lighted my pipe and sat down on a mossy bank to await developments.

In about half an hour I heard the bushes rustle, and Bill wabbled out into the little glade in front of the cave. Behind 300 him was the kid, stepping softly like a scout, with a broad grin on his face. Bill stopped, took off his hat, and wiped his face with a red handkerchief. The kid stopped about eight feet behind him.

"Sam," says Bill, "I suppose you'll think I'm a renegade, but I couldn't help it. I'm a grown person with masculine proclivities and habits of self-defense, but there is a time when all systems of egotism and predominance fail. The boy is gone. I sent him home. All is off. There was martyrs in old times,"

---

15. **hump:** here, hurry.

goes on Bill, "that suffered death rather than give up the
particular graft they enjoyed. None of 'em ever was subjugated
to such supernatural tortures as I have been. I tried to be
faithful to our articles of depredation;[16] but there came a limit."

"What's the trouble, Bill?" I asks him.

"I was rode," says Bill, "the ninety miles to the stockade,
not barring an inch. Then, when the settlers was rescued, I was
given oats. Sand ain't a <u>palatable</u> substitute. And then, for an
hour I had to try to explain to him why there was nothin' in
holes, how a road can run both ways, and what makes the
grass green. I tell you, Sam, a human can only stand so much.
I takes him by the neck of his clothes and drags him down the
mountain. On the way he kicks my legs black and blue from
the knees down; and I've got to have two or three bites on my
thumb and hand cauterized.[17]

"But he's gone"—continues Bill—"gone home. I showed
him the road to Summit and kicked him about eight feet nearer
there at one kick. I'm sorry we lose the ransom; but it was
either that or Bill Driscoll to the madhouse."

Bill is puffing and blowing, but there is a look of <u>ineffable</u>
peace and growing content on his rose-pink features.

"Bill," says I, "there isn't any heart disease in your family, is
there?"

"No," says Bill, "nothing chronic except malaria and
accidents. Why?"

"Then you might turn around," says I, "and have a look
behind you."

Bill turns and sees the boy, and loses his complexion and
sits down plump on the ground and begins to pluck aimlessly
at grass and little sticks. For an hour I was afraid of his mind.
And then I told him that my scheme was to put the whole job
through immediately and that we would get the ransom and be
off with it by midnight if old Dorset fell in with our <u>proposition</u>.

310
320
330
340

---

16. **depredation** (dep'rə·dā'shən): robbery; looting. The phrase *articles of
depredation* is a pun on *Articles of Confederation,* the name of the first U.S.
constitution.

17. **cauterized:** burned to prevent infection.

INTERPRET

Dramatic irony (that's the
third kind of irony) occurs
when the reader knows
something a character does
not know. Why is this
situation an example of
dramatic irony? What do we
know that Bill doesn't know
yet?

_____

_____

_____

_____

_____

_____

_____

_____

_____

_____

_____

WORDS TO OWN
palatable (pal'it·ə·bəl) *adj.:*
fit to eat.
ineffable (in·ef'ə·bəl) *adj.:*
too great to describe.
proposition (präp'ə·zish'ən)
n.: proposal; suggested plan.

INFER

The Russians were badly beaten in the Russo-Japanese War (1904–1905). What do you suppose will happen to Bill when he plays the Russian?

_____

_____

_____

_____

_____

_____

_____

_____

INTERPRET

Underline Mr. Dorset's "counterproposition." How is it **situational irony**—the opposite of the kind of proposal you might expect from a worried father?

_____

_____

_____

_____

_____

_____

So Bill braced up enough to give the kid a weak sort of a smile and a promise to play the Russian in a Japanese war with him as soon as he felt a little better.

I had a scheme for collecting that ransom without danger of being caught by counterplots that ought to commend itself to professional kidnappers. The tree under which the answer was to be left—and the money later on—was close to the road fence, with big, bare fields on all sides. If a gang of constables

350 should be watching for anyone to come for the note, they could see him a long way off crossing the fields or in the road. But no, sirree! At half-past eight I was up in that tree as well hidden as a tree toad, waiting for the messenger to arrive.

Exactly on time, a half-grown boy rides up the road on a bicycle, locates the pasteboard box at the foot of the fence post, slips a folded piece of paper into it, and pedals away again back toward Summit.

I waited an hour and then concluded the thing was square. I slid down the tree, got the note, slipped along the fence till I

360 struck the woods, and was back at the cave in another half an hour. I opened the note, got near the lantern, and read it to Bill. It was written with a pen in a crabbed hand,[18] and the sum and substance of it was this:

TWO DESPERATE MEN:

Gentlemen: I received your letter today by post, in regard to the ransom you ask for the return of my son. I think you are a little high in your demands, and I hereby make you a counterproposition, which I am inclined to believe you will accept. You bring Johnny home and pay me two hundred and

370 fifty dollars in cash, and I agree to take him off your hands. You had better come at night, for the neighbors believe he is lost, and I couldn't be responsible for what they would do to anybody they saw bringing him back. Very respectfully,

EBENEZER DORSET

---

18. **crabbed** (krab′id) **hand:** handwriting that is hard to read.

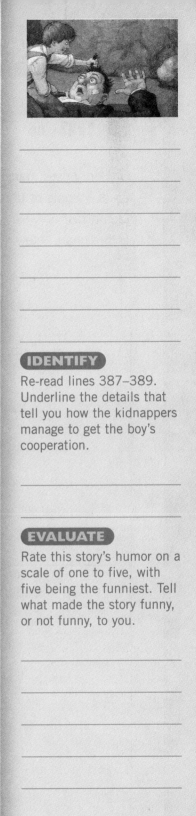

"Great Pirates of Penzance," says I; "of all the impudent—"

But I glanced at Bill, and hesitated. He had the most appealing look in his eyes I ever saw on the face of a dumb or a talking brute.

"Sam," says he, "what's two hundred and fifty dollars, after 380 all? We've got the money. One more night of this kid will send me to a bed in Bedlam.[19] Besides being a thorough gentleman, I think Mr. Dorset is a spendthrift for making us such a liberal offer. You ain't going to let the chance go, are you?"

"Tell you the truth, Bill," says I, "this little he–ewe lamb has somewhat got on my nerves too. We'll take him home, pay the ransom, and make our getaway."

We took him home that night. We got him to go by telling him that his father had bought a silver-mounted rifle and a pair of moccasins for him and we were to hunt bears the next day.

390 It was just twelve o'clock when we knocked at Ebenezer's front door. Just at the moment when I should have been abstracting the fifteen hundred dollars from the box under the tree, according to the original proposition, Bill was counting out two hundred and fifty dollars into Dorset's hand.

When the kid found out we were going to leave him at home, he started up a howl like a calliope[20] and fastened himself as tight as a leech to Bill's leg. His father peeled him away gradually, like a porous plaster.

"How long can you hold him?" asks Bill.

400 "I'm not as strong as I used to be," says old Dorset, "but I think I can promise you ten minutes."

"Enough," says Bill. "In ten minutes I shall cross the Central, Southern, and Middle Western States and be legging it trippingly for the Canadian border."

And as dark as it was, and as fat as Bill was, and as good a runner as I am, he was a good mile and a half out of Summit before I could catch up with him.

IDENTIFY

Re-read lines 387–389. Underline the details that tell you how the kidnappers manage to get the boy's cooperation.

EVALUATE

Rate this story's humor on a scale of one to five, with five being the funniest. Tell what made the story funny, or not funny, to you.

---

19. **Bedlam:** an insane asylum.
20. **calliope** (kə·lī′ə·pē′): keyboard instrument like an organ, with a series of whistles sounded by steam or compressed air.

Humor Chart

O. Henry uses many different techniques to make us laugh in "The Ransom of Red Chief." Some of these are **exaggeration** (overstatement), **understatement, situational irony** (a contrast between what we expect and what happens), and **high-falutin'** (fancy) **language.** In the chart below, list several examples of each kind of humor.

Exaggeration	Situational Irony
Understatement	High-falutin' Language

Vocabulary and Comprehension

A. Match words and definitions. Write the letter of the correct definition next to each word.

_____ **1.** diatribe   **a.** natural tendencies

_____ **2.** somnolent   **b.** proposal

_____ **3.** peremptory   **c.** consented

_____ **4.** acceded   **d.** indescribable

_____ **5.** surreptitiously   **e.** drowsy

_____ **6.** renegade   **f.** traitor

_____ **7.** proclivities   **g.** condemnation

_____ **8.** palatable   **h.** in a sneaky way

_____ **9.** ineffable   **i.** commanding

_____ **10.** proposition   **j.** acceptable

> **Word Bank**
> diatribe
> somnolent
> peremptory
> acceded
> surreptitiously
> renegade
> proclivities
> palatable
> ineffable
> proposition

B. Choose two words from the Word Bank. Use each word in a sentence.

1. _____

_____

2. _____

_____

C. Answer each question below.

1. Why did Sam and Bill's kidnapping scheme fail?

_____

2. How did Sam and Bill finally get away from the boy?

_____

The Cremation of Sam McGee

Make the Connection

Going to Extremes

"The Cremation of Sam McGee" is a tall tale in rhyme. A **tall tale** is an obviously untrue story told with a straight face, as though it should be believed. The key element of a tall tale is **exaggeration,** otherwise known as overstatement. When you exaggerate for comic effect, you stretch the truth as high and wide as it will go, like this:

- "We were so hungry we ate everything on the table, and then we ate the table."
- "It rained so hard, I had to swim to school."
- "My dog is so smart, he does my homework for me."

Now you try it. Complete the three starters below with humorous exaggerations. If you prefer, you can cross them out and make up some of your own. Try to exaggerate in a way that creates a funny or weird **image,** or picture. Then, draw a picture to illustrate one of your exaggerations.

Exaggeration	Draw the Image
• It was so cold _____ _____	
• It was so hot _____ _____	
• My backpack is so heavy _____ _____ _____	

The Cremation of Sam McGee

Robert W. Service

Background

In the 1890s, gold was discovered in the Klondike region of the Yukon Territory in northwestern Canada. The town of Dawson became the capital of the Yukon Territory. Thousands of fortune hunters braved the bitter cold and deep snow of the Klondike in hopes of striking it rich.

Like many gold seekers, Sam McGee was unprepared for the Klondike's seven-month winter, with its extreme temperatures falling as low as −68° F.

A *cremation* is the burning of a dead body. The *Northern Lights* are bands of lights that sometimes appear in the night sky of the Northern Hemisphere.

PREDICT

Based on this first stanza, lines 1–8, what do you predict the **mood** of this poem will be? Underline the details that suggest this mood to you.

_____

_____

INFER

Circle in lines 9–12 the place where Sam McGee came from. What kind of climate is he used to?

_____

_____

_____

_____

IDENTIFY

A **simile** is a comparison between two unlike things using _like_ or _as_. Circle the simile in line 14. Notice that this simile is also an **exaggeration,** an overstatement of the cold.

_____

_____

_____

_____

_____

_____

*T*here are strange things done in the midnight sun
    By the men who moil[1] for gold;
The Arctic trails have their secret tales
    That would make your blood run cold;
5   The Northern Lights have seen queer sights,
    But the queerest they ever did see
Was that night on the marge[2] of Lake Lebarge
    I cremated Sam McGee.

Now Sam McGee was from Tennessee, where the cotton blooms
    and blows.
Why he left his home in the South to roam 'round the
10   Pole, God only knows.
He was always cold, but the land of gold seemed to hold him
    like a spell;
Though he'd often say in his homely way that he'd "sooner live
    in hell."

On a Christmas Day we were mushing our way over the
    Dawson trail.
Talk of your cold! through the parka's fold it stabbed like a
    driven nail.
If our eyes we'd close, then the lashes froze till sometimes
15   we couldn't see;
It wasn't much fun, but the only one to whimper was Sam
    McGee.

And that very night, as we lay packed tight in our robes
    beneath the snow,
And the dogs were fed, and the stars o'erhead were dancing
    heel and toe,
He turned to me, and "Cap," says he, "I'll cash in this trip,
    I guess;
And if I do, I'm asking that you won't refuse my last
20   request."

---

1. **moil:** labor.
2. **marge:** edge.

Well, he seemed so low that I couldn't say no; then he says
    with a sort of moan:
"It's the cursèd cold, and it's got right hold till I'm chilled clean
    through to the bone.
Yet 'tain't being dead—it's my awful dread of the icy grave that
    pains;
So I want you to swear that, foul or fair, you'll cremate my last
    remains."

A pal's last need is a thing to heed, so I swore I would
25   not fail;
And we started on at the streak of dawn; but God! he looked
    ghastly pale.
He crouched on the sleigh, and he raved all day of his home in
    Tennessee;
And before nightfall a corpse was all that was left of Sam
    McGee.

There wasn't a breath in that land of death, and I hurried,
    horror-driven,
With a corpse half hid that I couldn't get rid, because of a
30   promise given;
It was lashed to the sleigh, and it seemed to say: "You may tax
    your brawn and brains,
But you promised true, and it's up to you to cremate those last
    remains."

Now a promise made is a debt unpaid, and the trail has its own
    stern code.
In the days to come, though my lips were dumb, in my heart
    how I cursed that load.
In the long, long night, by the lone firelight, while the huskies,
35   round in a ring,
Howled out their woes to the homeless snows—O God! how I
    loathed the thing.

IDENTIFY

Underline the words in lines 21–24 that tell about Sam's last request. What does he fear more than death?

_____

_____

_____

_____

IDENTIFY

Alliteration is the repetition of consonant sounds in words close together in a poem. Alliteration often involves sounds at the beginning of words ("hurried, horror-driven," line 29). It can also involve sounds inside or at the end of words ("promise made is a debt unpaid," line 33). Re-read line 35, and circle all the alliteration you find in it.

PREDICT

Will the narrator be able to keep his promise to Sam? Will the narrator also die? Predict what you think will happen.

_____

_____

_____

_____

RETELL

Pause at line 44. **Retell** what has happened to Sam and the narrator since Christmas Day (line 13).

And every day that quiet clay seemed to heavy and
    heavier grow;
And on I went, though the dogs were spent and the grub was
    getting low;
The trail was bad, and I felt half mad, but I swore I would not
    give in;
And I'd often sing to the hateful thing, and it hearkened[3] with
40   a grin.

Till I came to the marge of Lake Lebarge, and a derelict[4] there
    lay;
It was jammed in the ice, but I saw in a trice it was called the
    "Alice May."
And I looked at it, and I thought a bit, and I looked at my
    frozen chum;
Then "Here," said I, with a sudden cry, "is my cre-ma-tor-ium."

Some planks I tore from the cabin floor, and I lit the
45   boiler fire;
Some coal I found that was lying around, and I heaped the fuel
    higher;
The flames just soared, and the furnace roared—such a blaze
    you seldom see;
And I burrowed a hole in the glowing coal, and I stuffed in Sam
    McGee.

Then I made a hike, for I didn't like to hear him sizzle so;
And the heavens scowled, and the huskies howled, and the
50   wind began to blow.
It was icy cold, but the hot sweat rolled down my cheeks, and I
    don't know why;
And the greasy smoke in an inky cloak went streaking down
    the sky.

VISUALIZE

Re-read lines 45–52. Underline the **images,** details that appeal to your senses. Notice how they create a nightmarish scene. Circle the vivid verbs that appeal to your senses.

---

3. **hearkened** (härk′ənd): listened carefully.
4. **derelict** (der′ə·likt′): abandoned ship.

I do not know how long in the snow I wrestled with
    grisly[5] fear;
But the stars came out and they danced about ere again I
    ventured near;
I was sick with dread, but I bravely said: "I'll just take a peep
55   inside.
I guess he's cooked, and it's time I looked"; . . . then the door
    I opened wide.

And there sat Sam, looking cool and calm, in the heart of the
    furnace roar;
And he wore a smile you could see a mile, and he said: "Please
    close that door.
It's fine in here, but I greatly fear you'll let in the cold and
    storm—
Since I left Plumtree, down in Tennessee, it's the first time I've
60   been warm."

There are strange things done in the midnight sun
    By the men who moil for gold;
The Arctic trails have their secret tales
    That would make your blood run cold;
65 *The Northern Lights have seen queer sights,*
    But the queerest they ever did see
Was that night on the marge of Lake Lebarge
    I cremated Sam McGee.

---

5. grisly: here, caused by something horrible.

IDENTIFY

Look closely at lines 53–54. Notice that this poem uses **end rhymes,** rhymes at the ends of lines (fear/near), as well as **internal rhymes,** rhymes contained inside lines (know/snow; out/about). In lines 55–56, underline the two end rhymes, and circle the two pairs of internal rhymes.

INFER

What did Cap expect to see when he opened the door? What does he see instead?

_____

_____

_____

_____

BUILD FLUENCY

Read the boxed passage twice. Emphasize the strong, regular rhythm that thumps along throughout the poem. Try to capture Cap's tone of voice and his surprise when he opens the door. Notice and try to show with your voice where the mood of the poem suddenly changes. Try two or three ways of reading the **refrain**— the lines repeated at the beginning and end of the poem—to make them sound different from the other stanza in this passage.

Story Map

"The Cremation of Sam McGee" is a poem that tells a story, so it has a plot. Use the Story Map below to show how one plot element leads to another until you get to the resolution.

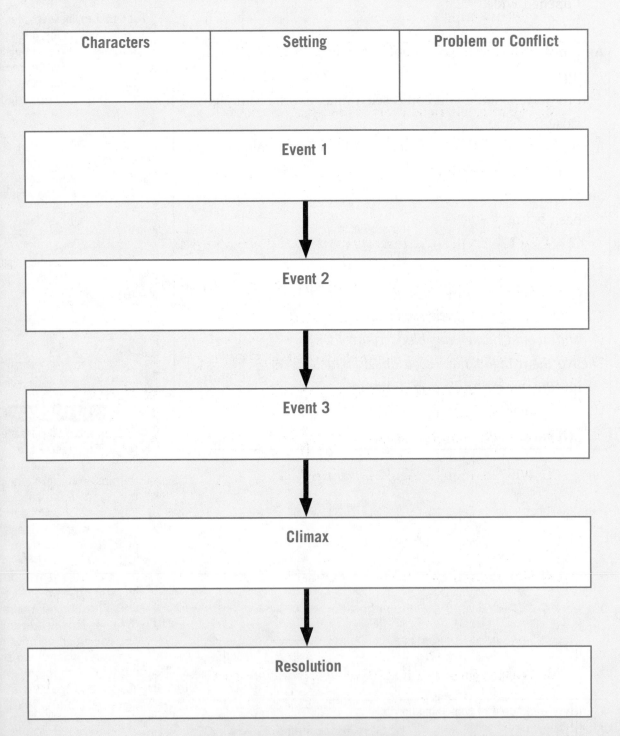

Characters	Setting	Problem or Conflict

Event 1

Event 2

Event 3

Climax

Resolution

Vocabulary and Comprehension

A. Complete each sentence with one of these words: *code, remains, ghastly, spell.*

1. Even though Sam McGee hated the cold, the Klondike gold seemed to hold him like a _____ .

2. When Sam was dying, he turned a horrible, _____ shade of blue.

3. He made his friend promise to cremate his dead _____ .

4. If his friend broke his promise, he would also break the rules, or the _____ , of the trail.

B. Write **T** or **F** next to each statement to tell if it is true or false.

_____**1.** The narrator promises to cremate Sam McGee if he dies.

_____**2.** Sam McGee loves cold weather.

_____**3.** The narrator never keeps his promises.

_____**4.** The narrator puts Sam on an abandoned ship and sets fire to it.

C. Answer each question below.

1. Why does Sam want to be cremated?

_____

_____

2. Give details from the poem that describe the cold.

_____

_____

3. What happens to Sam McGee when he is cremated?

_____

_____

Paul Revere's Ride

Make the Connection

Two Kinds of Heroes

Heroes are the men and women we admire. Some heroes are famous. They're given parades and medals that honor the important things they've done. Other heroes may be known to only a few people. They're everyday heroes, such as the patient coach who brought out the best in us, or the relative who helped us through a rough time. By being people we can look up to, heroes change our lives.

Imagine that you could award a medal to two heroes, one famous hero (living or dead), and one everyday hero. Write the name of your heroes inside the medals below. Then, give three reasons why you chose these people as your heroes.

Reasons: 1. _____   1. _____

_____   _____

2. _____   2. _____

_____   _____

3. _____   3. _____

_____   _____

Henry Wadsworth Longfellow

PAUL REVERE'S RIDE

Background

This poem is based loosely on historical events. On the night of April 18, 1775, Paul Revere, William Dawes, and Dr. Samuel Prescott set out from Boston to warn American colonists of a planned British raid on Concord, Massachusetts. The British wanted to arrest two Americans who were calling for armed resistance to England. The British also wanted to destroy a supply of arms in Concord. The next day armed volunteers known as minutemen confronted the British at Lexington and Concord. These were the first battles of the American Revolution.

RETELL

Pause at line 14. **Retell** in your own words the system of signals that Revere arranges with his friend, and the action he plans to take.

_____

_____

_____

_____

INFER

Re-read lines 15–23. Explain why it takes bravery for Revere to row to Charlestown. What could happen to him?

_____

_____

_____

IDENTIFY

Circle two details in lines 19–23 that describe the Somerset in a scary way.

_____

_____

_____

_____

Listen, my children, and you shall hear
Of the midnight ride of Paul Revere,
On the eighteenth of April, in Seventy-five;
Hardly a man is now alive
Who remembers that famous day and year.

He said to his friend, "If the British march
By land or sea from the town tonight,
Hang a lantern aloft in the belfry arch
Of the North Church tower as a signal light—
10 One, if by land, and two, if by sea;
And I on the opposite shore will be,
Ready to ride and spread the alarm
Through every Middlesex village and farm,
For the country folk to be up and to arm."

Then he said, "Good night!" and with muffled oar
Silently rowed to the Charlestown shore,
Just as the moon rose over the bay,
Where swinging wide at her moorings[1] lay
The Somerset, British man-of-war;
20 A phantom ship, with each mast and spar[2]
Across the moon like a prison bar,
And a huge black hulk, that was magnified
By its own reflection in the tide.

Meanwhile, his friend, through alley and street,
Wanders and watches with eager ears,
Till in the silence around him he hears
The muster[3] of men at the barrack door,
The sound of arms, and the tramp of feet,
And the measured tread of the grenadiers,[4]
30 Marching down to their boats on the shore.

---

1. **moorings:** cables holding a ship in place so that it doesn't float away.
2. **mast and spar:** poles supporting a ship's sails.
3. **muster:** assembly; gathering.
4. **grenadiers** (gren'ə·dirz'): foot soldiers who carry and throw grenades.

Then he climbed the tower of the Old North Church,

By the wooden stairs, with stealthy tread,

To the belfry chamber overhead,

And startled the pigeons from their perch

On the somber rafters, that round him made

Masses and moving shapes of shade—

By the trembling ladder, steep and tall,

To the highest window in the wall,

Where he paused to listen and look down

40 A moment on the roofs of the town,

And the moonlight flowing over all.

Beneath, in the churchyard, lay the dead,

In their night encampment on the hill,

Wrapped in silence so deep and still

That he could hear, like a sentinel's⁵ tread,

The watchful night wind, as it went

Creeping along from tent to tent,

And seeming to whisper, "All is well!"

A moment only he feels the spell

50 Of the place and the hour, and the secret dread

Of the lonely belfry and the dead;

For suddenly all his thoughts are bent

On a shadowy something far away,

Where the river widens to meet the bay—

A line of black that bends and floats

On the rising tide, like a bridge of boats.

Meanwhile, impatient to mount and ride,

Booted and spurred, with a heavy stride

On the opposite shore walked Paul Revere.

60 Now he patted his horse's side,

Now gazed at the landscape far and near,

Then, impetuous,⁶ stamped the earth,

And turned and tightened his saddle girth;

But mostly he watched with eager search

IDENTIFY

Alliteration is the repetition of consonant sounds in words that are close together. Underline two examples of alliteration in lines 31–41.

INTERPRET

The speaker uses a **metaphor,** a comparison without using *like* or *as*, to compare the graveyard to a military camp (line 43). Another metaphor compares the gravestones to soldiers' tents (line 47). Circle the **simile,** the comparison that does use *like* or *as*, in lines 45–48. What is the wind compared to?

_____

_____

INFER

What is the "shadowy something" (line 53) that Revere's friend sees from his lookout?

_____

_____

PREDICT

Pause at line 56. What do you think Revere's friend will do next? (Remember the plan!)

_____

_____

_____

INFER

Based on lines 57–72, describe Revere's **character.** Circle two details that lead you to that description.

_____

_____

_____

INFER

What do the two lamps (line 72) in the church belfry mean? How will the British be coming?

_____

_____

_____

BUILD FLUENCY

Read the boxed passage aloud. Then, read it aloud a second time. Try to capture the **rhythm** of galloping hooves. Notice how the **alliteration,** with its repeated consonant sounds, suggests the sound of hooves striking the ground.

IDENTIFY

In lines 81–92, circle one **image** that appeals to each sense: sight, hearing, and touch. Draw an arrow from each circled image, and write the sense the image appeals to.

_____

_____

_____

The belfry tower of the Old North Church,
As it rose above the graves on the hill,
Lonely and spectral[7] and somber and still.
And lo! as he looks, on the belfry's height
A glimmer, and then a gleam of light!
70 He springs to the saddle, the bridle he turns,
But lingers and gazes, till full on his sight
A second lamp in the belfry burns!

A hurry of hoofs in a village street,
A shape in the moonlight, a bulk in the dark,
And beneath, from the pebbles, in passing, a spark
Struck out by a steed flying fearless and fleet:
That was all! And yet, through the gloom and the light,
The fate of a nation was riding that night;
And the spark struck out by that steed, in his flight,
80 Kindled the land into flame with its heat.

He has left the village and mounted the steep,
And beneath him, tranquil and broad and deep,
Is the Mystic, meeting the ocean tides;
And under the alders that skirt its edge,
Now soft on the sand, now loud on the ledge,
Is heard the tramp of his steed as he rides.

It was twelve by the village clock,
When he crossed the bridge into Medford town.
He heard the crowing of the cock,
90 And the barking of the farmer's dog,
And felt the damp of the river fog,
That rises after the sun goes down.

It was one by the village clock,
When he galloped into Lexington.
He saw the gilded weathercock
Swim in the moonlight as he passed,

7. **spectral:** ghostly.

And the meetinghouse windows, blank and bare,

Gaze at him with a spectral glare,

As if they already stood aghast

100 At the bloody work they would look upon.

It was two by the village clock,

When he came to the bridge in Concord town.

He heard the bleating of the flock,

And the twitter of birds among the trees,

And felt the breath of the morning breeze

Blowing over the meadows brown.

And one was safe and asleep in his bed

Who at the bridge would be first to fall,

Who that day would be lying dead,

110 Pierced by a British musket ball.

You know the rest. In the books you have read,

How the British Regulars fired and fled—

How the farmers gave them ball for ball,

From behind each fence and farmyard wall,

Chasing the redcoats down the lane,

Then crossing the fields to emerge again

Under the trees at the turn of the road,

And only pausing to fire and load.

So through the night rode Paul Revere;

120 And so through the night went his cry of alarm

To every Middlesex village and farm—

A cry of defiance and not of fear,

A voice in the darkness, a knock at the door,

And a word that shall echo forevermore!

For, borne on the night wind of the Past,

Through all our history, to the last,

In the hour of darkness and peril and need,

The people will waken and listen to hear

The hurrying hoofbeats of that steed,

130 And the midnight message of Paul Revere.

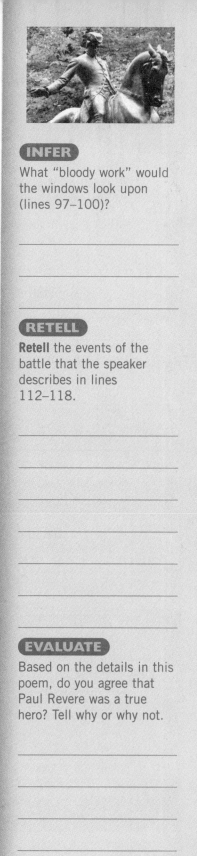

INFER

What "bloody work" would the windows look upon (lines 97–100)?

_____

_____

_____

RETELL

Retell the events of the battle that the speaker describes in lines 112–118.

_____

_____

_____

_____

_____

_____

EVALUATE

Based on the details in this poem, do you agree that Paul Revere was a true hero? Tell why or why not.

_____

_____

_____

_____

_____

_____

Character Traits Cluster

We learn a lot about Paul Revere from reading this poem. This graphic will help you create a profile of his character. Fill in details from the poem in the boxes below. At the end of the cluster, write your profile of Paul Revere's character.

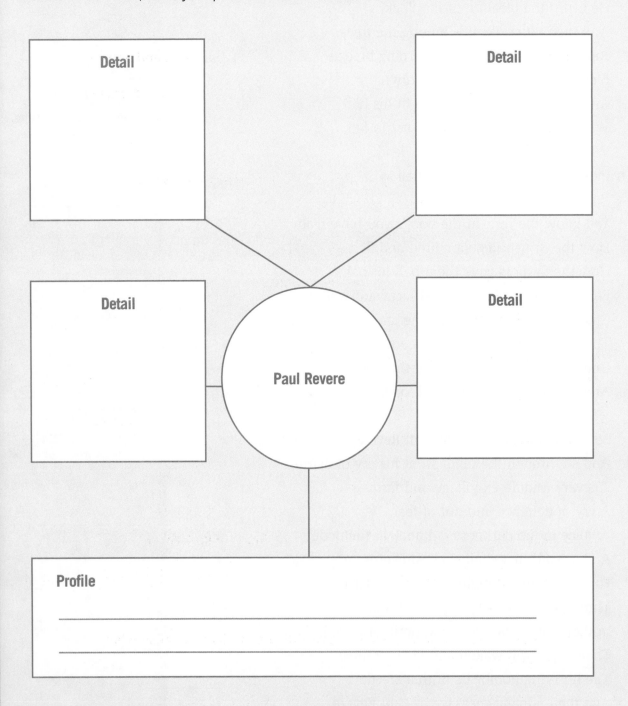

Detail

Detail

Detail

Paul Revere

Detail

Profile

_____

_____

Vocabulary and Comprehension

A. Complete each phrase with one of these words: *tranquil*, *defiance*, *muffled*, *stealthy*.

1. sneaking, secret, _____ footsteps

2. a soft, barely heard, _____ sound of oars

3. a calm, peaceful, _____ evening

4. a cry of challenge and _____

B. Match words and synonyms. Write the letter of the correct synonym next to each word.

_____**1.** somber   **a.** danger

_____**2.** peril   **b.** serious

_____**3.** gazes   **c.** eager

_____**4.** impatient   **d.** looks

C. Answer each question below.

1. What did the two lights in the church belfry signify?

_____

_____

2. Where does Revere ride after he sees the two lights in the belfry?

_____

_____

3. The poet says "the fate of a nation was riding that night." Explain what he meant.

_____

_____

from Harriet Tubman: Conductor on the Underground Railroad

Make the Connection

Honoring a Freedom Fighter

Throughout our country's history, men and women have fought for freedom. Some of them have even given their lives so others could be free. Imagine that you've been asked to design a Freedom Coin. You get to choose the Freedom Fighter whose face (in profile) will be on the coin. The graphic below shows the A and B sides of a coin. On the A side, write

- the name of the person who was (or is) an outstanding freedom fighter
- one word or phrase that you associate with freedom, and
- the year when this coin will be made

On the B side of the coin, write *United States of America*. Then, inside it, draw a symbol that means freedom to you. (You might want to look at real coins for ideas.)

On the lines below the coin, explain why you chose your freedom fighter, and why you chose the symbol.

A side   B side

I chose _____ as the Freedom Fighter

because _____ .

I chose _____ for a freedom symbol

because _____ .

Ann Petry

FROM Harriet Tubman: Conductor on the Underground Railroad

Background

In the Biblical Book of Exodus, God chooses Moses to lead the people of Israel out of slavery in Egypt. Pursued by the Egyptians, Moses takes his people on a long, perilous desert journey and leads them to the Promised Land. As you read about Harriet Tubman, ask yourself why she was called "the Moses of her people."

IDENTIFY

Circle the name of the "man" who was "running off slaves." Explain in your own words what this person was doing.

_____

_____

_____

_____

_____

INFER

Who or what do you think was making bird sounds? Underline the details in lines 17–20 that back up your **inference.**

_____

_____

_____

_____

IDENTIFY

In lines 25–32, circle the day when runaway slaves were usually missed. Underline the reasons why slaves usually left on that day.

_____

_____

_____

WORDS TO OWN
fugitives (fyo͞o′ji·tivz) _n._: people fleeing from danger.

Along the Eastern Shore of Maryland, in Dorchester County, in Caroline County, the masters kept hearing whispers about the man named Moses, who was running off slaves. At first they did not believe in his existence. The stories about him were fantastic, unbelievable. Yet they watched for him. They offered rewards for his capture.

They never saw him. Now and then they heard whispered rumors to the effect that he was in the neighborhood. The woods were searched. The roads were watched. There was
10 never anything to indicate his whereabouts. But a few days afterward, a goodly number of slaves would be gone from the plantation. Neither the master nor the overseer had heard or seen anything unusual in the quarter.[1] Sometimes one or the other would vaguely remember having heard a whippoorwill call somewhere in the woods, close by, late at night. Though it was the wrong season for whippoorwills.

Sometimes the masters thought they had heard the cry of a hoot owl, repeated, and would remember having thought that the intervals between the low moaning cry were wrong, that
20 it had been repeated four times in succession instead of three. There was never anything more than that to suggest that all was not well in the quarter. Yet, when morning came, they invariably discovered that a group of the finest slaves had taken to their heels.

Unfortunately, the discovery was almost always made on a Sunday. Thus a whole day was lost before the machinery of pursuit could be set in motion. The posters offering rewards for the <u>fugitives</u> could not be printed until Monday. The men who made a living hunting for runaway slaves were out of reach,
30 off in the woods with their dogs and their guns, in pursuit of four-footed game, or they were in camp meetings saying their prayers with their wives and families beside them.

Harriet Tubman could have told them that there was far more involved in this matter of running off slaves than

_____

1. **quarter:** area in a plantation where enslaved Africans lived. It consisted of windowless, one-room cabins made of logs and mud.

signaling the would-be runaways by imitating the call of a whippoorwill, or a hoot owl, far more involved than a matter of waiting for a clear night when the North Star[2] was visible.

In December 1851, when she started out with the band of fugitives that she planned to take to Canada, she had been in
40　the vicinity of the plantation for days, planning the trip, carefully selecting the slaves that she would take with her.

She had announced her arrival in the quarter by singing the forbidden spiritual[3]—"Go down, Moses, 'way down to Egypt Land"—singing it softly outside the door of a slave cabin, late at night. The husky voice was beautiful even when it was barely more than a murmur borne on the wind.

Once she had made her presence known, word of her coming spread from cabin to cabin. The slaves whispered to each other, ear to mouth, mouth to ear, "Moses is here."
50　"Moses has come." "Get ready. Moses is back again." The ones who had agreed to go North with her put ashcake[4] and salt herring in an old bandanna, hastily tied it into a bundle, and then waited patiently for the signal that meant it was time to start.

There were eleven in this party, including one of her brothers and his wife. It was the largest group that she had ever conducted, but she was determined that more and more slaves should know what freedom was like.

She had to take them all the way to Canada. The Fugitive
60　Slave Law[5] was no longer a great many incomprehensible words written down on the country's lawbooks. The new law had become a reality. It was Thomas Sims, a boy, picked up on the streets of Boston at night and shipped back to Georgia. It was Jerry and Shadrach, arrested and jailed with no warning.

---

2. **North Star:** Runaways fleeing north used the North Star (Polaris) to help them stay on course.
3. **forbidden spiritual:** Spirituals are religious songs, some of which are based on the Biblical story of the Israelites' escape from slavery in Egypt. Plantation owners feared that the singing of spirituals might lead to rebellion.
4. **ashcake:** cornmeal bread baked in hot ashes.
5. **Fugitive Slave Law:** harsh federal law passed in 1850 stating that slaves who escaped to free states could be forced to return to their owners. As a result, those who escaped were safe only in Canada. The law also made it a crime for a free person to help slaves escape or to prevent their return.

INFER

Why did Harriet Tubman wait for the North Star to be visible?

_____

_____

IDENTIFY

Underline the signal Tubman used to let slaves know she was in the area. What was the real name of "the man named Moses, who was running off slaves" (page 178, line 3)?

_____

_____

INFER

Why do the people put ashcake and salt herring in a bundle?

_____

_____

_____

_____

_____

_____

_____

WORDS TO OWN
incomprehensible
(in·käm′prē·hen′sə·bəl)
adj.: impossible to understand.

IDENTIFY

Re-read lines 65–77. Underline the details that tell you why this trip was different—and more difficult—for Tubman.

INFER

Pause at line 77. Circle the way Tubman would be punished if she and the slaves were caught. List below three **inferences** you can make about Tubman's **character** from the information you have read so far. Support each inference with one detail from the text.

_____

_____

_____

_____

_____

INFER

Re-read lines 85–98. Underline the details that tell you the runaways will not be welcomed at their first stop. Circle the two reasons the farmer turns them away.

WORDS TO OWN

incentive (in·sent′iv) *n.:* reason to do something; motivation.

disheveled (di·shev′əld) *adj.:* rumpled; untidy.

She had never been in Canada. The route beyond Philadelphia was strange to her. But she could not let the runaways who accompanied her know this. As they walked along, she told them stories of her own first flight; she kept painting vivid word pictures of what it would be like to be free.

70   But there were so many of them this time. She knew moments of doubt, when she was half afraid and kept looking back over her shoulder, imagining that she heard the sound of pursuit. They would certainly be pursued. Eleven of them. Eleven thousand dollars' worth of flesh and bone and muscle that belonged to Maryland planters. If they were caught, the eleven runaways would be whipped and sold South, but she— she would probably be hanged.

They tried to sleep during the day but they never could wholly relax into sleep. She could tell by the positions they
80   assumed, by their restless movements. And they walked at night. Their progress was slow. It took them three nights of walking to reach the first stop. She had told them about the place where they would stay, promising warmth and good food, holding these things out to them as an <u>incentive</u> to keep going.

When she knocked on the door of a farmhouse, a place where she and her parties of runaways had always been welcome, always been given shelter and plenty to eat, there was no answer. She knocked again, softly. A voice from within said, "Who is it?" There was fear in the voice.

90   She knew instantly from the sound of the voice that there was something wrong. She said, "A friend with friends," the password on the Underground Railroad.

The door opened, slowly. The man who stood in the doorway looked at her coldly, looked with unconcealed astonishment and fear at the eleven <u>disheveled</u> runaways who were standing near her. Then he shouted, "Too many, too many. It's not safe. My place was searched last week. It's not safe!" and slammed the door in her face.

She turned away from the house, frowning. She had
100   promised her passengers food and rest and warmth, and instead

of that, there would be hunger and cold and more walking over the frozen ground. Somehow she would have to <u>instill</u> courage into these eleven people, most of them strangers, would have to feed them on hope and bright dreams of freedom instead of the fried pork and corn bread and milk she had promised them.

They stumbled along behind her, half dead for sleep, and she urged them on, though she was as tired and as discouraged as they were. She had never been in Canada, but she kept painting wondrous word pictures of what it would be like. She 110 managed to <u>dispel</u> their fear of pursuit so that they would not become hysterical, panic-stricken. Then she had to bring some of the fear back, so that they would stay awake and keep walking though they drooped with sleep.

Yet, during the day, when they lay down deep in a thicket, they never really slept, because if a twig snapped or the wind sighed in the branches of a pine tree, they jumped to their feet, afraid of their own shadows, shivering and shaking. It was very cold, but they dared not make fires because someone would see the smoke and wonder about it.

120 She kept thinking, eleven of them. Eleven thousand dollars' worth of slaves. And she had to take them all the way to Canada. Sometimes she told them about Thomas Garrett, in Wilmington.[6] She said he was their friend even though he did not know them. He was the friend of all fugitives. He called them God's poor. He was a Quaker[7] and his speech was a little different from that of other people. His clothing was different, too. He wore the wide-brimmed hat that the Quakers wear.

She said that he had thick white hair, soft, almost like a baby's, and the kindest eyes she had ever seen. He was a big 130 man and strong, but he had never used his strength to harm anyone, always to help people. He would give all of them a new pair of shoes. Everybody. He always did. Once they reached his house in Wilmington, they would be safe. He would see to it that they were.

---

6. **Wilmington**: city in Delaware.
7. **Quaker**: member of the Society of Friends, a religious group active in the movement to end slavery.

INTERPRET
Why has the runaways' situation suddenly become more dangerous?

INTERPRET
How does Tubman keep up the runaways' courage? What does the narrator mean when she says that Tubman had to "bring some of the fear back" (lines 111–112)?

PREDICT
Pause at line 119. Things don't look good for the runaways. What do you think will happen to them?

WORDS TO OWN
instill (in·stil') v.: gradually put in.
dispel (di·spel') v.: drive away; scatter.

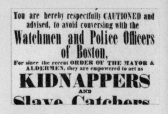

IDENTIFY

Circle three details from the text that tell you what Thomas Garrett does to help the fugitives.

INFER

Why does Tubman make the runaways hide behind trees? What does this action reveal about her character?

_____

_____

_____

_____

RETELL

Retell what happened at the first stop (page 180, lines 85–98) and at the second stop (lines 151-171) on Tubman's journey with the runaways.

_____

_____

_____

_____

_____

_____

_____

_____

_____

She described the house where he lived, told them about the store where he sold shoes. She said he kept a pail of milk and a loaf of bread in the drawer of his desk so that he would have food ready at hand for any of God's poor who should suddenly appear before him, fainting with hunger. There was a 140 hidden room in the store. A whole wall swung open, and behind it was a room where he could hide fugitives. On the wall there were shelves filled with small boxes—boxes of shoes—so that you would never guess that the wall actually opened.

While she talked, she kept watching them. They did not believe her. She could tell by their expressions. They were thinking. New shoes, Thomas Garrett, Quaker, Wilmington— what foolishness was this? Who knew if she told the truth? Where was she taking them anyway?

That night they reached the next stop—a farm that belonged 150 to a German. She made the runaways take shelter behind trees at the edge of the fields before she knocked at the door. She hesitated before she approached the door, thinking, suppose that he too should refuse shelter, suppose— Then she thought, *Lord, I'm going to hold steady on to You and You've got to see me through*—and knocked softly.

She heard the familiar guttural voice say, "Who's there?"

She answered quickly, "A friend with friends."

He opened the door and greeted her warmly. "How many this time?" he asked.

160 "Eleven," she said and waited, doubting, wondering.

He said, "Good. Bring them in."

He and his wife fed them in the lamp-lit kitchen, their faces glowing as they offered food and more food, urging them to eat, saying there was plenty for everybody, have more milk, have more bread, have more meat.

They spent the night in the warm kitchen. They really slept, all that night and until dusk the next day. When they left, it was with reluctance. They had all been warm and safe and well-fed. It was hard to exchange the security offered by 170 that clean, warm kitchen for the darkness and the cold of a December night.

"Go On or Die"

Harriet had found it hard to leave the warmth and friendliness, too. But she urged them on. For a while, as they walked, they seemed to carry in them a measure of contentment; some of the serenity and the cleanliness of that big, warm kitchen lingered on inside them. But as they walked farther and farther away from the warmth and the light, the cold and the darkness entered into them. They fell silent, sullen, suspicious. She waited for the moment when some one of them would turn

180 mutinous. It did not happen that night.

Two nights later, she was aware that the feet behind her were moving slower and slower. She heard the irritability in their voices, knew that soon someone would refuse to go on.

She started talking about William Still and the Philadelphia Vigilance Committee.[8] No one commented. No one asked any questions. She told them the story of William and Ellen Craft and how they escaped from Georgia. Ellen was so fair that she looked as though she were white, and so she dressed up in a man's clothing and she looked like a wealthy young planter.

190 Her husband, William, who was dark, played the role of her slave. Thus they traveled from Macon, Georgia, to Philadelphia, riding on the trains, staying at the finest hotels. Ellen pretended to be very ill—her right arm was in a sling and her right hand was bandaged because she was supposed to have rheumatism.[9] Thus she avoided having to sign the register at the hotels, for she could not read or write. They finally arrived safely in Philadelphia and then went on to Boston.

No one said anything. Not one of them seemed to have heard her.

200 She told them about Frederick Douglass, the most famous of the escaped slaves, of his eloquence, of his magnificent appearance. Then she told them of her own first, vain effort at running away, evoking the memory of that miserable life she had led as a child, reliving it for a moment in the telling.

---

8. **Philadelphia Vigilance Committee:** group that offered help to people escaping slavery. Still, a free African American, was chairman of the committee.

9. **rheumatism** (r$\overline{oo}$′mə·tiz′əm): painful swelling and stiffness of the joints or muscles.

PREDICT

Do you think the fugitives will really turn against Tubman (line 183)? What actions might they take?

_____

_____

_____

INTERPRET

Why does Tubman tell stories to the fugitives?

_____

_____

_____

_____

_____

_____

_____

_____

WORDS TO OWN

mutinous (my$\overline{oo}$t′'n·əs) *adj.:* rebellious; turning against a leader.

eloquence (el′ə·kwəns) *n.:* ability to speak and write convincingly.

IDENTIFY

Re-read lines 221–230. Circle the reason Tubman says no slave can return to the plantation. Then, underline the details that tell how one returned slave might ruin the whole operation for helping runaways.

INTERPRET

Explain what Tubman means when she says (lines 231–232), "We got to go free or die. And freedom's not bought with dust."

_____

_____

_____

_____

_____

_____

_____

_____

_____

_____

BUILD FLUENCY

Read the boxed passage aloud twice. See if you can read it more smoothly each time. Try to use a voice that will show Tubman's strong character.

But they had been tired too long, hungry too long, afraid too long, footsore too long. One of them suddenly cried out in despair, "Let me go back. It is better to be a slave than to suffer like this in order to be free."

She carried a gun with her on these trips. She had never 210 used it—except as a threat. Now, as she aimed it, she experienced a feeling of guilt, remembering that time, years ago, when she had prayed for the death of Edward Brodas, the Master, and then, not too long afterward, had heard that great wailing cry that came from the throats of the field hands, and knew from the sound that the Master was dead.

One of the runaways said again, "Let me go back. Let me go back," and stood still, and then turned around and said, over his shoulder, "I am going back."

She lifted the gun, aimed it at the despairing slave. She said, 220 "Go on with us or die." The husky, low-pitched voice was grim.

He hesitated for a moment and then he joined the others. They started walking again. She tried to explain to them why none of them could go back to the plantation. If a runaway returned, he would turn traitor; the master and the overseer would force him to turn traitor. The returned slave would disclose the stopping places, the hiding places, the corn stacks they had used with the full knowledge of the owner of the farm, the name of the German farmer who had fed them and sheltered them. These people who had risked their own security 230 to help runaways would be ruined, fined, imprisoned.

She said, "We got to go free or die. And freedom's not bought with dust."

This time she told them about the long agony of the Middle Passage[10] on the old slave ships, about the black horror of the holds, about the chains and the whips. They too knew these stories. But she wanted to remind them of the long, hard way they had come, about the long, hard way they had yet to go. She told them about Thomas Sims, the boy picked up on the

10. **Middle Passage:** route traveled by ships carrying captured Africans across the Atlantic Ocean to the Americas. The captives endured the horrors of the Middle Passage crammed into **holds,** airless cargo areas below decks.

streets of Boston and sent back to Georgia. She said when
240 they got him back to Savannah, got him in prison there, they
whipped him until a doctor who was standing by watching
said, "You will kill him if you strike him again!" His master
said, "Let him die!"

Thus she forced them to go on. Sometimes she thought she
had become nothing but a voice speaking in the darkness,
cajoling, urging, threatening. Sometimes she told them things to
make them laugh; sometimes she sang to them and heard the
eleven voices behind her blending softly with hers, and then
she knew that for the moment all was well with them.

250 She gave the impression of being a short, muscular,
indomitable woman who could never be defeated. Yet at any
moment she was liable to be seized by one of those curious fits
of sleep, which might last for a few minutes or for hours.[11]

Even on this trip, she suddenly fell asleep in the woods. The
runaways, ragged, dirty, hungry, cold, did not steal the gun as
they might have and set off by themselves or turn back. They
sat on the ground near her and waited patiently until she
awakened. They had come to trust her implicitly, totally. They,
too, had come to believe her repeated statement, "We got to go
260 free or die." She was leading them into freedom, and so they
waited until she was ready to go on.

Finally, they reached Thomas Garrett's house in
Wilmington, Delaware. Just as Harriet had promised, Garrett
gave them all new shoes, and provided carriages to take them
on to the next stop.

By slow stages they reached Philadelphia, where William
Still hastily recorded their names, and the plantations whence
they had come, and something of the life they had led in
slavery. Then he carefully hid what he had written, for fear it
270 might be discovered. In 1872 he published this record in book
form and called it *The Underground Railroad.* In the foreword to

---

11. Harriet's losses of consciousness were caused by a serious head injury that she
had suffered as a teenager. Harriet had tried to protect another slave from punishment, and an enraged overseer threw a two-pound weight at her head.

You are hereby respectfully CAUTIONED and
advised, to avoid conversing with the
Watchmen and Police Officers
of Boston,
For since the recent ORDER OF THE MAYOR &
ALDERMEN, they are empowered to act as
KIDNAPPERS
AND
Slave Catchers

IDENTIFY

Underline the words in lines
254–261 that tell you that
the runaways' attitude
toward Tubman has
changed.

_____

_____

_____

_____

INFER

William Still kept a record
book of the fugitives he had
met so that the fugitives
and their families would
have a way to find each
other. Why did Still's book
become even more
important than he realized
at the time that he kept it?

_____

_____

_____

_____

_____

WORDS TO OWN
cajoling (kə·jōl'iŋ) v. used
as *adj.:* coaxing.

EVALUATE

Evaluate Tubman as a leader. Consider at least two of the following questions in your evaluation: What advantage, if any, did being a woman give her? Why do you think she risked her own safety to help others escape to Canada?

_____

_____

_____

_____

_____

_____

_____

_____

_____

_____

_____

_____

_____

_____

_____

WORDS TO OWN
fastidious (fas·tid′ē·əs) adj.:
hard to please; fussy.

his book he said: "While I knew the danger of keeping strict records, and while I did not then dream that in my day slavery would be blotted out, or that the time would come when I could publish these records, it used to afford me great satisfaction to take them down, fresh from the lips of fugitives on the way to freedom, and to preserve them as they had given them."

280   William Still, who was familiar with all the station stops on the Underground Railroad, supplied Harriet with money and sent her and her eleven fugitives on to Burlington, New Jersey.

Harriet felt safer now, though there were danger spots ahead. But the biggest part of her job was over. As they went farther and farther north, it grew colder; she was aware of the wind on the Jersey ferry and aware of the cold damp in New York. From New York they went on to Syracuse,[12] where the temperature was even lower.

In Syracuse she met the Reverend J. W. Loguen, known as "Jarm" Loguen. This was the beginning of a lifelong friendship.

290   Both Harriet and Jarm Loguen were to become friends and supporters of Old John Brown.[13]

From Syracuse they went north again, into a colder, snowier city—Rochester. Here they almost certainly stayed with Frederick Douglass, for he wrote in his autobiography:

"On one occasion I had eleven fugitives at the same time under my roof, and it was necessary for them to remain with me until I could collect sufficient money to get them to Canada. It was the largest number I ever had at any one time, and I had some difficulty in providing so many with food and shelter, but,

300   as may well be imagined, they were not very fastidious in either direction, and were well content with very plain food, and a strip of carpet on the floor for a bed, or a place on the straw in the barn loft."

_____

12. **Syracuse:** city in central New York.
13. **Old John Brown** (1800–1859): abolitionist (opponent of slavery) who was active in the Underground Railroad. In 1859, Brown led a raid on the federal arsenal at Harpers Ferry, Virginia, in hopes of inspiring a slave uprising. Federal troops overpowered Brown and his followers, and Brown was convicted of treason and hanged.

Late in December 1851, Harriet arrived in St. Catharines, Canada West (now Ontario), with the eleven fugitives. It had taken almost a month to complete this journey.

You are hereby respectfully CAUTIONED and advised, to avoid conversing with the
Watchmen and Police Officers
of Boston,
For since the recent ORDER OF THE MAYOR & ALDERMEN, they are empowered to act as
KIDNAPPERS
AND
Slave Catchers

Beliefs Chart

Our actions and words can be strong proof of our beliefs. Harriet Tubman's willingness to risk her life showed how strongly she believed in freedom. In the graphic organizer below, list Harriet Tubman's actions and words as described in the selection. Then, based on these actions and words, fill in what you think are her beliefs about freedom and what battles for freedom she'd fight today.

Harriet Tubman's actions . . .
Harriet Tubman's words . . .

Harriet Tubman believed freedom meant . . .

_____

_____

_____

If Harriet Tubman were alive today she would probably fight for . . .

_____

_____

_____

Vocabulary and Comprehension

A. Match the words with their definitions. Write the letter of the correct definition next to each word.

_____ **1.** fugitives

_____ **2.** incomprehensible

_____ **3.** incentive

_____ **4.** disheveled

_____ **5.** instill

_____ **6.** dispel

_____ **7.** mutinous

_____ **8.** eloquence

_____ **9.** cajoling

_____ **10.** fastidious

a. rumpled

b. ability to speak convincingly

c. coaxing

d. gradually put in

e. rebellious

f. motivation

g. people fleeing danger

h. fussy

i. impossible to understand

j. scatter

Word Bank
fugitives
incomprehensible
incentive
disheveled
instill
dispel
mutinous
eloquence
cajoling
fastidious

B. Choose two words from the Word Bank. Use each word in a sentence.

1. _____

_____

2. _____

_____

C. Answer each question below.

1. What were some of the problems the fugitives were faced with on their journey to freedom?

_____

_____

2. How did Harriet Tubman's actions change history?

_____

_____

Barbara Frietchie

Make the Connection

Stars and Stripes Forever

To Barbara Frietchie, the hero of the next poem, our country's flag was more important than life itself. Wherever it's displayed, at home, around the world, or even on the moon, our red, white, and blue flag stands for the United States of America. In times of national crisis, the flag means even more.

What does our flag mean to you? Around the flag below, write words and phrases that tell the feelings, ideas, events, and hopes that you associate with our flag.

Barbara Frietchie

John Greenleaf Whittier

Background

"Barbara Frietchie" is set in 1862, during the Civil War. Led by Confederate Generals Robert E. Lee and Stonewall Jackson, the troops marched into the town of Frederick, Maryland, on September 6. The Confederates expected a warm welcome, but the people of Frederick were loyal to the Union. According to the poem, as the Confederate forces came into town, one person dared to display the U.S. flag.

VISUALIZE

Read lines 1–12. Circle the details that help you see where the town of Frederick is located in relation to the meadows, hills, orchards, and mountains. Underline the details that help you picture what these same features look like. Imagine this scene as the beginning of a movie. What do you see coming down from the hills?

_____

_____

_____

_____

_____

_____

IDENTIFY

Underline the words that reveal Frietchie's age. How old is she? (Look up "score" if you need to.)

_____

INFER

What happened to the forty flags that had been displayed in the morning?

_____

_____

_____

_____

Up from the meadows rich with corn,
Clear in the cool September morn,

The clustered spires of Frederick stand
Green-walled by the hills of Maryland.

Round about them orchards sweep,
Apple and peach tree fruited deep,

Fair as the garden of the Lord
To the eyes of the famished rebel horde,[1]

On that pleasant morn of the early fall
10   When Lee marched over the mountain wall;

Over the mountains winding down,
Horse and foot, into Frederick town.

Forty flags with their silver stars,
Forty flags with their crimson bars,

Flapped in the morning wind: the sun
Of noon looked down, and saw not one.

Up rose old Barbara Frietchie then,
Bowed with her fourscore years and ten;

Bravest of all in Frederick town,
20   She took up the flag the men hauled down

In her attic window the staff she set,
To show that one heart was loyal yet.

Up the street came the rebel tread,
Stonewall Jackson riding ahead.

---

1. **horde** (hôrd): moving crowd.

Under his slouched hat left and right
He glanced; the old flag met his sight.

"Halt!"—the dust-brown ranks stood fast.
"Fire!"—out blazed the rifle blast.

It shivered the window, pane and sash;
30 It rent the banner with seam and gash.

Quick, as it fell, from the broken staff
Dame Barbara snatched the silken scarf.

She leaned far out on the windowsill,
And shook it forth with a royal will.

"Shoot, if you must, this old gray head,
But spare your country's flag," she said.

A shade of sadness, a blush of shame,
Over the face of the leader came;

The nobler nature within him stirred
40 To life at that woman's deed and word;

"Who touches a hair of yon gray head
Dies like a dog! March on!" he said.

All day long through Frederick street
Sounded the tread of marching feet:

All day long that free flag tossed
Over the heads of the rebel host.

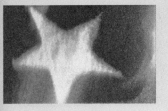

INFER

Why does Stonewall Jackson order his troops to shoot at the flag?

_____

_____

_____

INTERPRET

"Barbara Frietchie" is a **narrative poem,** a poem that tells a story. Like most stories, it contains **dialogue,** the words that characters speak. Circle the dialogue. What does this dialogue reveal about Frietchie's character and about Jackson's character?

_____

_____

BUILD FLUENCY

Re-read the boxed lines aloud until you can read them smoothly. Then, try to read the words of Frietchie, Jackson, and the narrator in the tone of voice they might have used. List one emotion you'll try to express when you read the words of

Frietchie:

_____

Jackson:

_____

The narrator:

_____

Ever its torn folds rose and fell
On the loyal winds that loved it well;

And through the hill gaps sunset light
50 Shone over it with a warm good night.

Barbara Frietchie's work is o'er,
And the Rebel rides on his raids no more.

Honor to her! and let a tear
Fall, for her sake, on Stonewall's bier.[2]

Over Barbara Frietchie's grave,
Flag of Freedom and Union, wave!

Peace and order and beauty draw
Round thy symbol of light and law;

And ever the stars above look down
60 On thy stars below in Frederick town!

IDENTIFY

In lines 55–60, circle the seven words that the narrator associates with our country's flag.

EVALUATE

Years ago, many school children had to memorize and recite this poem. What values does this poem teach? Tell why you agree or disagree that this was a good poem for children to memorize.

---

2. **bier** (bir): coffin and the platform on which it rests. Stonewall Jackson died in 1863 after being wounded in battle.

Text Reformulation: News Article

"Barbara Frietchie" is a **narrative poem,** which means it tells a story. Reformulate this story of this woman's bravery against Confederate forces as a news article.

A news article is usually described as an inverted pyramid. The most important information about the story is at the top of the inverted pyramid. This is called the **lead.** The lead paragraph usually answers *who, what, when, where, and why.* The rest of the article adds less important details.

Fill in the information for your news article in the graphic organizer below.

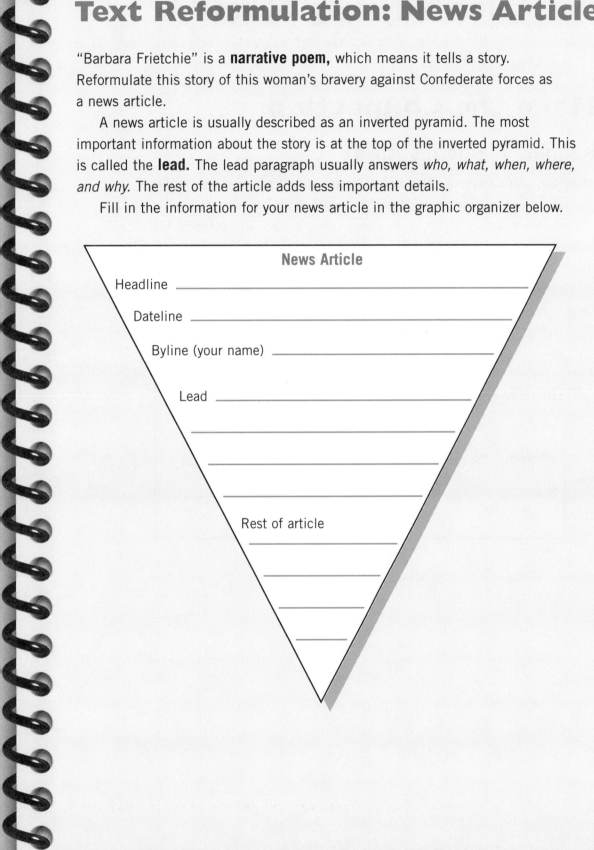

News Article

Headline _____

Dateline _____

Byline (your name) _____

Lead _____

_____

_____

_____

Rest of article

_____

_____

_____

_____

The Gettysburg Address

Make the Connection

Keeping Memories Alive

When you visit Gettysburg National Military Park, the site of the battle that was a turning point in the Civil War, you see more than a thousand monuments standing in the fields where soldiers died. Gravestones, statues, buildings, scholarship funds, and national holidays all serve as memorials to honor people or events that we want never to forget.

Think of a heroic group of people, battle, or event that you hope Americans will never forget. Then, suggest an appropriate memorial.

Group or event to be remembered: _____

Why remembering it is important: _____

Where the memorial would be located: _____

Words for the memorial: _____

Draw a picture of it below:

The Gettysburg Address

Abraham Lincoln

Background

The Battle of Gettysburg, which took place in Pennsylvania in 1863, was a turning point of the Civil War. In that bloody three-day battle, Union forces prevented Confederate forces from moving north, thus confining the war mainly to the South. The battle left at least 51,000 soldiers dead, wounded, or missing. On November 19, 1863, part of the battlefield was dedicated as a military cemetery. President Abraham Lincoln was asked to make some remarks at the dedication. Although very brief, Lincoln's Gettysburg Address is considered one of the greatest speeches by a U.S. political leader. It is notable especially for its vision of American democracy.

IDENTIFY

Underline the "proposition," the big idea, that the civil war tested.

INTERPRET

Notice how Lincoln uses **refrains,** repeated words and phrases, to build rhythm and emphasize certain points. Circle one refrain in lines 4–9. Tell what idea he emphasizes.

_____

_____

INTERPRET

What challenge does Lincoln propose for "us the living" (line 15)?

_____

_____

_____

EVALUATE

In lines 13–14, Lincoln says "the world will little note nor long remember" his speech. Why do you think people still read—and even memorize—it today? How is this speech a kind of memorial?

_____

_____

_____

_____

_____

_____

Four score and seven years ago our fathers brought forth on this continent a new nation, conceived in liberty, and dedicated to the proposition that all men are created equal.

Now we are engaged in a great civil war, testing whether that nation, or any nation so conceived and so dedicated, can long endure. We are met on a great battlefield of that war. We have come to dedicate a portion of that field, as a final resting place for those who here gave their lives that that nation might live. It is altogether fitting and proper that we should do this.

10 But, in a larger sense, we cannot dedicate—we cannot consecrate—we cannot hallow[1]—this ground. The brave men, living and dead, who struggled here, have consecrated it, far above our poor power to add or detract. The world will little note nor long remember what we say here, but it can never forget what they did here. It is for us the living, rather, to be dedicated here to the unfinished work which they who fought here have thus far so nobly advanced. It is rather for us to be here dedicated to the great task remaining before us—that from these honored dead we take increased devotion to that cause
20 for which they gave the last full measure of devotion—that we here highly resolve that these dead shall not have died in vain—that this nation, under God, shall have a new birth of freedom—and that government of the people, by the people, for the people, shall not perish from the earth.

---

1. **Consecrate** and **hallow** are synonyms meaning "make or declare holy." Lincoln is using repetition to create rhythm and emphasize his point.

Repetition Chart

Nonfiction works like "The Gettysburg Address" often contain **literary devices.** Speeches, especially, use repetition of words, sounds, structures, and ideas. The use of repetition helps emphasize the writer's ideas and fixes those ideas in the listeners' minds. Fill out the following Repetition Chart with details from "The Gettysburg Address."

Repetition of Sounds	Repetition of Words	Repetition of Structures

Camp Harmony *and* In Response to Executive Order 9066

Make the Connection

Interrupted Lives

Imagine that your family has been told that you all must leave your home tomorrow. The government has decided that everyone of your ethnic background is a threat to your country. Your family has been assigned to a camp in the desert where you will live in an army barracks behind barbed wire. You don't know for how long. It may be months or even years. Besides a bag for bedding and two suitcases for clothes, you can take only your school backpack. What would you take in your backpack?

In the graphic below, list four things you would especially want to put into your backpack. (Choose four things you won't mind talking about in class.) Then, tell why you chose each item.

My Backpack

Item

1. _____
2. _____
3. _____
4. _____

Why I Packed It

1. _____
2. _____
3. _____
4. _____

Camp Harmony
Monica Sone

In Response to Executive Order 9066
Dwight Okita

Background

In 1942, many thousands of Japanese Americans living on the West Coast were sent to internment camps. They had committed no crime, but the United States had gone to war with Japan. Executive Order 9066 made their confinement legal. Ironically, many of the evacuated families had sons or brothers serving with the U.S. Army in the war overseas. Most of the 120,000 Japanese Americans detained spent three years behind barbed wire. Released in 1945, at the end of World War II, they returned home to find their property stolen and their livelihoods gone. They had to wait more than forty years for an apology and compensation from the U.S. government.

IDENTIFY

An **autobiography** is a writer's account of his or her own life. Circle the pronouns in the first sentence that tell you that this true story is told from the **first-person point of view.**

_____

_____

_____

_____

INFER

In lines 16–28, the narrator admires the scenery, but is she really enjoying the ride? How does she feel about this trip? Underline the details that led to your conclusion.

_____

_____

_____

_____

_____

_____

_____

_____

WORDS TO OWN
palled (pôld) v.: became boring.
tersely (turs′lē) adv.: briefly and clearly.

Camp Harmony

When our bus turned a corner and we no longer had to smile and wave, we settled back gravely in our seats. Everyone was quiet except for a chattering group of university students, who soon started singing college songs. A few people turned and glared at them, which only served to increase the volume of their singing. Then suddenly a baby's sharp cry rose indignantly above the hubbub. The singing stopped immediately, followed by a guilty silence. Three seats behind us, a young mother held a wailing red-faced infant in her arms,

10 bouncing it up and down. Its angry little face emerged from multiple layers of kimonos, sweaters, and blankets, and it, too, wore the white pasteboard tag[1] pinned to its blanket. A young man stammered out an apology as the mother gave him a wrathful look. She hunted frantically for a bottle of milk in a shopping bag, and we all relaxed when she had found it.

We sped out of the city southward along beautiful stretches of farmland, with dark, newly turned soil. In the beginning we devoured every bit of scenery which flashed past our window and admired the massive-muscled workhorses plodding along

20 the edge of the highway, the rich burnished copper color of a browsing herd of cattle, the vivid spring green of the pastures, but eventually the sameness of the country landscape <u>palled</u> on us. We tried to sleep to escape from the restless anxiety which kept bobbing up to the surface of our minds. I awoke with a start when the bus filled with excited buzzing. A small group of straw-hatted Japanese farmers stood by the highway, waving at us. I felt a sudden warmth toward them, then a twinge of pity. They would be joining us soon.

About noon we crept into a small town. Someone said,

30 "Looks like Puyallup, all right." Parents of small children babbled excitedly, "Stand up quickly and look over there. See all the chick-chicks and fat little piggies?" One little city boy stared hard at the hogs and said <u>tersely</u>, "They're bachi—dirty!"

---

1. **white pasteboard tag:** All Japanese American families registering for evacuation were given numbered tags to wear and to attach to their luggage. Monica's family became family #10710.

Our bus idled a moment at the traffic signal, and we noticed at the left of us an entire block filled with neat rows of low shacks, resembling chicken houses. Someone commented on it with awe, "Just look at those chicken houses. They sure go in for poultry in a big way here." Slowly the bus made a left turn, drove through a wire-fence gate, and to our dismay, we were
40 inside the oversized chicken farm. The bus driver opened the door, the guard stepped out and stationed himself at the door again. Jim, the young man who had shepherded us into the buses, popped his head inside and sang out, "OK, folks, all off at Yokohama, Puyallup."

We stumbled out, stunned, dragging our bundles after us. It must have rained hard the night before in Puyallup, for we sank ankle deep into gray, <u>glutinous</u> mud. The receptionist, a white man, instructed us courteously, "Now, folks, please stay together as family units and line up. You'll be assigned your
50 apartment."

We were standing in Area A, the mammoth parking lot of the state fairgrounds. There were three other separate areas, B, C, and D, all built on the fairgrounds proper, near the baseball field and the racetracks. This camp of army barracks was hopefully called Camp Harmony.

We were assigned to apartment 2–I–A, right across from the bachelor quarters. The apartments resembled <u>elongated</u>, low stables about two blocks long. Our home was one room, about eighteen by twenty feet, the size of a living room. There was
60 one small window in the wall opposite the one door. It was bare except for a small, tinny wood-burning stove crouching in the center. The flooring consisted of two-by-fours laid directly on the earth, and dandelions were already pushing their way up through the cracks. Mother was delighted when she saw their shaggy yellow heads. "Don't anyone pick them. I'm going to cultivate them."

Father snorted, "Cultivate them! If we don't watch out, those things will be growing out of our hair."

INTERPRET

Yokohama is a seaport city south of Tokyo, Japan. Puyallup is a city in Washington state, near Tacoma. Why do you think Jim identifies their destination as Yokohama, Puyallup?

_____

_____

_____

_____

VISUALIZE

Underline the details in lines 56–66 that help you picture the room. Sketch the room in the space below.

WORDS TO OWN
glutinous (glōōt′'n·əs) *adj.*: sticky, gluey.
elongated (ē·loŋ′gāt′id) *v.* used as *adj.*: lengthened; extended.

INFER

What do the mother's comments about the dandelions reveal about her **character**?

_____

_____

_____

_____

_____

INTERPRET

How does the author's poem, created quickly and meant as a joke, relate to her family's situation?

_____

_____

_____

_____

_____

_____

_____

_____

WORDS TO OWN

laconically (lə·kän′ik·lē)
adv.: with few words.

70 Just then Henry stomped inside, bringing the rest of our baggage. "What's all the excitement about?"

Sumi replied <u>laconically</u>, "Dandelions."

Henry tore off a fistful. Mother scolded, "Arra! Arra! Stop that. They're the only beautiful things around here. We could have a garden right in here."

"Are you joking, Mama?"

I chided Henry, "Of course she's not. After all, she has to have some inspiration to write poems, you know, with all the 'nari keri's.'[2] I can think of a poem myself right now:

Oh, Dandelion, Dandelion,
80 Despised and uprooted by all,
Dance and bob your golden heads
For you've finally found your home
With your yellow fellows, nari keri, amen!"

Henry said, thrusting the dandelions in Mother's black hair, "I think you can do ten times better than that, Mama."

Sumi reclined on her sea bag[3] and fretted, "Where do we sleep? Not on the floor, I hope."

"Stop worrying," Henry replied disgustedly.

Mother and Father wandered out to see what the other folks 90 were doing and they found people wandering in the mud, wondering what other folks were doing. Mother returned shortly, her face lit up in an ecstatic smile, "We're in luck. The latrine is right nearby. We won't have to walk blocks."

We laughed, marveling at Mother who could be so poetic and yet so practical. Father came back, bent double like a woodcutter in a fairy tale, with stacks of scrap lumber over his shoulder. His coat and trouser pockets bulged with nails. Father dumped his loot in a corner and explained, "There was a pile of wood left by the carpenters and hundreds of nails scattered

2. **nari keri's:** _Nari keri_ (nä·rē ke·rē) is a phrase used to end many Japanese poems. It is meant to convey wonder and awe.
3. **sea bag:** large canvas bag like the ones sailors use to carry their personal belongings. Each person was allowed to bring only one sea bag of bedding and two suitcases of clothing to the internment camps.

100 loose. Everybody was picking them up, and I hustled right in
with them. Now maybe we can live in style, with tables and
chairs."

The block leader knocked at our door and announced
lunchtime. He instructed us to take our meal at the nearest
mess hall. As I untied my sea bag to get out my pie plate, tin
cup, spoon, and fork, I realized I was hungry. At the mess hall
we found a long line of people. Children darted in and out of
the line, skiing in the slithery mud. The young stood
impatiently on one foot, then the other, and scowled, "The food

110 had better be good after all this wait." But the issei stood
quietly, arms folded, saying very little. A light drizzle began to
fall, coating bare black heads with tiny sparkling raindrops. The
chow line inched forward.

Lunch consisted of two canned sausages, one lob of boiled
potato, and a slab of bread. Our family had to split up, for the
hall was too crowded for us to sit together. I wandered up and
down the aisles, back and forth along the crowded tables and
benches, looking for a few inches to squeeze into. A small issei
woman finished her meal, stood up, and hoisted her legs

120 modestly over the bench, leaving a space for one. Even as I
thrust myself into the <u>breach</u>, the space had shrunk to two
inches, but I worked myself into it. My dinner companion,
hooked just inside my right elbow, was a baldheaded, gruff-
looking issei man who seemed to resent nestling at mealtime.
Under my left elbow was a tiny, mud-spattered girl. With busy,
runny nose, she was belaboring her sausages, tearing them into
shreds and mixing them into the potato gruel which she had
made with water. I choked my food down.

We cheered loudly when trucks rolled by, distributing

130 canvas army cots for the young and hardy, and steel cots for
the older folks. Henry directed the arrangement of the cots.
Father and Mother were to occupy the corner nearest the wood
stove. In the other corner, Henry arranged two cots in an L
shape and announced that this was the combination living
room–bedroom area, to be occupied by Sumi and myself. He
fixed a male den for himself in the corner nearest the door. If I

INTERPRET

Pause at line 128. Based on what you've read so far, what conclusion can you draw about conditions in Japanese internment camps? If you had been assigned to Camp Harmony, list three complaints you might have about conditions there.

_____

_____

_____

_____

VISUALIZE

In the space below, redraw the room you sketched earlier. This time, show the door, window, and stove, as well as the arrangement of the cots. On each cot, write the name of the person assigned to it.

WORDS TO OWN
breach (brēch) *n.:* opening; usually refers to a breakthrough in a line of defense.

had had my way, I would have arranged everyone's cots in one neat row, as in Father's hotel dormitory.

We felt fortunate to be assigned to a room at the end of the barracks, because we had just one neighbor to worry about. The partition wall separating the rooms was only seven feet high, with an opening of four feet at the top, so at night, Mrs. Funai next door could tell when Sumi was still sitting up in bed in the dark, putting her hair up. "Mah, Sumi-chan," Mrs. Funai would say through the plank wall, "are you curling your hair tonight, again? Do you put it up every night?" Sumi would put her hands on her hips and glare defiantly at the wall.

The block monitor, an impressive nisei who looked like a star tackle, with his crouching walk, came around the first night to tell us that we must all be inside our room by nine o'clock every night. At ten o'clock, he rapped at the door again, yelling, "Lights out!" and Mother rushed to turn the light off not a second later.

Throughout the barracks, there was a medley of creaking cots, whimpering infants, and explosive night coughs. Our attention was riveted on the intense little wood stove, which glowed so violently I feared it would melt right down to the floor. We soon learned that this condition lasted for only a short time, after which it suddenly turned into a deep freeze. Henry and Father took turns at the stove to produce the harrowing blast which all but singed our army blankets but did not penetrate through them. As it grew quieter in the barracks, I could hear the light patter of rain. Soon I felt the *splat! splat!* of raindrops digging holes into my face. The dampness on my pillow spread like a mortal bleeding, and I finally had to get out and haul my cot toward the center of the room. In a short while, Henry was up. "I've got multiple leaks, too. Have to complain to the landlord first thing in the morning."

All through the night I heard people getting up, dragging cots around. I stared at our little window, unable to sleep. I was glad Mother had put up a makeshift curtain on the window, for I noticed a powerful beam of light sweeping across it every few seconds. The lights came from high towers placed around the

camp, where guards with tommy guns kept a twenty-four-hour vigil. I remembered the wire fence encircling us, and a knot of anger tightened in my breast. What was I doing behind a fence, like a criminal? If there were accusations to be made, why hadn't I been given a fair trial? Maybe I wasn't considered an American anymore. My citizenship wasn't real, after all. Then 180 what was I? I was certainly not a citizen of Japan, as my parents were. On second thought, even Father and Mother were more alien residents of the United States than Japanese nationals, for they had little tie with their mother country. In their twenty-five years in America, they had worked and paid their taxes to their adopted government as any other citizen.

Of one thing I was sure. The wire fence was real. I no longer had the right to walk out of it. It was because I had Japanese ancestors. It was also because some people had little faith in the ideas and ideals of democracy. They said that after all these 190 were but words and could not possibly ensure loyalty. New laws and camps were surer devices. I finally buried my face in my pillow to wipe out burning thoughts and snatch what sleep I could.

INTERPRET

How would you describe the speaker's tone in lines 1–5? How does the tone change in these few lines? What is the "invitation" she has received?

_____

_____

INTERPRET

Why do you think the speaker describes herself this way (lines 6–9)? What kind of teenager does she seem to be?

_____

_____

INFER

Why has Denise moved to a different seat? Why do you think she speaks so cruelly to her former friend?

_____

_____

_____

EVALUATE

What do you think of the way the speaker responds to Denise's verbal attack? How would you have advised her to respond? Why?

_____

_____

_____

_____

In Response to
Executive Order 9066:
All Americans of Japanese Descent
Must Report to Relocation Centers

Dear Sirs:
Of course I'll come. I've packed my galoshes
and three packets of tomato seeds. Denise calls them
"love apples." My father says where we're going
they won't grow.

I am a fourteen-year-old girl with bad spelling
and a messy room. If it helps any, I will tell you
I have always felt funny using chopsticks
and my favorite food is hot dogs.
10 My best friend is a white girl named Denise—
we look at boys together. She sat in front of me
all through grade school because of our names:
O'Connor, Ozawa. I know the back of Denise's head very well.
I tell her she's going bald. She tells me I copy on tests.
We're best friends.

I saw Denise today in Geography class.
She was sitting on the other side of the room.
"You're trying to start a war," she said, "giving secrets away
to the Enemy. Why can't you keep your big mouth shut?"
20 I didn't know what to say.
I gave her a packet of tomato seeds
and asked her to plant them for me, told her
when the first tomato ripened
she'd miss me.

Description Drawing

The author of "Camp Harmony" includes many vivid **descriptions** of the things she sees and experiences on the bus ride to the internment camp. In the graphic organizer below, draw (or write, if you prefer) what she describes inside the bus and what she observes outside of the bus.

Comparison Chart

The details in a literary selection work together to create a theme, or message about life. Different writers may explore the same theme but use different topics and details to convey that theme. Writers might also explore the same topic but convey very different themes.

Fill in the following chart with important details from "Camp Harmony" and "In Response to Executive Order 9066." Then, write the theme of each piece in the last cell of each column. Finally, write a generalization about the similiarities in the themes.

Important Details from "Camp Harmony"	Important Details from "In Response to Executive Order 9066"
Theme	Theme

Generalization:

_____

_____

Vocabulary and Comprehension

A. Match words and definitions. Write the letter of the correct definition next to each word.

_____ **1.** palled

_____ **2.** tersely

_____ **3.** glutinous

_____ **4.** elongated

_____ **5.** breach

_____ **6.** medley

_____ **7.** riveted

_____ **8.** harrowing

_____ **9.** vigil

a. distressing

b. jumble

c. with few words

d. watch

e. sticky

f. fastened

g. became boring

h. opening

i. extended

Word Bank
palled
tersely
glutinous
elongated
breach
medley
riveted
harrowing
vigil

B. Answer each question about "Camp Harmony."

1. How big was the room of the Sone family?

_____

_____

2. How was the camp like a prison? Use details from the story in your answer.

_____

_____

C. The following statements refer to "In Response to Executive Order 9066." Write **T** or **F** next to each statement to tell if it is true or false.

_____ **1.** The speaker is a fourteen-year-old boy.

_____ **2.** The speaker is being sent away to a relocation center.

_____ **3.** The speaker likes to use chopsticks.

_____ **4.** Denise decides not to be friends with the speaker anymore.

_____ **5.** The speaker gives Denise a packet of tomato seeds.

from I Have a Dream

Make the Connection

Time to Think

Before you start reading, take a moment to think about these important ideas that Dr. Martin Luther King, Jr. talks about in his "I Have a Dream" speech.

- freedom
- equality
- justice
- American dream

Then, choose one of these ideas and write it in the center circle of the cluster map below. In the surrounding circles, write or draw anything you associate with that idea. It could be a definition, example, symbol, or anything else you think of. For instance, for *justice*, you might write *courts, law, punishments,* and *rewards,* and then draw a scale. You can add additional circles if you want.

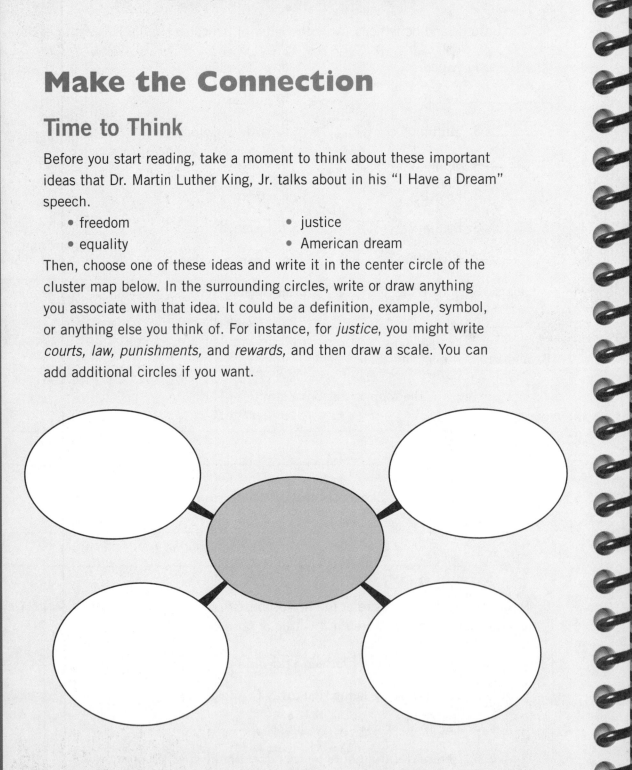

from *I Have a Dream*

Dr. Martin Luther King, Jr.

Background

On August 28, 1963, more than 200,000 Americans took part in a march in Washington, D.C. The marchers called on Congress to pass a civil rights bill proposed by President John F. Kennedy, and they demanded full equality for African Americans. People of all races, from almost every state in the Union, gathered in front of the Lincoln Memorial to sing and listen to speeches.

Late in the day, Dr. Martin Luther King, Jr., rose to speak. He began by describing how the promise of America had not yet been realized for African Americans. Then, setting aside his prepared speech, he improvised. His speech, which was heard by people across the country on TV and radio, deeply moved his listeners. Dr. King's concluding words, with their powerful rhythm and vivid images, are reprinted here as "I Have a Dream."

IDENTIFY

Underline the two
metaphors in lines 10–13.
What does King compare
Mississippi to? What does
he want Mississippi to
become?

_____

_____

_____

INTERPRET

An **allusion** is a reference to
someone or something from
literature, religion, history,
or culture. In lines 18–22,
King **alludes** to the Book of
Isaiah (40:4–5) in the
Bible. What nonreligious
meaning might King also
have had in mind when he
said these lines? Write this
meaning in one sentence,
substituting the word *nation*
for *Lord*.

_____

_____

_____

WORDS TO OWN
creed (krēd) *n.*: statement
of belief or principles.
oasis (ō·ā′sis) *n.*: place in a
desert with plants and a
supply of water; place or
thing offering relief.
exalted (eg·zôlt′id) *v.*:
raised; lifted up.
discords (dis′kôrdz′) *n.*:
conflicts; disagreements.
prodigious (prō·dij′əs) *adj.*:
huge; amazing.

I say to you today, my friends, that in spite of the difficulties and frustrations of the moment I still have a dream. It is a dream deeply rooted in the American Dream.

I have a dream that one day this nation will rise up and live out the true meaning of its creed: "We hold these truths to be self-evident; that all men are created equal."

I have a dream that one day on the red hills of Georgia the sons of former slaves and the sons of former slaveowners will be able to sit down together at the table of brotherhood.

10   I have a dream that one day even the state of Mississippi, a desert state sweltering with the heat of injustice and oppression, will be transformed into an oasis of freedom and justice.

I have a dream that my four little children will one day live in a nation where they will not be judged by the color of their skin but by the content of their character.

I have a dream today.

I have a dream that one day every valley shall be exalted, every hill and mountain shall be made low, the rough places
20   will be made plain, and the crooked places will be made straight, and the glory of the Lord shall be revealed, and all flesh shall see it together.

This is our hope. This is the faith with which I return to the South. With this faith we will be able to hew out of the mountain of despair a stone of hope. With this faith we will be able to transform the jangling discords of our nation into a beautiful symphony of brotherhood. With this faith we will be able to work together, to pray together, to struggle together, to go to jail together, to stand up for freedom together, knowing
30   that we will be free one day.

This will be the day when all of God's children will be able to sing with new meaning "My country 'tis of thee, sweet land of liberty, of thee I sing. Land where my fathers died, land of the pilgrim's pride, from every mountainside, let freedom ring."

And if America is to be a great nation, this must become true. So let freedom ring from the prodigious hilltops of New Hampshire. Let freedom ring from the mighty mountains of

New York. Let freedom ring from the heightening Alleghenies of Pennsylvania!

Let freedom ring from the snowcapped Rockies of Colorado!

Let freedom ring from the curvaceous peaks of California!

But not only that; let freedom ring from Stone Mountain of Georgia!

Let freedom ring from Lookout Mountain of Tennessee!

Let freedom ring from every hill and molehill of Mississippi. From every mountainside, let freedom ring.

When we let freedom ring, when we let it ring from every village and every hamlet, from every state and every city, we will be able to speed up that day when all of God's children, black men and white men, Jews and Gentiles, Protestants and Catholics, will be able to join hands and sing in the words of the old Negro spiritual, "Free at last! Free at last! Thank God almighty, we are free at last!"

EVALUATE

In lines 36–46, King **alludes** to the patriotic song "My Country 'Tis of Thee." How does this **allusion** add to the effectiveness of his speech?

_____

_____

_____

_____

INTERPRET

What is King's hope? State the **main idea** of this speech in one sentence.

_____

_____

_____

_____

BUILD FLUENCY

Re-read the boxed lines until you can read them smoothly and with feeling. Remember that King wanted this speech to arouse the emotions of his listeners. So put all the passion you can into your reading. Let your voice flow with the rhythm of the powerful repetitions. Don't be afraid to let your voice rise with the feelings. Let yourself go and enjoy it. Rouse your audience to their feet, and leave them cheering!

Allusion Listing

Dr. Martin Luther King, Jr.'s, "I Have a Dream" speech is full of allusions. **Allusions** are references to experiences that people share. An allusion may refer to a person or a place, or to an event from literature, history, religion, politics, sports, or science. Re-read Dr. King's famous speech, and fill in the chart below with allusions you find. In the column to the right, explain where the allusion comes from.

Allusion in "I Have a Dream"		Where the Allusion Comes From
	↔	
	↔	
	↔	
	↔	

Vocabulary and Comprehension

A. Match words and definitions. Write the letter of the correct definition next to each word.

Word Bank
creed
oasis
exalted
discords
prodigious

_____ **1.** oasis   **a.** conflicts

_____ **2.** discords   **b.** principles

_____ **3.** prodigious   **c.** lifted up

_____ **4.** creed   **d.** place in desert

_____ **5.** exalted   **e.** huge

B. Choose three words from the Word Bank. Use each word in a sentence.

1. _____

_____

2. _____

_____

3. _____

_____

C. Answer the following questions.

1. In the list below, circle the sentence that best expresses the main idea of Dr. King's speech.

   a. Freedom must ring from every mountaintop.

   b. People should love one another.

   c. Freedom and equality should be given to all Americans.

2. Why did you pick that sentence and not the others?

_____

_____

Road Warriors, Listen Up: Some Rules for Streetwise Biking

Proposition and Support

The author of this article is trying to persuade you to ride your bike safely. You will have to decide if her argument is convincing or not.

The writer of a persuasive article usually begins with a **proposition,** which is an important idea or an opinion that the writer wants you to agree with. Then, the writer will support the proposition with **reasons.** Reasons may be

- **facts**—statements that can be proved true
- **statistics**—facts in the form of numbers
- **anecdotes**—very brief stories, sometimes from personal experience
- **examples**—illustrations of the reasons

On the chart below, you'll find a proposition that you'll probably agree with. Try out your own persuasive skills: Write down some reasons to support the proposition.

Proposition: Kids should be paid for chores.
Reason:
Reason:
Reason:

Road Warriors, Listen Up: Some Rules for Streetwise Biking

Madeline Travers Hovland

IDENTIFY

Re-read the first paragraph. Then, underline the **proposition** of this article.

IDENTIFY

Pause at line 19. The author has cited three **statistics** to support her **proposition** so far. Underline them.

IDENTIFY

Pause at line 33. Underline one **fact** in the paragraph you have just read that supports the author's **proposition.**

When you ride a bike on city streets, you share the road with speeding fire engines, ambulances, and police cars. You see—but can't see around—giant-sized trucks with eighteen wheels instead of your two. Sports cars and SUVs zip in and out of lanes. Everyone's in a hurry, and there you are, with less protection than anyone else in a moving vehicle. Your best defense is your good sense. To ride a bike safely—on highways or byways—you've got to know and follow the rules of the road.

10   The consequences of not following bike-safety rules can be painful, if not fatal. Every year in the United States there are about eight hundred deaths due to bike accidents. More than half a million people end up in emergency rooms because of bike injuries.

To protect yourself against serious injury, wear a bike helmet whenever you hop on a bike, even for a short ride. A helmet that meets safety standards may seem expensive, but your intact brain is worth the investment. Bike helmets can reduce head injuries by as much as 80 percent.

20   To ride safely, you need to hear approaching traffic, barking dogs, and shouting drivers. Therefore, you should never ride wearing headphones. Wait to listen to music till you get where you're going. If you carry a cell phone or a pager, pull over to the side of the road before you take or make a call or check your beeper.

Biking safely also means obeying traffic signs and signals. Stop signs and red lights apply to everyone on the road, not just cars. State laws—and common sense—dictate that bicyclists ride on the right side of the road, in the same direction as all 30   other traffic, not against it. When you come to an intersection, wait for the green light before you ride across. Remember that pedestrians always have the right of way, whether they are on the sidewalk or in the street.

Watch out for road hazards. (There are even more obstacles to worry about than cars and trucks and people.) Steer around potholes, bumps, gravel, piles of leaves, and grates covering storm drains. Use hand signals to alert drivers to your

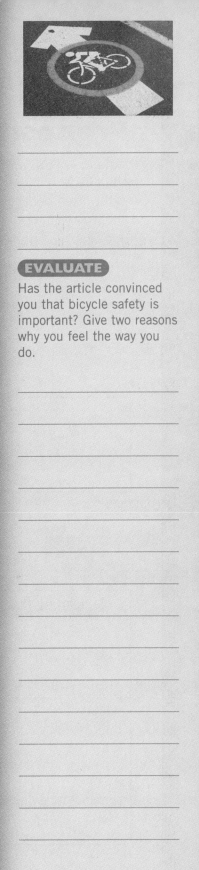

intentions. When you're not making a hand signal, be sure to keep both hands on your handlebars.

40   Biking is excellent practice for driving later on. Safe biking will help prepare you to be a safe driver. Even when you're old enough to drive a car, however, you'll probably still go biking. It's fun. It's an inexpensive way to travel. And it's great exercise. Whatever your age, always remember to follow the rules for streetwise biking. The life you save may be your own!

EVALUATE

Has the article convinced you that bicycle safety is important? Give two reasons why you feel the way you do.

Proposition and Support Chart

The proposition is the most important point the writer is making about a subject. In a well-written persuasive article, the proposition is clearly supported by reasons.

   After you read "Road Warriors, Listen Up," fill out this graphic organizer. First, write the subject of the article. Then, write down the proposition. Finally, fill in the reasons the writer provides to support the proposition.

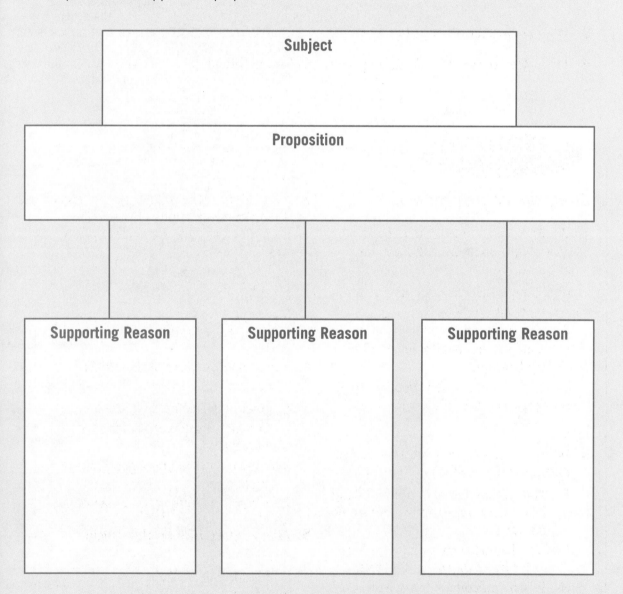

Subject

Proposition

Supporting Reason

Supporting Reason

Supporting Reason

Reading Check

1. According to the writer, what can happen if you don't follow bike-safety rules?

   _____

2. Why should you wear a bike helmet? _____

   _____

3. Who always has the right of way? _____

4. How does streetwise biking prepare riders for the future? _____

   _____

Test Practice

Circle the correct answer.

1. Which sentence best states the writer's **proposition,** the main idea of the article?

   A Biking safely means obeying traffic signs and signals.

   B Watch out for road hazards.

   C Biking is excellent practice for driving later on.

   D To ride a bike safely, you've got to know and follow the rules of the road.

2. Which of the following is a statistic used to support the main idea of the article?

   F The consequences of not following bike-safety rules can be painful, if not fatal.

   G Bike helmets can reduce head injuries by as much as 80 percent.

   H When you come to an intersection, wait for the green light before you ride across.

   J Safe biking will help prepare you to be a safe driver.

3. "More than half a million people end up in emergency rooms because of bike injuries." This sentence is an example of a —

   A personal experience

   B proposition

   C supporting detail

   D main idea

4. The overall **purpose** of the article is to —

   F discourage bikers

   G convince readers that bike safety is important

   H explain how to buy a good bike helmet

   J get readers interested in bike riding

5. Another good **title** for this article might be —

   A "Walk, Don't Bike"

   B "My Experiences as a Cyclist"

   C "Bike Now, Drive Later"

   D "Biking Safety: Your Best Defense on Two Wheels"

An Example of Fallacious Reasoning

EDGAR ALLAN POE:
HIS LIFE REVEALED IN HIS WORK

Fallacious (fə·lā′shəs) **reasoning** means simply "false thinking." People reason fallaciously when they draw incorrect or false conclusions. Such conclusions may be illogical, or they may be based on incomplete information.

"Because the world is flat, you'll fall off if you sail to the end of it" sounds funny today, but centuries ago uneducated people in Europe believed this fallacy. It was considered fact because, after all, when you looked at the world, it was flat for as far as you could see. This is the problem with fallacious reasoning: People believe it because they do not realize that it is based on incomplete or incorrect information.

For an argument to be convincing, it must be based on **logic,** or correct reasoning. Opinions should be supported by reasons and evidence, such as **facts, statistics, examples,** or **expert testimony.** When you decide whether or not you agree with an argument, you probably look automatically for reasons that you can agree or disagree with. Are you also on the lookout for **fallacious reasoning**? Fallacious, or faulty, reasoning can be hard to spot, so it's important to watch for it whenever you evaluate an argument. Here are some common kinds of logical fallacies. Which ones do you recognize?

- **Hasty generalization**—a conclusion drawn from weak or insufficient evidence: *Harry and Joe didn't help when I dropped my books. Everyone in my school is so rude and uncaring.*

- **False cause and effect**—assuming that event A caused event B simply because A came first: *After I wore my new shirt to school, Mary invited me to her party. New clothes will make me more popular.*

- **Either/or fallacy**—the assumption that a problem or situation has only one possible cause or resolution when there may be several: *If we don't elect Jane class president, girls will have no say in running the school.*

- **Stereotyping**—believing that all members of a group share a certain characteristic: *All teenagers are angry and rebellious, and they all sleep late, too.*

- **Name-calling** or **attacking the person**—attacking the person who's making the argument rather than the argument itself: *Ray's in favor of school uniforms. Big surprise—we all know how badly he dresses.*

- **Begging the question**—assuming that everyone agrees that something is true: *We all know that Samantha is the nicest girl in school.*

Now see if you can identify types of fallacious reasoning. Read the statements in the chart below, and identify the type of fallacious reasoning each represents.

I'll be a failure for the rest of my life unless I win the contest.	
Julio forgot to study last night, but he still got a higher score on the test than I did. Studying just doesn't help me.	
Everybody knows Mrs. Fernandez is the nicest math teacher in the world.	
Jennifer thinks our meetings should be scheduled earlier, but she only feels that way because she's lazy.	

IDENTIFY

Pause at line 6. Underline at least one example of **fallacious reasoning** you've read so far. What type(s) of **fallacious reasoning** did you underline?

_____

_____

_____

IDENTIFY

Pause at line 15. Underline the second sentence of this paragraph. What type of **fallacious reasoning** does this sentence represent?

_____

_____

_____

IDENTIFY

Underline an example of **false cause and effect** in the third paragraph.

_____

_____

_____

IDENTIFY

Underline the **hasty generalization** at the end of the selection. Why is it a hasty generalization?

_____

_____

_____

Grade F

An Example of Fallacious Reasoning

Edgar Allan Poe: His Life Revealed in His Work

Edgar Allan Poe was a very, very disturbed man. Every single story and poem he ever wrote is about disturbed, usually insane people. He writes about murderers, people buried alive, people being tortured, people killed by the Black Death. His characters imagine weird things, like a raven that croaks in English and plunges his beak into someone's heart.

No one could write stories like this without being crazy. How else could Poe have known what it is like to be insane? The only way he could have known is by being insane himself.

10   Poe's stories also show that he was a drug addict or an alcoholic. We know that he was always drunk. That probably accounts for the strange style of his writing. His stories are often very choppy. They use a lot of dashes and exclamation points, which suggests that a very nervous person wrote them, or someone on drugs.

We know that all writers are strange anyway, especially writers who specialize in horror.

I hope I have convinced you that Poe's writing reflects his sick mind.

20   (Despite all this, I love Poe's stories!)

Test Practice

Circle the correct answer.

1. "Every single story and poem he ever wrote is about disturbed, usually insane people" is a **hasty generalization** because the writer —

   A probably hasn't read everything Poe wrote

   B was in a hurry when he or she wrote it

   C is not of Poe's generation

   D carefully considered the evidence

2. "The only way he could have known is by being insane himself" is another **hasty generalization** because —

   F the statement shows how insane the writer is

   G there is insufficient evidence to support the statement

   H the statement assumes we all agree on something

   J the statement is an unfair attack on Poe

3. By saying that Poe's use of dashes and exclamation points suggests that a very nervous person or someone on drugs wrote the text, the writer is —

   A using the either/or fallacy

   B using false cause and effect

   C stereotyping

   D begging the question

4. By implying that we shouldn't take Poe's stories seriously because he was always drunk, the writer is —

   F using false cause and effect

   G begging the question

   H name-calling

   J using the either/or fallacy

5. Which two **fallacies** does the writer use in the statement "We know that all writers are strange anyway"?

   A false cause and effect and name-calling

   B hasty generalization and stereotyping

   C stereotyping and name-calling

   D begging the question and stereotyping

Fallacy Chart

Re-read the selection, and find six or more examples of faulty reasoning. (To review types of faulty reasoning, see pages 226–227 of *The Holt Reader*.) Write each example in the box under the appropriate heading, and explain what makes each example flawed. Try to find at least one example of each flaw.

Edgar Allan Poe: His Life Revealed in His Work		
Begging the Question	**Hasty Generalization**	**False Cause and Effect**

Fallacy Chart continues

Fallacy Chart continues

Edgar Allan Poe: His Life Revealed in His Work		
Name-calling	**Stereotyping**	**Either/Or Fallacy**

An Example of Unsupported Inferences

OLYMPIC GAMES *AND* THE OLD OLYMPIC GAMES: A REPORT

"Hi, Mrs. Johnson. Got a minute?"

"Sure, Ted. What's up?"

"I was just wondering about this grade on my essay. I thought I did better than that."

"Well, Ted, you really went out on a limb with unsupported inferences."

"Unsupported what?"

"Inferences. You know, when you take the writer's clues and put two and two together."

"I did it wrong?"

"Well, in this essay you sometimes took two and two and came up with twenty-two. At other times you took two and two into orbit."

An **inference** is an educated guess. When you read, you make inferences by combining information in the text with what you already know. When you're evaluating a text or presenting an argument, make sure your inferences are supported—make sure you base them on information in the text and on reasonable prior knowledge.

Supported inferences are based on details in a writer's text. You can pose any number of possibilities as long as you can find evidence in the text to support your ideas. When making inferences about a character in a story, you cannot ignore facts in the text.

Unsupported inferences are not based on details in the text. They might ignore facts or misinterpret details. They might draw conclusions that are not logical. Unsupported inferences can also go too far. Carrying inferences too far from the text is what Mrs. Johnson, in the dialogue above, means by going into orbit.

You'll find two readings in the pages that follow. One is an encyclopedia article about the Olympic Games. The second, a report based on the first article, is full of **unsupported inferences.**

An Encyclopedia Article

OLYMPIC GAMES

T HE ANCIENT GAMES. Athletics played an important role in the religious festivals of ancient Greece. Historians believe the ancient Greeks first organized athletic games as part of funeral ceremonies for important people. This practice probably existed by the 1200s B.C. Later, games became part of religious festivals honoring the gods. Many Greek cities held festivals every two or four years.

Over time, four great religious festivals developed that brought together people from throughout the Greek world.
10 These festivals were the Isthmian, Nemean, Pythian, and Olympic games. The Olympic Games, which ranked as the most important, honored Zeus, the king of the gods.

The first recorded Olympic contest took place in 776 B.C. at Olympia in western Greece. The first winner was Koroibos (later spelled Coroebus), a cook from Elis. The Olympic Games were held every four years. They were so important to the ancient Greeks that time was measured in *Olympiads*, the four-year intervals between games. The only event in the first thirteen games was the *stadion*, a running race of 192 meters (210 yards).
20 Through the years, longer running races were added.

Other types of competition became part of the ancient Olympics. In 708 B.C., wrestling and the pentathlon were added. The pentathlon was a combination of jumping, running, the discus throw, the javelin throw, and wrestling. Boxing joined the program in 688 B.C., and the four-horse chariot race was added in 680 B.C. Horse racing was included in 648 B.C., as was the *pancratium* (also spelled *pankration*), a combination of boxing, wrestling, and kicking. Some unusual events were included in the Olympics, such as a race in armor, a chariot
30 race called the *apene*, in which two mules pulled the chariot, and a competition for trumpeters. . . .

INTERPRET

The writer says that the Olympic Games were the most highly regarded event in ancient Greece. Underline the details in the first two paragraphs that **support** that **inference.**

IDENTIFY/INFER

Pause at line 20. How did the ancient Greeks measure time? What **inference** can you make from this information?

INFER

Pause at line 34, and make an **inference** of your own: Why do you think the Romans banned the games after they conquered Greece? Circle the details in the text that support your **inference**.

The Romans conquered Greece during the 140s B.C., and the games soon lost their religious meaning. In A.D. 393, Emperor Theodosius I banned the games.

THE MODERN GAMES. In 1857, a group of German archaeologists began to excavate the ruins of the stadium and temples of Olympia, which had been destroyed by an earthquake and buried by a landslide and floods. Their discoveries inspired Baron Pierre de Coubertin, a French

40 educator, to organize a modern international Olympics. He first proposed the idea publicly in 1892. In 1894, the first IOC was formed.

The first modern Olympic Games were held in Athens, Greece, in 1896. The athletes competed in nine sports: (1) cycling, (2) fencing, (3) gymnastics, (4) lawn tennis, (5) shooting, (6) swimming, (7) track and field, (8) weight lifting, and (9) wrestling. James B. Connolly of the United States became the first modern Olympic champion, winning the triple jump (then known as the hop, step, and jump).

—from *The World Book Encyclopedia*

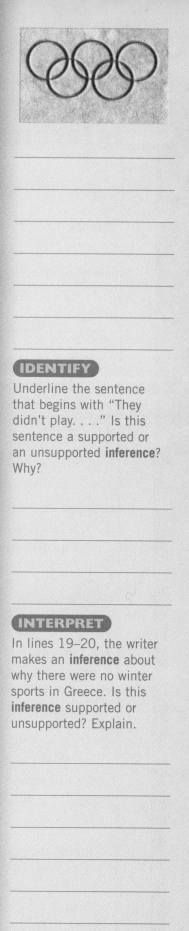

An Example of Unsupported Inferences

Grade F

The Old Olympic Games: A Report

The Olympic Games began in Greece a long time ago, before anyone knew how to write or play basketball. People weren't as smart back then as we are today. They played games for dead people, and they believed in lots of gods. They even thought the gods had a king, named Zeus. They didn't have clocks or watches, either, so they told time by counting games.

At first the only thing the old Greeks could do was race. They weren't very strong, so they could run only 210 yards. Later they got stronger and ran farther. Then they learned
10 how to wrestle, jump, and throw things. They didn't play fair, though, and kicked each other when they were boxing and wrestling. They also raced chariots using four horses, which seems like three too many to me. Some of them raced chariots using mules! If they were that silly, it's no wonder the Romans conquered them and banned the games.

An earthquake and a landslide buried the old stadium. After a German dug it up, for some reason—I don't know what—a Frenchman decided to hold games again. The modern games began in 1896. They had nine cool events but no winter sports
20 because it is too hot in Greece. An American won the hop, step, and jump. It's nice that an American won, but I don't get why winning a dance contest made him a champion.

IDENTIFY

Underline the sentence that begins with "They didn't play. . . ." Is this sentence a supported or an unsupported **inference**? Why?

INTERPRET

In lines 19–20, the writer makes an **inference** about why there were no winter sports in Greece. Is this **inference** supported or unsupported? Explain.

Inference Chart

In the chart below, factual statements from the encyclopedia article "Olympic Games" are listed in the left column. In the middle column, next to each fact, is an **unsupported inference** made by the writer of "The Old Olympic Games: A Report" using that fact. The right column has been left blank for you to fill in with a **supported inference** based on the factual statement.

The Olympics

Factual Statement from "Olympic Games"	Unsupported Inference from "The Old Olympic Games"	Supported Inference
The first recorded Olympic contest took place in 776 B.C.	The Olympic games began a long time ago, before anyone knew how to write.	
The only event in the first thirteen games was a running race of 210 yards.	The only thing the old Greeks could do was race. They weren't very strong, so they could only run 210 yards.	
In 708 B.C. wrestling and pentathlon (jumping, running, the discus throw, the javelin throw, and wrestling) were added.	Then they learned how to wrestle, jump, and throw things.	
In 648 B.C. the pancratium was added, a combination of boxing, wrestling, and kicking	They didn't play fair though, and kicked each other when they were boxing and wrestling.	
The Romans conquered Greece during the 140s B.C. . . . In A.D. 393, Emperor Theodosius I banned the games.	Some of them raced chariots using mules! If they were that silly, it's no wonder the Romans conquered them.	

Reading Check

Base your answers to the following questions on "Olympic Games," the article from *The World Book Encyclopedia*.

1. When was the first recorded Olympic contest held? _____

2. List four events in the ancient Olympic Games. _____

_____

3. Why did the ancient Olympic Games end? _____

_____

Test Practice

Circle the correct answer.

1. Which of the following statements from the report can be **supported** by details in the encyclopedia article?

A "The Olympic Games began in Greece. . . ."

B "People weren't as smart back then. . . ."

C "They played games for dead people. . . ."

D "They didn't have clocks or watches. . . ."

2. Which of the following statements from the report is an **unsupported inference**?

F "The only thing the old Greeks could do was race."

G "They also raced chariots using four horses. . . ."

H "The Romans conquered them. . . ."

J "The modern games began in 1896."

3. The following statements from the report are all **unsupported inferences** *except*—

A "They even thought the gods had a king, named Zeus."

B "They told time by counting games."

C "They weren't very strong. . . ."

D "They didn't play fair, though. . . ."

4. The report ends with the **unsupported inference** that the hop, step, and jump was—

F a triple jump

G a track-and-field event

H a dance contest

J won by an American

Destination: Mars

Text Structures: Magazines

Some magazines—like *Time* and *Newsweek*—cover a broad range of topics. Others deal specifically with a popular sport or hobby. No matter what you're interested in, you can probably find a magazine devoted to it.

All About Magazines

Magazines have structural features that tell you what's inside:

- **The cover**. A magazine's cover art and its main headline tell you what the lead article is. Often the cover will have one or two smaller headlines that announce other featured stories.

- **The contents page.** Usually found within the first few pages of a magazine, the contents page lists articles and regular features and tells you what pages they are on. *National Geographic World,* the magazine that "Destination: Mars" comes from, calls its contents page "Inside this issue."

Before you read your next magazine article, take some time to look at the way it's structured. Along with the text, a magazine article may include the following features:

- **A title.** A magazine article usually has a title that is cleverly worded to get your attention.

- **A subtitle.** An article often has a subtitle—a secondary title that tells you more about the article.

- **Illustrations.** An article is usually illustrated with art or photographs that explain or enrich the text. **Captions** usually explain illustrations.

- **Sidebars.** Many articles feature a sidebar or two, short articles set off within the main article that focus on a topic related to the main story.

IDENTIFY

In the first paragraph, underline the reasons humans have not gone to Mars.

IDENTIFY

Underline the experiment scientists designed in 1997 (lines 12–15).

EVALUATE

Can you think of reasons why *you* would want to visit Mars? What are they?

So far only robots have visited Mars. Robots are safer and cheaper than manned missions. Scientists used to think sending humans would require hauling three years' worth of oxygen and water (for the round trip as well as the time spent on Mars) and enough rocket fuel to get them home. That's a bulky and expensive way to travel.

However, scientists are studying new ideas that would be less costly and also allow astronauts to "pack light." Using inflatable habitats, producing oxygen and rocket fuel on Mars 10 instead of lugging it all from Earth, and recycling air and water would all lighten the load.

In 1997, engineer John Lewis took part in an experiment designed to see whether four people could survive in a closed-loop life-support system. That means nothing goes to waste—not even a drop of water—no matter where it comes from.

For about three months the crew was sealed inside a three-story chamber at Johnson Space Center in Houston, Texas. They washed their hands in recycled sweat, measured and weighed

The Earthlings are coming! The Earthlings are coming!

Engineers at the National Aeronautics and Space Administration (NASA), in Houston, Texas, are preparing to send people to Mars. The mission is not official yet. "But it will happen," says John Connolly, NASA mission designer. "Probably before 2020."

Scientists give many reasons for going: to explore, to learn new things, to find important minerals, and maybe eventually to establish colonies so people can live there. But perhaps the most exciting reason to go is to search for evidence of past or present life, probably microscopic, on Mars.

"I want to believe it's there," says Connolly. "But the surface of Mars is a pretty nasty place. We may have to dig down to where we think it's wetter and warmer."

The mission will require an extended stay on a frozen planet that lacks breathable oxygen and has only trace amounts of water on its surface. Keep reading to learn how NASA is planning to get humans there and then keep them alive and safe.

how much they went to the bathroom, and even drank each
20 other's urine! Sounds disgusting, right? It wasn't. All the body
wastes were collected and purified. "Our drinking water was
cleaner than water out of a tap," says Lewis. . . .

"Our eventual goal," explains aerospace engineer Scott
Baird, "is to live off the land." In preparation for the astronauts'
arrival, a cargo carrier will reach Mars first and drop off a large
chemical maker[1] and inflatable habitat.

It will take six months for astronauts to travel to Mars.
Once there, they will study and explore Mars for 500 days
before returning to Earth. Their landing craft, expanded with
30 the attached inflatable habitat, will serve as their home away
from home.

"It'll be a blast," says Baird. "And by the time the kids of
today grow up, they may be able to go."

Inside the "can," the nickname for the simulated capsule, the crew lived as they would during a long space voyage. Cut off from the world, they kept busy by exercising, maintaining the life-support systems, and keeping written logs.

COMPARING EARTH AND MARS

Nickname: the Blue Planet
Length of day: 23 hours, 56 minutes
Length of year: 365 days
Moons: one
Planet surface: mostly wet and warm
Atmosphere: 98 percent oxygen and nitrogen mix
Weather highlights: temperatures range from below −100°F to above 120°F; most storms wet

Nickname: the Red Planet
Length of day: 24 hours, 37 minutes
Length of year: 687 Earth days
Moons: two
Planet surface: cold and dry
Atmosphere: 95 percent carbon dioxide
Weather highlights: almost always below freezing; dry dust storms

---

1. **chemical maker:** device that produces oxygen and fuel.

IDENTIFY
Underline the goal of engineer Scott Baird (lines 23–24).

IDENTIFY
Circle the **caption** on this page.

RETELL
Write down a fact about Earth or Mars that you learned in the **sidebar** Comparing Earth and Mars.

Matching Chart

Magazines are built around design features that make it easy for the reader to see quickly the highlights. If done well by the publisher, those same design features can lead to increased sales of the magazine.

Read the following definitions of design features. Then, match the design feature to its use in "Destination Mars." Write the letter of the example from the right column next to the correct label in the left column.

Design	Design Examples from "Destination Mars"

Design

_____ **Decorative typefaces** have elaborately designed characters that convey a distinct mood. They are often used in titles.

_____ **Contrast** refers to the visual effect of using different typefaces in an article. There might be one kind of typeface in the body of the article, and another typeface with more emphasis in the beginning.

_____ **Symbols** help draw the eye to the special features like charts or drawings.

_____ **Rule lines** draw your eye to something on the page. Rule lines can be thick or thin, plain or fancy, vertical or horizontal.

_____ Another kind of graphic is a **table** that provides information in an organized way.

Design Examples from "Destination Mars"

a. **SO FAR** only robots have visited Mars.

b. ◄ Inside the "can," the nickname for the simulated capsule, the crew

c. Destination MARS

d. The Earthlings are coming! The Earthlings are coming!

e. EARTH

Nickname: the Blue Planet
Length of day: 23 hours, 56 minutes
Length of year: 365 days
Moons: one
Planet surface: mostly wet and warm
Atmosphere: 98 percent oxygen and nitrogen mix

Reading Check

1. According to information in the **sidebar,** when is it likely that people will land on Mars?

_____

_____

2. Give some reasons for scientists' wanting to travel to Mars. Where do you find this information?

_____

_____

3. Name three differences between Earth and Mars. Where do you find this information?

_____

_____

Test Practice

Circle the correct answer.

1. In what part of "Destination: Mars" do you learn that the surface of Mars is "a pretty nasty place"?

  A the title
  B the subtitle
  C the caption
  D the sidebar

2. The explanation that accompanies the photo of the "can" is called —

  F a caption
  G a subtitle
  H an illustration
  J a sidebar

3. It is clear that the author of the article got some information from —

  A personal experience
  B interviews
  C photographs
  D travel magazines

4. All of the following statements about Mars are true *except* —

  F it lacks breathable oxygen
  G its surface is warm
  H it has more than one moon
  J it's nicknamed "the Red Planet"

Fast, Strong, and Friendly Too

Text Structure: Comparison and Contrast

In "The Dogs Could Teach Me" (page 81), Gary Paulsen describes his dogs as a team and also as individuals. Think for a moment about the dogs you have known. Do you agree that no two dogs are ever alike in personality, even those that have been raised together? Take a moment to complete a Venn diagram for two dogs—or cats or cows—you have known. In each circle, note the animals' differences. In the center, where the circles overlap, note the similarities.

When you note similarities, you are **comparing** features. When you note differences, you are **contrasting** features.

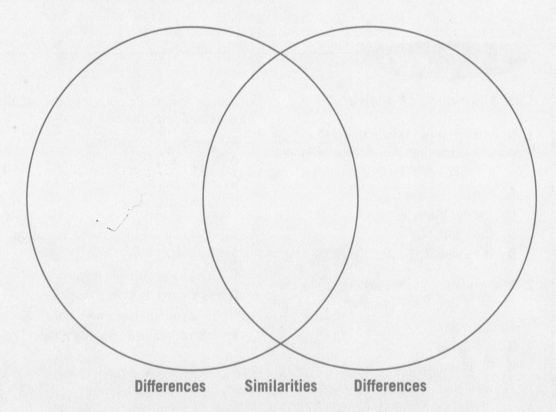

Differences   **Similarities**   **Differences**

As you read the next selection, watch for the ways in which the writer provides you with information about each breed. Where is comparison used? Where is contrast used?

Fast, Strong, and Friendly Too

Flo Ota De Lange

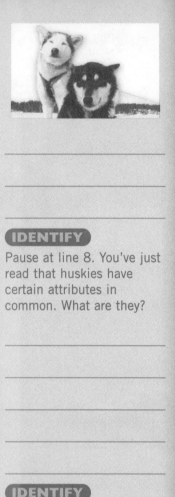

IDENTIFY

Pause at line 8. You've just read that huskies have certain attributes in common. What are they?

IDENTIFY

Pause at line 20, and underline three facts you have learned about Siberian huskies.

INTERPRET

Re-read lines 21–27. What is one **difference** between the Samoyed and the Siberian husky?

In October 1999, a team of 230 huskies hauled a big-rig Kenworth flatbed truck with a huge load up Front Street in Whitehorse, Yukon Territory, Canada. The truck and load weighed 110,000 pounds.

Who were these dogs that performed this amazing feat? Huskies are thick-coated working dogs of the Arctic, often used as sled dogs. They can be of a number of breeds, including Siberian husky, Samoyed, and Alaskan malamute.

Siberian huskies are the typical sled dog. They were bred
10 originally by the Chukchi people of Siberia, in northeastern Asia. The Chukchi trained them to run at a fast pace over great distances. That background probably accounts for the ability of the Siberian huskies to win races. For many years they won most of the dog-team-racing titles in Alaska. Their great endurance makes them ideally suited to take on the rugged terrain of the North.

The Chukchi upbringing may also account for the dogs' friendly nature. Siberian huskies are particularly good with children, and Chukchi tots were encouraged to play with
20 the dogs.

Of all modern dog breeds the Samoyed is the one most closely related to the first ancestor dog. No wolf or fox bloodlines run in the Samoyed strain. For centuries the Samoyed has been bred true in its homeland—the vast stretches of tundra reaching from the White Sea to the Yenisei River in central Siberia. There they served as sled dogs, reindeer guards, and household companions.

Many dog lovers believe the Samoyed to be the ultimate canine companion. After centuries of living with humankind,
30 this white-furred, smiling-faced dog has developed an almost uncanny understanding of people. Samoyeds are intelligent and good-natured; they always protect and never hurt their human families. Some people consider Samoyeds to be the most beautiful dogs in existence.

Alaskan malamutes are the largest of the sled dogs, standing some twenty-four inches high. These powerful-looking dogs

have remarkable endurance and fortitude. They were bred in upper western Alaska by an Inuit people called Mahlemuts, or Malemutes. Like Siberian huskies and Samoyeds, Alaskan
40 malamutes are known for their loyalty, understanding, and intelligence.

While Alaskan malamutes are the largest of the sled dogs, the smallest dog that *looks* like one is the American Eskimo dog. No one knows why the Eskie is called an Eskimo dog. This miniature animal probably couldn't find its way out of a tall northern snowbank. At nine inches short, the toy-sized Eskie looks like a full-sized sled dog in the same way that a toy version of a big-rig Kenworth flatbed truck looks like a full-sized one. Can't you just see it? Two hundred thirty less-
50 than-one-foot-tall Eskies hauling a toy-sized big rig up Front Street in Whitehorse, Yukon Territory, Canada.

IDENTIFY

Pause at line 41. Underline the ways Alaskan malamutes are **similar** to the other breeds you've read about so far.

_____

_____

_____

INFER

Which breed of husky would you use to protect your home? Which would you use to win a dog-racing title? Give reasons from the text to justify your responses.

_____

_____

_____

_____

_____

_____

_____

_____

_____

_____

Compare-and-Contrast Chart

Compare and **contrast** the characteristics of the three breeds of dog you've just read about by filling in the chart below. Look back through the article and the notes you took as you read to help complete the chart.

Breed of Dog	Where Bred	Appearance	Demeanor	Abilities
Siberian husky				
Samoyed				
Alaskan malamute				

Test Practice

Circle the correct answer.

1. The writer says that all the following breeds have been used as sled dogs *except* the —

A Alaskan malamute
B Siberian husky
C Samoyed
D American Eskimo dog

2. Samoyeds are different from Siberian huskies and Alaskan malamutes in that they —

F have no wolf bloodlines in their strain
G are intelligent and loyal
H are strong and hardworking
J like to play with children

3. The largest sled dog is the —

A Alaskan malamute
B Siberian husky
C Samoyed
D American Eskimo dog

4. The smallest dog that looks like a sled dog is the —

F Siberian husky
G Samoyed
H Alaskan malamute
J American Eskimo dog

5. Which breed of husky has won the most dog-team-racing titles in Alaska?

A Samoyed
B American Eskimo dog
C Siberian husky
D Alaskan malamute

6. The dog breed most closely related to the first ancestor dog is the —

F American Eskimo dog
G Alaskan malamute
H Siberian husky
J Samoyed

7. According to the article, the Samoyed and Siberian husky breeds are **similar** in what way?

A Both were bred by the Chukchi people of Siberia.
B Both are friendly to humans by nature.
C Both served as reindeer guards.
D Both are encouraged to play with tots.

Union Pacific Railroad Poster
and Home, Sweet Soddie

Comparing Texts: Treatment and Scope of Ideas

Home on the Range
Oh give me a home
Where the buffalo roam
Where the deer and the antelope play
Where seldom is heard
A discouraging word
And the skies are not cloudy all day

"Home on the Range" makes the prairie sound like a paradise, doesn't it? That must have been another prairie, not the one Mary encountered. Perhaps the ballad was written by a lonesome cowboy long after he'd left the prairie for the comforts of running tap water and home cooking.

But let's not be too hard on our singing cowboy, even though he has given us a **biased,** or one-sided treatment of his subject. He has conveniently forgotten all unpleasant memories in order to paint a beautiful picture of the life he longs for.

An **objective,** or balanced, treatment presents all sides of a subject so that readers can draw their own conclusions. When the treatment covers many aspects of a topic, it is said to have a **broad scope,** unlike our ballad, which has a **limited scope.**

As you read the poster from the Union Pacific Railroad and the article "Home, Sweet Soddie," think about what they say and how they say it.

- Is there evidence of bias, or is the treatment balanced and objective?
- Is the focus on the big picture or on a small snapshot?
- How are the selections similar in their scope and treatment of ideas?
- How are they different?

Union Pacific Railroad Poster

Home, Sweet Soddie

Flo Ota De Lange

RICH FARMING LANDS!

ON THE LINE OF THE

Union Pacific Railroad!

Located in the GREAT CENTRAL BELT of POPULATION, COMMERCE and WEALTH, and adjoining the WORLD'S HIGHWAY from OCEAN TO OCEAN.

12,000,000 ACRES!

3,000,000 Acres in Central and Eastern Nebraska, in the Platte Valley, now for sale!

We invite the attention of all parties seeking a HOME, to the

IDENTIFY

Re-read lines 1–11. Circle where the land for sale is located. Then, underline the description of the location.

_____

_____

_____

_____

_____

_____

_____

_____

IDENTIFY

Exaggeration is overstating something for effect. Advertisers may sometimes exaggerate the good points of a product so it will seem more attractive than it actually is. Underline three examples of exaggeration in lines 12–24.

_____

_____

_____

_____

_____

RICH FARMING LANDS!

ON THE LINE OF THE

Union Pacific Railroad!

Located in the GREAT CENTRAL BELT of POPULATION, COMMERCE and WEALTH, and adjoining the WORLD'S HIGHWAY from OCEAN TO OCEAN.

12,000,000 ACRES!

3,000,000 Acres in Central and Eastern Nebraska, in the Platte Valley, now for sale!

10 We invite the attention of all parties seeking a HOME, to the LANDS offered for sale by this Company.

The Vast Quantity of Land from which to select enables everyone to secure such a location as he desires, suitable to any branch of farming or stock raising.

The Prices are Extremely Low. The amount of land owned by the Company is so large that they are determined to sell at the cheapest possible rates, ranging from $1.50 to $8.00 per acre.

The Terms of Payment are Easy. Ten years' credit at six 20 percent interest. A deduction of ten percent for cash.

The Location is Central, along the 41st parallel, the favorite latitude of America. Equally well adapted to corn or wheat; free from the long, cold winters of the Northern, and the hot, unhealthy influences of the Southern States.

The Face of the Country is diversified with hill and dale, grain land and meadow, rich bottoms, low bluffs, and undulating tables, all covered with a thick growth of sweet nutritious grasses.

The Soil is a dark loam, slightly impregnated with lime, free 30 from stone and gravel, and eminently adapted to grass, grain, and root crops; the subsoil is usually light and porous, retaining moisture with wonderful tenacity.

The Climate is mild and healthful; the atmosphere dry and pure. Epidemic diseases never prevail; Fever and Ague are

unknown. The greatest amount of rain falls between March and October. The Winters are dry with but little snow.

Timber is found on the streams and grows rapidly.

The Title given the purchaser is absolute, in fee simple, and free from all encumbrances, derived directly from the United
40 States.

Soldiers of the Late War are entitled to a Homestead of one hundred and sixty acres, within Railroad limits, which is equal to a bounty of $400.

Persons of Foreign Birth are also entitled to the benefits of the Free Homestead Law, on declaring their intentions of becoming citizens of the United States; this they may do immediately on their arrival in this country. . . .

Full information in regard to lands, prices, terms of sale, etc., together with pamphlets, circulars and maps, may be
50 obtained from the Agents of the Department, also the

"PIONEER."

A handsome Illustrated Paper, with maps, etc., and containing the Homestead Law. Mailed free to all applicants. Address

O. F. DAVIS,

Land Commissioner, U. P. R. R.

OMAHA, NEB.

IDENTIFY

Loaded words are words that evoke a strong emotional reaction in a reader. Sometimes these words are not really relevant to the topic being discussed. Underline two loaded words in lines 25–40.

_____

_____

_____

_____

INTERPRET

What do you think is the **main point** of the Union Pacific Railroad poster?

_____

_____

_____

_____

_____

_____

_____

_____

_____

_____

IDENTIFY

Underline two examples of **exaggeration** in lines 1–9.

_____

_____

_____

_____

_____

_____

_____

_____

_____

_____

IDENTIFY

Underline the reason that the first houses on the prairie were built of sod. List the advantages of living in a sod house (lines 23–34).

_____

_____

_____

_____

_____

_____

_____

_____

_____

_____

_____

Home, Sweet Soddie

Here you are, a pioneer on the prairie, settled for your first night in your new Home Sweet Home. After you've traveled overland so many miles that it felt as though you'd gone halfway around the world, your straw mattress feels like heaven. But it sure is dark in here. Even though your fingers are right in front of your nose, you can't see them. The dark here is absolutely dark. There are no lights from other houses or from a town or city to reflect on the horizon. Outside there might be stars, but inside there is nothing but the velvety-black black.

10 **Thousands of Worms**

So when the first crack of dawn comes, you're anxious to check out your new world. But what's that? It looks like the ceiling above your head is moving. No, it couldn't be. Look again. Now it looks like the wall is moving too. Shut those eyes quick! While you're lying there trying to muster your forces to take another look, your parents wake up. Your mother exclaims, "This place is alive with worms!" You look again, and, sure enough, there are worms suspended from the ceiling, worms waving at you from the walls, and—what's

20 that all over the floor? More worms! Hundreds—no, thousands of worms!

Houses Built of Soil

Where did all those worms come from? Since there are hardly any trees out on the prairie, the pioneers built their first houses out of sod bricks cut from the surface layer of soil and including all the grasses and roots growing in it. It wasn't easy to build a house of sod. A twelve-by-fourteen-foot shelter required an acre of sod and a great deal of hard work. Because of the thick root system in the prairie grassland, walls built

30 of sod were strong and long lasting. This was one of the advantages. Other advantages of sod houses included the fact that they were better insulated than wood houses, so they were cooler in summer and warmer in winter. They also offered more protection from tornadoes, wind, and fire.

No Sense Cleaning It!

What were the disadvantages? These: Sod blocks were essentially compacted soil, which tended to sift down from the ceiling and walls, making it hard, if not impossible, to keep the house clean. Sod also wasn't waterproof. In fact, it was quite
40 the opposite. Whenever there was a heavy rain, water followed the root systems in the sod bricks right on down through the sod ceiling, soaking everything in the room and turning the sod floor to mud. All this dripping didn't stop when the rains stopped either. The roof could leak for days, and that meant people sometimes had to use boots and umbrellas indoors while the sun was shining brightly outside!

Bugs and Weather

The drawbacks of sod houses were not the only difficulties you would have faced as a pioneer on the prairie. Others
50 included the unaccustomed vastness of the wide-open spaces, the endless blue sky, and the almost total lack of neighbors. There were also fleas, flies, mosquitoes, moths, bedbugs, field mice, rattlesnakes, grasshoppers, tornadoes, floods, hail, blizzards, prairie fires, dust storms, and drought. In summer the ground baked, and in winter it froze. The wind blew constantly, and water was as scarce as hens' teeth. One pioneer who couldn't take it anymore left this hard-earned lesson scrawled across the cabin door of his deserted homestead: "250 miles to the nearest post office, 100 miles to wood, 20 miles to water, 6
60 inches to hell. Gone to live with wife's folks."

No Warranties

Yes, sirree, homesteading on the prairie was hard work, and there were no warranties on claimed land. The buyers had to take all the risks upon themselves. The term for this arrangement is *caveat emptor*—"let the buyer beware." So what can you do but sweep all those worms out the front door and back onto the prairie? What else can happen, after all?

Well, newly cut sod is home to fleas, and bedbugs come crawling out of it at night. So every morning you have to take
70 your bitten self and your infested bedding out-of-doors and pick off all those bugs. Then you head back inside armed

IDENTIFY

Circle some of the disadvantages of a sod house.

_____

_____

_____

_____

INTERPRET

Compare the treatment of ideas in "Home, Sweet Soddie" to the poster on pages 252–253. Write two specific differences in the treatment of ideas you've noticed so far.

_____

_____

_____

_____

INTERPRET

Underline the meaning of *caveat emptor* (line 65). Explain how this saying applies to life on the prairie.

_____

_____

_____

_____

INTERPRET

What is the **main point** of this article?

EVALUATE

Do you feel that this article is a **biased** or **objective** view of life on the prairie? Explain. Is the life described in the article anything like the life described in the land advertisement on pages 252–253?

with chicken feathers dipped in kerosene to paint every crack and every crevice in every bit of that sod ceiling, wall, and floor.

Blizzards of Grasshoppers

One creature that doesn't come *out of* the sod, but instead comes *onto* the sod, is the grasshopper. You know, of course, about blizzards of snow. But what about a blizzard of grasshoppers? Enough grasshoppers to block out the sun? So
80 many millions of grasshoppers that they can strip a farm bare in a matter of hours? Did you know that grasshoppers can chew their way through a plow handle? Did you know that grasshoppers are capable of eating almost everything in sight, including fences, bark, and that bedding that you just picked clean of fleas and bedbugs? If a pioneer family had dug 150 feet down for a well—the height of a thirteen-story building— grasshoppers falling into it could sour the water for weeks upon weeks. Grasshoppers could even stop a Union Pacific Railroad train from running. Piled some six inches deep on the
90 tracks, their bodies so greased the rails that a train's wheels would spin but not move.

So, welcome to the good life out on the prairie, where "the skies are not cloudy all day." By the way, do you know what constantly blue skies mean for the average farmer?

— Flo Ota De Lange

Comparison Chart

Compare the Union Pacific Railroad advertisement and the article "Home, Sweet Soddie" by filling out the chart below.

	Union Pacific Railroad Poster	Home, Sweet Soddie
Who were the writers?		
What was each writer's purpose?		
Who was it written for?		
In your opinion, was bias shown?		
List details that show bias.		

Main-Idea Chart

Home, Sweet Soddie

The **main idea** of an article is the most important point the writer makes about the topic, or subject. In a well-written article, the main idea is supported by details.

After you read "Home, Sweet Soddie," fill out this chart. First, record the supporting details that the article provides about life on the prairie. Then, think about these details and write a statement that expresses the main idea.

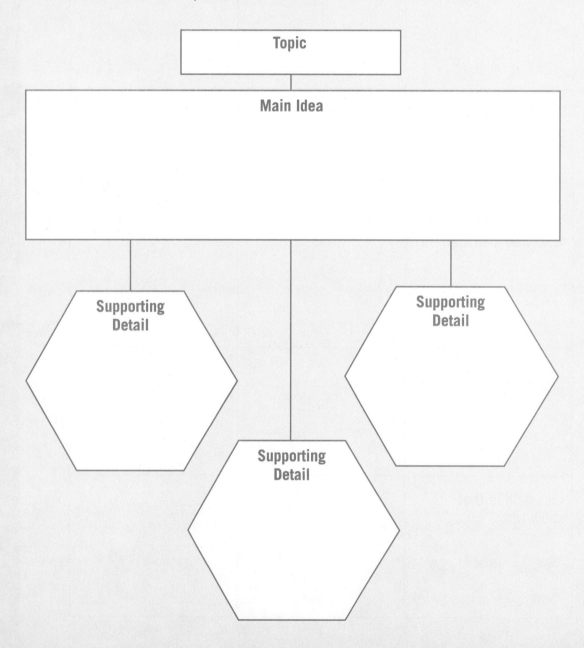

Topic

Main Idea

Supporting Detail

Supporting Detail

Supporting Detail

Reading Check

1. Find at least five details in the poster that would have motivated pioneers to buy

land in Nebraska. _____

_____

2. Find at least five details in "Home, Sweet Soddie" that might have discouraged

pioneers from buying land in Nebraska. _____

_____

Test Practice

Circle the correct answer.

1. The **purpose** of the Union Pacific Railroad poster was to —

  A entertain railroad travelers passing through Nebraska

  B persuade people to buy land in Nebraska

  C provide information on Nebraska to scientists

  D describe the good and bad qualities of Nebraska

2. The **purpose** of "Home, Sweet Soddie" is to —

  F encourage people to move to the prairie

  G praise the heroism of pioneers

  H teach people how to build sod houses

  J describe some of the difficulties of life on the prairie

3. The poster and the article are **similar** in that they both offer —

  A an unbiased treatment

  B a biased treatment

  C an objective treatment

  D a discouraging word

4. Which statement accurately describes the **tone** of these texts—that is, their attitudes toward their topics?

  F "Home, Sweet Soddie" is humorous; the poster is enthusiastic.

  G "Home, Sweet Soddie" is romantic; the poster is satiric.

  H Both are romantic.

  J Both are sarcastic.

5. The Union Pacific Railroad poster was intended as —

  A a newspaper editorial

  B an encyclopedia entry

  C a travel magazine article

  D an advertisement

Cesar Chavez: He Made a Difference

Text Structure: Cause and Effect

Think about a time when you or someone you know had a disagreement that turned into a fight or a shoving match. Jot down the details of that experience on a sheet of paper.

Finished? Whatever else you had to say about the incident, chances are you wrote down what started it (the **cause**) and what happened next (the **effect**). Human beings are naturally curious (OK, nosy). We like to know the reason (**cause**) for an action or reaction (**effect**). We want to know why (**cause**) something happened (**effect**). We make sense of events (**effects**) by looking carefully at what caused them. We sometimes even want to know what caused our mistakes.

Cause and Effect: It Happens in Real Life

Many years ago, thousands of migrant farmworkers in California had to endure many hardships, including poor working and living conditions, low wages, and lack of education. One of those thousands of workers, Cesar Chavez, set out to change things for the farmworkers by forming a union in order to fight for fair wages and better working conditions. In 1962, he organized the National Farm Workers Association (later called the United Farm Workers of America). It took years of difficult and sometimes frightening struggles, but the farmworkers eventually prevailed.

Why did the farmworkers succeed despite all the odds against them? There was no single cause, but a major one was Chavez's belief in the power of nonviolence. Think back to the disagreement you wrote about at the start of this lesson. Did resorting to violence help things? Probably not. Chavez knew that resorting to violence would lead to defeat for the farmworkers. His decision to use nonviolent means was important to their success.

We might also wonder, "Why was Cesar Chavez so determined to change things, even to the point of risking his life? Why, out of the thousands of migrant farmworkers in California, did this man make a difference? What goes into the making of such a person?" As you read the following biographical article, see if you can spot some causes of his actions.

Flo Ota De Lange

Cesar Chavez:
He Made a Difference

IDENTIFY

In the second paragraph, circle the name of the person who is the subject of this biographical article. Draw arrows to the words that describe his family.

VISUALIZE

Underline the words in the story that help create an image of the life of a migrant farmworker. Circle one way that this life is like or unlike your life (lines 4–11).

RETELL

In your own words, describe the agreement between Cesar's father and the landowner. Do you think it was a fair agreement? Why?

_____

_____

_____

_____

_____

_____

INTERPRET

What **caused** Cesar Chavez to establish a union for farmworkers (lines 28–32)?

_____

_____

_____

_____

What is it about the personal experience of injustice that makes some people decide to help others while other people help only themselves?

One of the people who decided to help others was Cesar Chavez (1927–1993). When Chavez was growing up, his family members were migrant farmworkers. They traveled from region to region in California and worked long hours picking crops in the hot sun for very low wages. Since the whole family had to work to make enough money to survive, Chavez was able to go

10 to school only when the harvests were in, and he had to quit school after eighth grade.

One year his father saw an opportunity to own his own land. He made an agreement with a landowner to clear eighty acres of the man's land and to take forty other acres of the man's land as payment for his work. Chavez's father cleared the eighty acres as promised, but when the time came for him to be paid, the landowner refused to give him the deed to the promised forty acres. Instead, he sold the land to another person.

20 When Cesar Chavez's father saw a lawyer about the matter, the lawyer advised him to borrow some money and buy the land from the other person. Chavez's father did just that. But cash was a difficult thing for his father to come by, and one day he didn't have the money to make an interest payment. The lawyer not only took the forty acres back but also sold it to the original owner—the man who had cheated Chavez's father in the first place.

Cesar Chavez says that he never forgot the injustice those men did to his father. For more than a hundred years, people

30 like his father had been allowed to toil in the fields but had not been allowed to enjoy the fruits of their toil. Chavez hoped to change this, a task many regarded as hopeless.

Chavez believed that migrant farmworkers needed a union to help them get fair wages and better working conditions. In 1962, he organized the National Farm Workers Association, later called the United Farm Workers of America. The union's five-year strike against California's grape growers drew support

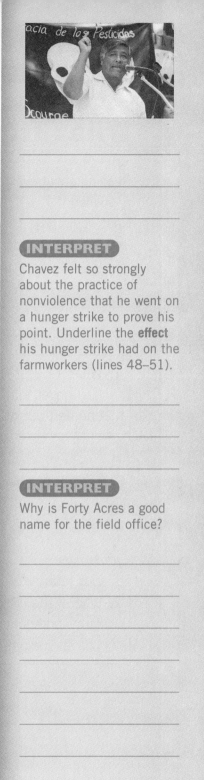

from around the country. Many people across the United States refused to buy or eat grapes until the strike was settled.

40   The union's actions were based on the non-violent principles of Mohandas K. Gandhi and Martin Luther King, Jr. However, many farmworkers were angry and believed that they could not win against the growers without violence. After all, the growers were using scare tactics and violence against them. Chavez met the threat of violence with a radical plan. He was willing to sacrifice his own life by going on a hunger strike to prevent violence and to ensure that the union would continue. His example won the angry workers over. By practicing nonviolence himself, Chavez inspired others in the

50 farmworkers' movement to recommit themselves to the struggle for justice through nonviolence.

When Cesar Chavez died in 1993, more than fifty thousand mourners gathered to honor him at the United Farm Workers' field office in Delano, California. The field office is called Forty Acres.

INTERPRET

Chavez felt so strongly about the practice of nonviolence that he went on a hunger strike to prove his point. Underline the **effect** his hunger strike had on the farmworkers (lines 48–51).

INTERPRET

Why is Forty Acres a good name for the field office?

What If? Chart

Reading about events in history gives us a chance to ask the question, "What would have happened if . . . ?" After you read "Cesar Chavez: He Made a Difference," think about what would have happened if certain events had *not* taken place. Write your responses in the boxes provided.

What If? (Cause)

Possible Effects

1. **What if** Cesar Chavez's father had never told him about being cheated out of his land?

2. **What if** the majority of the farmworkers had not followed Cesar Chavez's example of nonviolence?

3. **What if** the majority of the farmworkers had been too scared of losing their wages to form a union?

Test Practice

Circle the correct answer.

1. Which of the following situations was *not* a **cause** of Cesar Chavez's dedication to bettering the lives of migrant workers?

   A The way the landowner treated Chavez's father.

   B The way the lawyer treated Chavez's father.

   C The opportunity to purchase the Forty Acres field office.

   D The possibility of achieving justice through nonviolent means.

2. An **effect** of Cesar Chavez's dedication to bettering the lives of farmworkers was that the —

   F United Farm Workers was formed

   G farmworkers became angry

   H landowner cheated his father

   J lawyer gave his father advice

3. An **effect** of the United Farm Workers of America's strike against California grape owners was that —

   A Cesar Chavez's father lost his land

   B Cesar Chavez earned lower wages

   C many Americans refused to eat grapes

   D farmworkers used violent tactics against growers

4. The **cause** of Cesar Chavez's hunger strike was —

   F imprisonment of strikers

   G possibility of violence from farmworkers

   H love of his father

   J deep religious beliefs

5. An **effect** of Cesar Chavez's commitment to nonviolence was that farmworkers —

   A received a fair wage from growers

   B recommitted themselves to nonviolence

   C were praised by Martin Luther King, Jr.

   D quit the farmworkers' union

6. *Nonviolence* means —

   F "being too afraid to fight"

   G "being afraid of violence"

   H "refusing to use violence on principle"

   J "not wanting to be caught"

7. Cesar Chavez gave the name Forty Acres to the site of the United Farm Workers' field office at Delano. The name was —

   A symbolic

   B offensive

   C literal

   D humorous

Picking Strawberries: Could You Do It?

Guesses, Inferences, Conclusions, and Generalizations

Take A Guess

> Lance opened his eyes, glanced lazily at the clock, and was suddenly wide awake. Nine-thirty! Good grief, he must have overslept. . . . A slow smile spread across Lance's face and turned into a wide grin, which soon turned into a yawn. He stretched once, turned over, and thought, "Two weeks! No alarms, no bus, no homework." Ahhhhh . . . mmmmmmm . . . zzzzzzzzz.

Even though the writer of the passage above has left out quite a few details, it isn't difficult to figure out the situation. You don't need to have every fact spelled out to understand what is happening. That is because, like any good reader, you have made inferences and generalizations and drawn conclusions on your own.

Drawing Inferences

When you draw **inferences,** you make educated guesses based on the clues the writer gives and your own experience or knowledge. Try to supply the following information about the passage above even though the writer has not given it to you directly:

- What time of year might it be?

  _____

  _____

  _____

- What do you think Lance's situation is?

  _____

  _____

  _____

- Why doesn't Lance have to worry?

_____

_____

_____

- How do you think Lance feels?

_____

_____

_____

Reaching Conclusions

A **conclusion** is your final thought or judgment about what you have read. It takes into account all the facts and all your inferences. A conclusion is **valid** (both true and logical) if it can be supported with information from the text and if no information in the text contradicts it. Let's return to Lance. You probably concluded that Lance is enjoying the first day of a two-week vacation. Absolutely.

Making Generalizations

A **generalization** is a broad statement that can apply to many situations. To be valid, generalizations, like conclusions, have to be supported by facts. For the "story" about Lance, one generalization might be "Waking up on the first morning of a two-week vacation is a pleasure." Generalizations unsupported by facts are untrue. "All vacations are relaxing" would be too general, since some vacations are hectic.

As you read the following article, think about the inferences you might draw from it. Also think about any conclusions or generalizations you might make based on facts in the article.

Picking Strawberries:
Could You Do It?

Flo Ota De Lange

The following experiment will give you an idea of what it is like to pick strawberries for a living. One problem with picking a strawberry is that a ripe berry is easily bruised by handling, and if it is bruised, no one will buy it. So the strawberry picker must find a way to pluck the berry off the plant without hurting it. Sound easy? Well, maybe so—if you have all the time in the world and are picking only one berry. But what if, in order to earn enough money to provide your family with the basics, you have to pick about ten thousand strawberries in a twelve-hour
10 workday? That increase in numbers turns strawberry picking into a very different situation, doesn't it?

To pick ten thousand strawberries in twelve hours, you have to pick about

- 1 strawberry every four seconds
- 14 strawberries every minute
- 840 strawberries every hour

So how can we get an idea of what the strawberry picker's hands are doing as she or he picks a berry? In the absence of a real strawberry plant, let's settle for a twelve-inch length of
20 string. Anchor this piece of string around something stable, like a chair back or a door handle. Then, tie a granny knot. Have someone time you while you are doing it. How fast can you tie it? Practice doing it until you can tie a granny knot in four seconds or less. Then, try doing the same thing with fourteen separate lengths of twelve-inch string. The idea is to get fourteen separate knots tied in less than a minute. Now, imagine tying 840 knots in an hour and 10,080 knots in twelve hours. Are you getting an idea of what strawberry picking is like?

INFER

Re-read lines 1–11. Then, state the article's **main idea** in a sentence.

_____

_____

_____

EVALUATE

Re-read lines 1–11. Is strawberry picking easier or harder than you thought it would be?

_____

_____

_____

IDENTIFY

Describe the comparison that the author makes in lines 17–28.

_____

_____

_____

INFER

What **conclusion** can you draw about picking strawberries based on the information in the text?

_____

_____

_____

_____

Conclusions Chart

When you reach a **conclusion** about something, your conclusion should be supported by evidence. The suspicious character in a murder mystery with no alibi but a huge motive leads you to conclude that she is guilty. Using a conclusions chart helps you evaluate the evidence that leads you to a logical conclusion.

After you have read "Picking Strawberries: Could You Do It?," think about the conclusion you would draw about strawberry picking. Write your conclusion in the last box, below. In the Evidence boxes, write four pieces of evidence which lead you to this conclusion.

Evidence	Evidence	Evidence	Evidence

Conclusion

Reading Check

1. How many strawberries must a worker pick in an hour to support his or her family?

   _____

   _____

2. Why does the writer suggest that you try tying the knots? _____

   _____

Test Practice

Circle the correct answer.

1. "But what if, in order to earn enough money to provide your family with the basics, you have to pick about ten thousand strawberries in a twelve-hour workday?" One **inference** that can be made from this sentence is that —

   A strawberry pickers and their families are wealthy

   B strawberry picking is slow and leisurely

   C strawberry pickers are paid by quantity

   D strawberry pickers are paid by the hour

2. All of the following **inferences** can be made from the knot-tying experiment *except* —

   F a strawberry picker needs to know many knot-tying styles

   G a strawberry picker must have good coordination

   H strawberry picking is repetitive work

   J a strawberry picker must be fast

3. Which of the following **conclusions** about strawberry picking could be drawn from this text?

   A It is easy money.

   B It is harder than you might think.

   C It requires maturity and strength.

   D It is impossible.

4. One **generalization** that could be made from this reading is that —

   F strawberries taste good

   G strawberry picking is hard

   H strawberries are hard to grow

   J strawberry pickers are nice

5. Based on this article, which **conclusion** could you make about the writer's beliefs?

   A Strawberry pickers work too hard.

   B Strawberry pickers could work harder.

   C Strawberry pickers should seek other work.

   D Management takes unfair advantage of strawberry pickers.

Langston Hughes: A Biography *and* "Langston Hughes": A Summary

What Goes into a Summary?

Writing a good summary of an informational text is not easy. You have to restate the main ideas, include critical details, and sum up the underlying meaning of the text. The following is a checklist of what to look for in a good summary of informational nonfiction. Read the biography of Langston Hughes and the summary that follows. As you read "Langston Hughes": A Summary, place a check next to the items if they appear.

1. The summary should open with the **title** and author of the **text.**

2. The summary should state the **topic** of the text.

3. The summary should state the **main ideas** in the **order** in which they occur in the text.

4. The summary should include important **supporting details.**

5. Quotation marks should be put around any words from the text that are quoted exactly.

Langston Hughes:

A Biography

IDENTIFY

Circle the year Langston Hughes was born. Underline where he spent most of his childhood.

Langston Hughes was born in 1902 in Joplin, Missouri, but he spent most of his childhood in Lawrence, Kansas, with his grandmother. When he was twelve, he moved to Lincoln, Illinois, and then to Cleveland, Ohio, to live with his mother and stepfather. Hughes died in 1967 in his home in his beloved Harlem, in New York City.

According to a popular story, Langston Hughes first tasted fame when he was twenty-three years old. When the poet Vachel Lindsay came to dine at the Wardman Park Hotel in
10 Washington, D.C., where Hughes was working as a busboy, Hughes left three poems by Lindsay's plate. Lindsay was so impressed by the poems that he presented them that night at a reading, saying he had discovered a true poet, a young black man who was working as a busboy in a nearby restaurant. For the next few days, newspapers up and down the East Coast ran articles acclaiming the "busboy poet."

That story is a good one, but it's a little misleading. Hughes was not really an overnight success. He had already put in a long apprenticeship as a writer. He had written his first poem
20 when he was in eighth grade and was first published in his high school literary magazine. Hughes had also read a great

RETELL

Circle the name of the author who is said to have "discovered" Langston Hughes. In your own words, **retell** the story about Langston Hughes' first taste of fame (7–16).

IDENTIFY

Underline some of Langston Hughes's accomplishments on his journey to success (lines 17–42).

IDENTIFY

What did Langston Hughes write about in his poetry?

INTERPRET

What do you learn about Langston Hughes's **character** from this biography?

deal of poetry, especially the works of Edgar Lee Masters, Vachel Lindsay, Amy Lowell, Carl Sandburg, and Walt Whitman. Whitman and Sandburg had a strong influence on Hughes because they celebrated the humanity of all people regardless of age, gender, race, or class. Hughes had already seen many of his own poems published in journals and magazines. What's more, a book of his poetry, *The Weary Blues*, was soon to be published by a famous New York publisher.

30   As the anecdote about Vachel Lindsay shows, Hughes was energetic and ambitious. Before he met Lindsay, he had attended Columbia University and had worked as a crew member on a freighter crossing the Atlantic to Africa and back. He spoke German and Spanish and had lived in Mexico (where his father also lived), France, and Italy. After meeting Lindsay, Hughes went on to earn a college degree at Lincoln University and to write fifteen volumes of poetry, six novels, three books of short stories, eleven plays, and a variety of nonfiction works. Hughes worked in Harlem during the heady

40 days of the Harlem Renaissance, when that New York City neighborhood was teeming with talent—poets, musicians, artists.

About his poetry, Hughes said, "Perhaps the mission of an artist is to interpret beauty to the people—the beauty within themselves." Hughes also interpreted—and celebrated—the experiences of African Americans. Some of his most famous poems imitated jazz rhythms and the repetitive structure of the blues. Later in life he wrote poems specifically designed for jazz accompaniment. He also helped found several black theater

50 companies and wrote and translated plays for them to perform. Langston Hughes is perhaps the most famous and original of all African American poets. He said his work was an attempt to "explain and illuminate the Negro condition in America." Hughes succeeded in that and more: His work illuminates the condition of all people everywhere.

"Langston Hughes": A Summary

"Langston Hughes: A Biography" focuses on the life and works of the poet Langston Hughes. The main point made in this biographical sketch is that Langston Hughes wrote about the experiences of African Americans but his work "illuminates the condition of all people everywhere." Hughes became famous when he was twenty-three, when the poet Vachel Lindsay read his poems at a poetry reading. Hughes had been writing since eighth grade, however, and had published a poem in a high school literary magazine. He was especially influenced

10 by Whitman and Sandburg because they celebrated all humanity. Hughes accomplished a lot both before and after meeting Lindsay. He attended Columbia and graduated from Lincoln University. He traveled widely and spoke three languages. He was part of the Harlem Renaissance and published many books of poetry, plays, fiction, and nonfiction. Langston Hughes is probably the most famous and original of all African American poets.

IDENTIFY

List one **main idea** in "Langston Hughes": A Summary.

INTERPRET

Explain why there are quotation marks around "illuminates the condition of all people everywhere" (lines 4–5).

Summary-Notes Chart

When you write a summary of an informational text you must include all the main ideas along with their important supporting details. Minor details should be left out. In the graphic organizer below, write notes for a summary of "Langston Hughes: A Biography," by filling in the main idea and supporting details for each paragraph.

Title: Langston Hughes: A Biography
Author: unknown
Topic:

	Main Idea	Supporting Details
1		
2		
3		
4		
5		

Reading Check

1. According to the biography, which poets most influenced Hughes?

_____

_____

2. What did Hughes say was the mission of an artist?

_____

_____

_____

Test Practice

Circle the correct answer.

1. Which of the following **details** is included in *both* the summary and the biography?

A Hughes was influenced by Whitman and Sandburg.

B Hughes read Masters, Lindsay, Lowell, Sandburg, and Whitman.

C Hughes spoke German and Spanish.

D Hughes traveled to Africa, Mexico, France, and Italy.

2. Which detail in the summary is probably *not* important and could have been omitted?

F Hughes became famous at age twenty-three.

G Hughes was part of the Harlem Renaissance.

H Hughes wrote about African Americans.

J Hughes was published in a high school literary magazine.

3. Which **critical details** from the biography does the summary omit?

A Hughes's birth and death dates

B influences on Hughes

C colleges Hughes attended

D Hughes's subject matter

4. Which passage in the summary should be placed in **quotation marks** because it uses the exact words of the writer of the biography?

F attended Columbia and graduated from Lincoln University

G accomplished a lot both before and after meeting Lindsay

H traveled widely and spoke three languages

J the most famous and original of all African American poets

from The Power of Nonviolence

Taking Notes and Outlining

Good informational material is fascinating when you read it, but when you try to share your interest with a friend, you often cannot remember the details. You might even have forgotten the writer's main idea. Here are two good ways to keep track of important ideas and interesting details: (1) take notes, and (2) make an outline.

Notecards. Gather a stack of three-by-five-inch index cards. (You can substitute slips of paper of a similar size.)

Main ideas. As you read each paragraph, stop and ask yourself, "What is the main idea?" Some paragraphs may offer a new idea, while others will offer supporting evidence for an idea presented in a previous paragraph. Write each main idea at the top of a notecard.

Details. On each card containing a main idea, write all the important supporting details. Try to use your own words. If you do use the writer's words, put quotation marks around them.

Outline. Once your cards are filled, you can organize your notes in an outline. Here is how an **informal outline** is set up:

> **Informal Outline**
> I. First main idea
>   A. Supporting detail
>   B. Supporting detail
>   C. Suppporting detail
> II. Second main idea
> [Etc.]

A formal outline is useful when you are preparing notes for a composition of your own, especially a research paper. Here is how a **formal outline** is set up:

Formal Outline
I. First main idea
    A. Supporting point
        1. Detail
        2. Detail
    B. Supporting point
II. Second main idea
    A. Supporting point
        1. Detail
        2. Detail
    B. Supporting point
[Etc.]

A formal outline must always have at least two items at each level. That is, if there is a *I*, there must be at least a *II*, if not a *III*; if there is an *A*, there must be at least a *B*, and so on.

John Lewis was a civil rights activist who helped plan a lunch-counter sit-in in 1960. Here's the start of an informal outline of the interview with Lewis that you are about to read. It's up to you to outline the rest.

I. Childhood experience of segregation
    A. Encountered separate water fountains
    B. Encountered separate seating in movie theaters
    C. Found experience differed from religious teaching

from John Lewis

The Power of Nonviolence

WE WANT TO SIT DOWN

When I was a boy, I would go downtown to the little town of Troy, and I'd see the signs saying "White" and "Colored" on the water fountains. There'd be a beautiful, shining water fountain in one corner of the store marked "White," and in another corner was just a little spigot marked "Colored." I saw the signs saying "White Men," "Colored Men," and "White Women," "Colored Women." And at the theater we had to go upstairs to go to a movie. You bought your ticket at the same window that the white people did, but they could sit downstairs, and you had to go upstairs.

I wondered about that, because it was not in keeping with my religious faith, which taught me that we were all the same in the eyes of God. And I had been taught that all men are created equal.

It really hit me when I was fifteen years old, when I heard about Martin Luther King, Jr., and the Montgomery bus boycott. Black people were walking the streets for more than a year rather than riding segregated buses. To me it was like a great sense of hope, a light. Many of the teachers at the high school that I attended were from Montgomery, and they would tell us about what was happening there. That, more than any other event, was the turning point for me, I think. It gave me a way out. . . .

Lewis went on to college, where he attended workshops and studied the philosophy of nonviolence.

In February 1960, we planned the first mass lunch-counter sit-in. About five hundred students, black and white, from various colleges showed up and participated in a nonviolent workshop the night before the sit-in. Some of them came from as far away as Pomona College in California and Beloit College in Wisconsin.

We made a list of what we called the "Rules of the Sit-in"—the do's and don'ts—and we mimeographed it on an old machine and passed it out to all the students. I wish I had a copy of this list today. I remember it said things like, "Sit up straight. Don't talk back. Don't laugh. Don't strike back." And

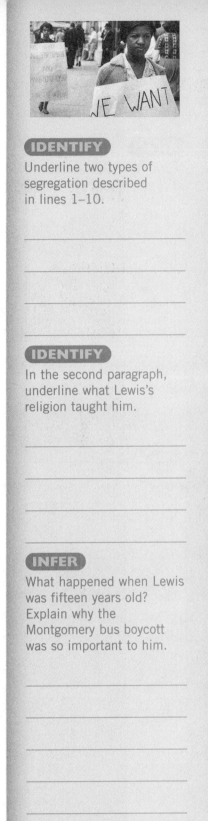

IDENTIFY

Underline two types of segregation described in lines 1–10.

_____

_____

_____

IDENTIFY

In the second paragraph, underline what Lewis's religion taught him.

_____

_____

_____

INFER

What happened when Lewis was fifteen years old? Explain why the Montgomery bus boycott was so important to him.

_____

_____

_____

_____

_____

_____

_____

_____

INFER

Why were the store chains such as Woolworth's, Kresge's, and Walgreen's primary targets for the lunch-counter sit-ins?

_____

_____

_____

_____

_____

_____

_____

_____

_____

_____

_____

_____

_____

_____

_____

_____

_____

IDENTIFY

Re-read lines 62–72. Underline the actions of the young white men. Circle the response of the police.

at the end it said, "Remember the teachings of Jesus, Gandhi, Thoreau, and Martin Luther King, Jr."

40 Then the next day it began. We wanted to make a good impression. The young men put on their coats and ties, and the young ladies their heels and stockings. We selected seven stores to go into, primarily the chain stores—Woolworth's, Kresge's, and the Walgreen drugstore—and we had these well-dressed young people with their books going to the lunch counters. They would sit down in a very orderly, peaceful, nonviolent fashion and wait to be served. They would be reading a book or doing their homework or whatever while they were waiting.

I was a spokesperson for one of these groups. I would ask to be served, and we would be told that we wouldn't be served. 50 The lunch counter would be closed, and they would put up a sign saying "Closed—not serving." Sometimes they would lock the door, leave us in there, and turn out all the lights, and we would continue to sit.

After we had been doing this for a month, it was beginning to bother the business community and other people in Nashville. We heard that the city had decided to allow the police officials to stand by and allow the hoodlum element to come in and attack us—and that the police would arrest us—to try to stop the sit-ins. We had a meeting after we heard that, to 60 decide did we still want to go down on this particular day. And we said yes.

I was with the group that went into the Woolworth's there. The lunch counter was upstairs—just a long row of stools in front of a counter. My group went up to sit there, and after we had been there for half an hour or so, a group of young white men came in and began pulling people off the lunch-counter stools, putting lighted cigarettes out in our hair or faces or down our backs, pouring ketchup and hot sauce all over us, pushing us down to the floor and beating us. Then the police 70 came in and started arresting _us_. They didn't arrest a single person that beat us, but they arrested all of us and charged us with disorderly conduct.

That was the first mass arrest of students in the South for participating in a sit-in. Over one hundred of us were arrested that day. We were sentenced, all of us, to a fifty-dollar fine or thirty days in jail, and since we wouldn't pay the fine, we were put in jail. . . .

Lewis and his fellow students were jailed, but they continued their protests when they were released. In April 1960, the mayor of 80 *Nashville agreed that the lunch counters should be desegregated.*

And so Nashville became the first major city in the South to desegregate its downtown lunch counters and restaurants. That was the power of nonviolence. . . .

I think one thing the movement did for all of us in the South, black and white alike, was to have a cleansing effect on our psyche. I think it brought up a great deal of the dirt and a great deal of the guilt from under the rug to the top, so that we could deal with it, so that we could see it in the light. And I think that in a real sense, we are a different people. We are 90 better people. It freed even those of us who didn't participate— black people, white people alike—to be a little more human.

IDENTIFY

What happened to the students who were arrested?

_____

_____

_____

_____

_____

_____

_____

INTERPRET

Explain how the effects of "the power of nonviolence" helped make people a little more human.

_____

_____

_____

_____

_____

_____

_____

_____

_____

_____

_____

Main-Idea Note Cards

Clarify your understanding of the excerpt from "The Power of Nonviolence" by taking notes on what you read. Fill in the note cards below with the main ideas from the text. Review your notes to clarify your understanding of the writer's ideas.

Note Card 1

Note Card 2

Note Card 3

Note Card 4

Note Card 5

Note Card 6

Reading Check

1. What were the "Rules of the Sit-in"? _____

_____

2. How did the city officials respond to the sit-ins? _____

_____

3. What was the result of the sit-ins? _____

_____

Test Practice

Circle the correct answer.

1. Suppose an **outline** of this article listed these main ideas:

   I   Experiences of segregation
   II
   III Lunch-counter sit-ins
   IV   Effect of the movement

   Which **main idea** should be II?

   A Segregated water fountains
   B Montgomery bus boycott
   C Rules of the sit-in
   D Woolworth's lunch counter

2. Suppose an **outline** of this article has a main heading that reads "Hoodlums Attack Demonstrators." Which of these details does *not* support that main idea?

   F pulled demonstrators off stools
   G poured hot sauce on demonstrators
   H beat up demonstrators
   J fined demonstrators fifty dollars

3. Which of the following is the *best* statement of John Lewis's **main idea** in this article?

   A Nonviolence makes us all better people.
   B All men are created equal.
   C Police arrest protesters unfairly.
   D Injustice can be overcome with nonviolence.

Leash-Free Dog Run Documents

Reading for Life

Read All About It

Life today can get pretty complicated as we race down the information superhighway. Let's say you want to do something easy, like go to a movie. There's nothing complicated about that. All you need to know is where and when the movie is playing. Actually there are many other choices you can make. Besides learning the time and place, you can read reviews by critics or by "regular" people like you, get in-depth information about the cast and director, reserve seats for yourself and your friends, view film clips and ads, purchase tie-in items like T-shirts, and even join a fan club. To do all this, you might use the telephone, TV, the Internet, e-mail, snail mail, instant messaging, or a fax. You might browse through a newspaper or magazine, a bookstore, a library, or a mall. In the process you would be reading a variety of information-based documents. Our world is full of them, and they come in three basic types.

Workplace Documents

The odds are good that in the next thirty years you will hold a variety of jobs. The job you volunteer for at age thirteen will probably be very different from the one you accept at age forty-three. Whether you are taking orders for fast food or giving orders to a staff of a thousand, your job will probably require you to **read for information.** When earning a living is involved, that information is important. **Workplace documents** serve two basic functions:

- **Communication.** E-mail, memorandums (memos), and reports will tell you about upcoming meetings, changes in policy, and other information you need to know in order to do your job. You will need to take precise and careful note of the information conveyed.
- **Instruction.** Employee manuals tell what is expected of you on the job. User's guides teach you how to operate the equipment you use. These, too, will be essential to your success at work.

Public Documents

Public documents consist of information concerning public agencies and not-for-profit groups. They can be about voting issues, health concerns, community decisions, and a host of other subjects. Public documents inform people of situations, decisions, responsibilities, schedules, occasions, and events that may interest them. Public documents exist to tell people what is happening in their own community, city, state, and nation and even on the planet.

Consumer Documents

A **consumer** is someone who buys something or uses what someone else buys. That covers just about everyone: you, your friends—even a baby. The things we—consumers—buy fall into two basic categories: goods (stuff) and services (help). Many goods are simple to use. More complicated goods may not be so easy to use. You buy a computer. Now what? You'll need some information to get your computer up and running. Therefore, your computer package will include some or all of the following documents:

- **product information** that tells what the computer will do
- a **contract** that spells out exactly what services will and will not be provided
- a **warranty** that spells out exactly what happens if the computer doesn't work properly and what you are required to do to receive service
- an **instruction manual** that tells how to set up and use the computer
- **technical directions** that give precise technical information about installing and assembling the computer and any peripheral devices, like printers

These **consumer documents** give you the information you need to select, purchase, and use your computer. They also define legal rights and responsibilities: yours, those of the company that made the computer, and those of the company that sold it.

Take the Time to Read It

Reading an owner's manual and the fine print in a warranty and a contract requires discipline when you are just itching to use your new purchase and start having fun with it. Patience! Perseverance! It's better to spend a few minutes slogging through difficult reading than to get stuck with an item that doesn't suit your needs, costs more than it has to, or gets broken right out of the box.

You can see how important information-based documents are. The pages that follow will give you some practice with them. Remember: Patience! Perseverance! This is *your* life—and perhaps your allowance.

Sheri Henderson

Leash-Free Dog Run Documents

SouthPaws

Welcome to the SouthPaws Web site. SouthPaws is a not-for-profit group dedicated to creating and maintaining a leash-free space on the south side of our city for its 165,000 canine (that's dog) citizens. Please consider joining our 3,300 + members. Your membership fees are tax-deductible and will help give our dogs their own space! If you are interested in volunteering, please check out Volunteer Want Ads. Finally, you might
10 want to consider SouthPaws T-shirts, sweats, caps, or leashes as a gift or for yourself. All proceeds support SouthPaws.

What's New?

Congratulations to the hundreds of volunteers who gathered signatures on the SouthPaws petition. All that hard work last spring paid off! The residents of our city have voted to establish a park or a beach where our dogs can run unleashed. This space will be jointly funded by the city and SouthPaws donations. SouthPaws volunteers will supervise the space during daylight hours and will be empowered to ticket dog owners who do not observe cleanup and safety rules. We will have one
20 trial year after the space officially opens to prove that the idea works. Now we need your help more than ever.

We are working with the city Parks and Recreation Department to choose a location. These are the most likely locations:

Cameo Park	Rocky Point Beach	Main Beach
Pro	**Pro**	**Pro**
• is centrally located	• is little used	• is centrally located
• has convenient access roads	• consists of 5 nonresidential acres	• consists of 7.3 nonresidential acres
• has street parking	• has ample parking	• has sand beach
Con	• will incur low start-up and maintenance costs	**Con**
• will incur high maintenance costs	**Con**	• is heavily used all year
• is smallest, at 1.2 residential acres	• is inconveniently located	• may cause conflicts with businesses
• is now a popular family park	• has small sand beach and a larger area of smooth but potentially slippery rocks	• has limited, costly parking
• may lead nearby residents to object to noise, nuisances		• will require 24-hour security and maintenance staffing
		• will incur high maintenance costs

Pick a Site
Click here to cast your vote in our survey.

INTERPRET

Why is Volunteer Want Ads underlined (line 9) ?

_____

_____

IDENTIFY

In the first paragraph, underline the sentence that describes the type of Web site SouthPaws is. Circle the items SouthPaws sells. Why does SouthPaws sell these things?

_____

_____

INFER

What issue do you think the SouthPaws petition addressed? Underline the information in lines 12–21 that supports your **inference**.

_____

_____

_____

EVALUATE

Which site do you think is the best choice for the "unleashed" location? Underline the "pros" and circle the "cons" that lead you to make that decision.

_____

_____

_____

IDENTIFY

What organization does the letter writer represent? To whom is the letter addressed? What is her position?

_____

_____

_____

INFER

What problems arise if a site that is already popular for sports, family activities, and tourism is chosen for a dog run?

_____

_____

_____

EVALUATE

Do you think that this letter was written with the best interests of the dogs, dog owners, or the community in mind? Underline the words that support your decision.

_____

_____

INTERPRET

Based on the concerns in this letter, do you still feel the park/beach you chose on page 289 is the best choice? If not, what choice would be better?

_____

_____

SouthPaws

SouthPaws • 1111 South P Street • South City, CA • 90123

December 12, 2002

Ms. T. Wagger
Director of Parks and Recreation
2222 Central Avenue
South City, CA 90123

Dear Ms. Wagger,

SouthPaws members would like you to take their concerns into account when choosing the site of the proposed dog run. Here they are, in order of importance:

10 **1. Space.** Healthy dogs need ample space in which to run. The park needs to be large enough for a fair number of dogs to run around in it without colliding with one another. Ample size will minimize the possibility of dogfights.

2. Conflicts. A site that is already popular for sports, family activities, or tourism will likely be a problem.

3. Site. Our research shows that dog beaches are preferable to dog parks. Dogs are hard on park grass, which quickly turns to mud in rainy weather. Sand or shells can be brushed off a dog, but mud requires a bath. Dog beaches are also easier to supervise and clean.

20 Thank you for working with us to find a solution that is in the best interests of the most people. We are looking forward to meeting with you next week.

Sincerely,

A. K. Nine

A. K. Nine
Chairperson
SouthPaws Site Committee

SouthPaws

Did You Know?

- In our city there are 165,000 licensed dogs.
- The city devotes a total of 10 acres to leash-free dog areas.
- The city devotes 1,050 acres to softball, 1,040 acres to golf, 287 acres to tennis.
- Eastside Leash-Free Dog Park accommodates 2,000 dogs per week on its 1-acre site.

10

SouthPaws Membership Information
Annual Tax-Deductible Membership Fees

Basic: $15 per year; entitles you to newsletter and voting rights

Deluxe: $25 per year; entitles you to the above plus one T-shirt or cap

Sponsor: $100 per year; entitles you to all of the above plus discounted dog-obedience classes and merchandise from local

20   merchants

Angel: $250 per year; entitles you to all of the above plus your name on our Wall of Fame

New!

Help SouthPaws while you tell the world about your best friend. Buy a brick in the new Dog Walk of Fame. Your pet's name and a short message will be inscribed. Be sure to provide your pet's name, your name, and your message (up to 45 letter spaces). (Available to SouthPaws members only; $50 per pet's name.)

30   Membership in SouthPaws makes a great gift. Print out a membership application, complete it, and mail it with your donation. Don't want to join? Then how about making a donation? We appreciate contributions in any amount.

INFER

Review the statistics in lines 1–10. Do you feel that the city is a dog-friendly place? Circle the reasons that support your **inference**.

_____

_____

_____

IDENTIFY

Circle the items you would receive if you joined SouthPaws as an "angel" (lines 21–22).

_____

_____

_____

INTERPRET

Imagine you are buying a brick for your dog in the new "Dog Walk of Fame" (line 25). What message would you write? Remember your message can only be 45 letter spaces long.

_____

_____

_____

_____

_____

_____

Business Letter Template

Imagine that you are T. Wagger, Director of Parks and Recreation. You want to respond to the Chairperson of the Site Committee of SouthPaws. To do this, use this business letter template. State your preferred site on the line provided. Then, write your reasons in the boxes labeled Space, Conflicts, and Type of Area.

2222 Central Avenue
South City, CA 90123

December 14, 2002

A. K. Nine
Chairperson, Site Committee
SouthPaws
1111 South P Street
South City, CA 90123

Dear A. K. Nine:

Thank you for your letter of December 12. It is important for us to work with the community in deciding where to put the dog park. Therefore, I would like to inform you that we favor the site at _____. Our reasons, in order of importance, are:

1. Space: _____

_____

2. Conflicts: _____

_____

3. Type of Area: _____

_____

Thank you for continuing to work with us on this issue. I look forward to seeing you at the upcoming meeting.

Sincerely,

T. Wagger
Director, Parks and Recreation

Reading Check

1. What problem is the SouthPaws Web site concerned with?

_____

_____

2. What three concerns do SouthPaws members have?

_____

_____

3. Which proposed site addresses *most* of SouthPaws' concerns? Why?

_____

_____

Test Practice

Circle the correct answer.

1. The decision to build the dog run was made by —

  A the city council
  B Parks and Recreation
  C SouthPaws
  D voters

2. If you were not a SouthPaws member but wanted to buy a brick in the new Dog Walk of Fame, it would cost you a minimum of —

  F $15
  G $25
  H $50
  J $65

3. How many acres are already devoted to leash-free zones?

  A 1
  B 10
  C 287
  D 1,050

4. SouthPaws members are *most* concerned about —

  F access
  G conflicts
  H space
  J type of area

5. The site that *best* meets the needs and concerns of SouthPaws members is —

  A Cameo Park
  B Rocky Point Beach
  C Main Beach
  D either Rocky Point or Main Beach

Computers
from Holt Science and Technology

Following Technical Directions

When you want to make or do something new, you usually consult directions. To find out how long to boil spaghetti, you would read directions on the box. For yoga exercises you might follow the directions on a videotape. The directions for performing scientific and mechanical activities or for operating mechanical devices are called **technical directions.** You rely on technical directions to do many things: to use your latest electronic gadget, program your thermostat, operate the microwave, build a robot or a radio-controlled model.

Technical directions are often included when an item is complicated or mechanical in nature. They lay out the steps you must follow to assemble or operate a device. If a step is skipped or performed out of order, the device may not work or may even break. When you're following technical directions, it's a good idea to

- read the directions all the way through
- check off the steps one by one as you complete them
- compare your work with the diagrams and drawings for each step

The pages that follow will provide some information on computers, as well as directions for setting up a computer.

COMPUTERS

from **Holt Science and Technology**

IDENTIFY

Pause at line 6. Why is an alarm clock a computer?

_____

_____

_____

_____

IDENTIFY

Underline the definition of *computer* (lines 8–9).

_____

_____

_____

_____

_____

INTERPRET

Re-read lines 13–25. Circle the four basic functions of a computer. Give a brief definition for each.

_____

_____

_____

_____

_____

_____

Did you use a computer to wake up this morning? You might think of a computer as something you use to send e-mail or surf the Net, but computers are around you all the time. Computers are in automobiles, VCRs, and telephones. Even an alarm clock is a computer! An alarm clock lets you program the time you want to wake up, and it will wake you up at that time.

What Is a Computer?

A **computer** is an electronic device that performs tasks by processing and storing information. A computer performs a task
10 when it is given a command and has the instructions necessary to carry out that command. Computers do not operate by themselves, or "think."

Figure 1
The Functions of a Computer

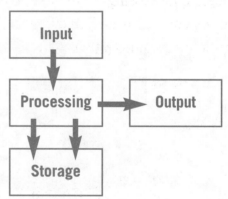

Basic Functions The basic functions a computer performs are shown in **Figure 1.** The information you give to a computer is called *input*. Setting your alarm clock is a type of input. To perform a task, a computer *processes* the input, changing it to a desirable form. Processing could mean adding a list of numbers, executing a drawing, or even moving a piece of equipment. Input doesn't have to be processed immediately; it can be
20 stored until it is needed. Computers store information in their *memory*. For example, your alarm clock stores the time you want to wake up. It can then process this stored information by going off at the programmed time. *Output* is the final result of the task performed by the computer. What's the output of an alarm clock? The sound that wakes you up!

Computer Hardware

For each function of a computer, there is a corresponding part of the computer where each function occurs. **Hardware** refers to the parts, or equipment, that make up a computer. As you
30 read about each piece of hardware, refer to **Figure 2.**

Input Devices   Instructions given to a computer are called input. An *input device* is the piece of hardware that feeds information to the computer. You can enter information into a computer using a keyboard, a mouse, a scanner, a digitizing pad and pen—even your own voice!

Central Processing Unit   A computer performs tasks within an area called the *central processing unit,* or CPU. In a personal computer, the CPU is a microprocessor. Input goes through the CPU for immediate processing or for storage in memory. The
40 CPU is where the computer does calculations, solves problems, and executes the instructions given to it.

Figure 2 Computer Hardware

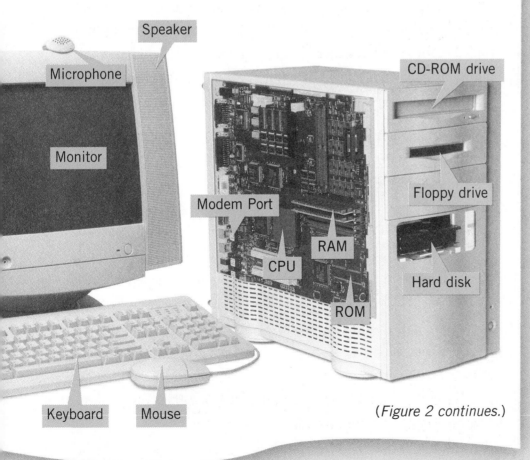

(*Figure 2 continues.*)

INFER
Pause at line 30. Can you guess which pieces of hardware will be discussed? Write your guesses on the lines below. If any of your guesses are mentioned, circle them in the text.

IDENTIFY
Pause at line 41. Underline what the computer does within the CPU.

IDENTIFY

Re-read lines 47–54. What are two differences between *RAM* and *ROM*?

_____

_____

_____

_____

_____

_____

_____

IDENTIFY

What can a modem permit computers to do?

_____

_____

_____

_____

_____

_____

_____

_____

_____

_____

Memory   Information can be stored in the computer's memory until it is needed. Hard disks inside a computer and floppy disks or CD-ROMs inserted into a computer have memory to store information. Two other types of memory are *ROM* (read-only memory) and *RAM* (random-access memory).

ROM is permanent. It handles functions such as computer start-up, maintenance, and hardware management. ROM normally cannot be added to or changed, and it cannot be lost
50 when the computer is turned off. On the other hand, RAM is temporary. It stores information only while that information is being used. RAM is sometimes called working memory. Large amounts of RAM allow more information to be input, which makes for a more powerful computer.

Output Devices   Once a computer performs a task, it shows the results on an *output device.* Monitors, printers, and speaker systems are all examples of output devices.

Modems   One piece of computer hardware that serves as an input device as well as an output device is a *modem.* Modems
60 allow computers to communicate. One computer can input information into another computer over a telephone line, as long as each computer has its own modem. As a result, modems permit computers to "talk" with other computers.

Figure 2 Computer Hardware (*continued*)

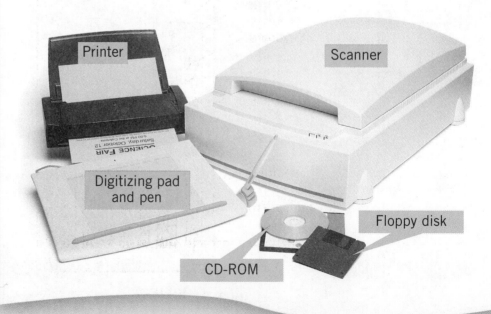

How to Set Up a Computer

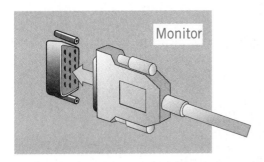

Step 1

Connect the monitor to the computer.

The monitor has two cords: One cord, the **monitor interface cable,** lets the computer communicate with the monitor. It connects to the video port (the port designated for monitors) at
70 the back of the computer. The connector on this cord is a plug with pins in it; the pins correspond to holes in the video port on the computer. This cable probably has screws to secure the connection. The other cord is the **monitor's power cord,** which plugs into the wall outlet or **surge protector,** a plug-in device that protects electronic equipment from high-voltage electrical surges (see Step 5).

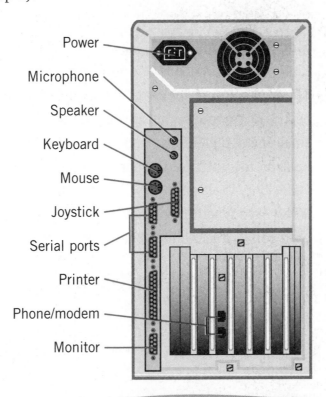

- Power
- Microphone
- Speaker
- Keyboard
- Mouse
- Joystick
- Serial ports
- Printer
- Phone/modem
- Monitor

IDENTIFY

Pause at line 76. Circle the name of each of the monitor's two cords. Then, underline each cord's function.

IDENTIFY

Look at the illustration of the back of the computer. Circle the outlets you are familiar with.

IDENTIFY

Pause at line 83. What tells you where to plug in the printer's cable on the back of a computer?

_____

_____

_____

_____

_____

_____

_____

_____

_____

INTERPRET

Pause at line 93. If you are having trouble connecting your mouse to its labeled port, what should you do?

_____

_____

_____

_____

_____

_____

_____

_____

_____

_____

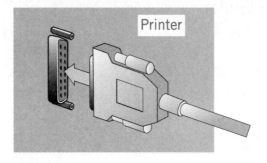
Printer

Step 2
Connect the printer to the computer.

The cable connectors that fit parallel ports, which your printer
80 uses, have pins like those on the monitor cable and are usually
secured with screws. Connect one end to the back of your
printer and then connect the other end to the back of your
computer where you see a **printer icon.**

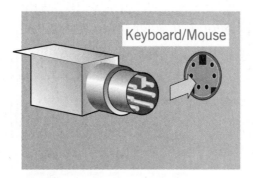
Keyboard/Mouse

Step 3
Connect the keyboard and mouse.

The connectors at the ends of the cords for the mouse and
keyboard are round, and if you look inside them, you'll see
small metal pins. These must be lined up correctly with the
holes in the ports for the parts to fit together. Do not force the
90 connectors together if they are not fitting properly; take another
look to see whether you have them lined up correctly. Plug
each connector into its labeled port on the back of your
computer.

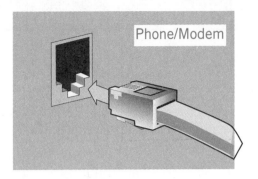

Phone/Modem

Step 4

Connect the phone line and phone to the modem.

Most computers come with **internal modems.** All you need to do is bring a line from the wall phone jack to the phone jack on the modem, which is visible on the back of your computer, and plug your telephone into the other jack on the modem.

Power cord

100 ## Step 5

Connect the power cords.

The **power cord** is a three-prong, grounded cord you attach to your computer. Attach the power cord to the computer first; then, plug it into a surge protector. Do the same with the monitor's power cord. The surge protector then plugs into a grounded wall outlet. Turn on the monitor first, then the computer, and you're ready to go!

INTERPRET

Re-read lines 100–107. You probably noticed that Step 5 is actually a series of smaller steps you must take before you can use your computer. Restate each step below.

1) _____

2) _____

3) _____

4) _____

5) _____

6) _____

7) Turn on your computer.

Directions Check

Any time you set up complex equipment, be sure to read the directions slowly and carefully. "Computers" contains a set of directions for setting up a computer. Re-read these directions to clarify any questions you may have. Also, take note of things you are told *not* to do.

Fill in the chart below to be sure you understand the procedure for computer setup.

1. What does the illustration next to Step 1 provide?

_____

_____

2. According to Step 1, which cord is to be plugged into the surge protector?

_____

_____

3. Step 3 contains a warning. What are you told *not* to do?

_____

_____

4. At what point do you connect the phone line and phone to the computer's modem?

_____

_____

5. In Step 5, you are given specific instructions on when to do certain things. Number the following steps in their correct order:

_____ Plug the power cord into a surge protector.

_____ Turn on the monitor.

_____ Plug the surge protector into the wall outlet.

_____ Turn on the computer.

_____ Attach the power cord to the computer.

Reading Check

1. According to the chart on page 296, what are the four functions of a computer?

_____

_____

2. What is computer hardware? _____

_____

Test Practice

1. What is the *best* answer to this question: Can computers operate by themselves?

   A No, because they need a command and instructions in order to operate.

   B Yes, because they can operate without a command.

   C No, because they can't get information stored in their memory.

   D Yes, because they can check spelling and count words.

2. Which of the following parts is *not* an example of an **output device**?

   F monitor

   G printer

   H speaker system

   J mouse

3. According to the illustration on page 297, which of the following is *not* housed with the central processing unit?

   A modem port

   B monitor

   C RAM

   D CD-ROM drive

4. What is the first thing you should do when you set up a computer?

   F connect the keyboard and mouse

   G connect the phone line to the modem

   H connect the monitor to the computer

   J connect the power cords

5. Why is it important to plug in the **surge protector**?

   A It connects the keyboard to the mouse.

   B It protects electronic equipment from high-voltage electrical surges.

   C It hooks up the phone line to the modem.

   D It turns the power off.

6. Which components of your computer do you *not* have to connect before you can use the Internet?

   F monitor to computer

   G printer to computer

   H keyboard and mouse

   J telephone line to modem

PART 3 STANDARDIZED TEST PRACTICE

Literature

Informational Materials

DIRECTIONS
Read the story. Then, read each question that follows on page 308 and circle the best response.

Those Three Wishes

Judith Gorog

No one ever said that Melinda Alice was nice. That wasn't the word used. No, she was clever, even witty. She was called— never to her face, however—Melinda Malice. Melinda Alice was clever and cruel. Her mother, when she thought about it at all, hoped Melinda would grow out of it. To her father, Melinda's very good grades mattered.

It was Melinda Alice, back in the eighth grade, who had labeled the shy, myopic[1] new girl "Contamination" and was the first to pretend that anything or anyone touched by the new girl had to be cleaned, inoculated,[2] or avoided. High school had merely given Melinda Alice greater scope for her talents.

The surprising thing about Melinda Alice was her power; no one trusted her, but no one avoided her either. She was always included, always in the middle. If you had seen her, pretty and witty, in the center of a group of students walking past your house, you'd have thought, "There goes a natural leader."

Melinda Alice had left for school early. She wanted to study alone in a quiet spot she had because there was going to be a big math test, and Melinda Alice was not prepared. That A mattered; so Melinda Alice walked to school alone, planning her studies. She didn't usually notice nature much, so she nearly stepped on a beautiful snail that was making its way across the sidewalk.

"Ugh. Yucky thing," thought Melinda Alice, then stopped. Not wanting to step on the snail accidentally was one thing, but now she lifted her shoe to crush it.

"Please don't," said the snail.

"Why not?" retorted Melinda Alice.

"I'll give you three wishes," replied the snail evenly.

"Agreed," said Melinda Alice. "My first wish is that my next," she paused a split second, "my next thousand wishes come true." She smiled triumphantly and opened her bag to take out a small notebook and pencil to keep track.

Melinda Alice was sure she heard the snail say, "What a clever girl," as it made

---

1. **myopic** (mī·äp′ik) *adj.:* nearsighted.
2. **inoculated** (i·näk′yə·lāt·id) *v.:* vaccinated.

it to the safety of an ivy bed beside the sidewalk.

During the rest of the walk to school, Melinda was occupied with wonderful ideas. She would have beautiful clothes. "Wish number two, that I will always be perfectly dressed," and she was just that. True, her new outfit was not a lot different from the one she had worn leaving the house, but that only meant that Melinda Alice liked her own taste.

After thinking awhile, she wrote, "Wish number three. I wish for pierced ears and small gold earrings." Her father had not allowed Melinda to have pierced ears, but now she had them anyway. She felt her new earrings and shook her beautiful hair in delight. "I can have anything: stereo, tapes, TV videodisc, moped, car, anything! All my life!" She hugged her books to herself in delight.

By the time she reached school, Melinda was almost an altruist;[3] she could wish for peace. Then she wondered, "Is the snail that powerful?" She felt her ears, looked at her perfect blouse, skirt, jacket, shoes. "I could make ugly people beautiful, cure cripples . . ." She stopped. The wave of altruism had washed past. "I could pay people back who deserve it!" Melinda Alice looked at the school, at all the kids. She had an enormous sense of power. "They all have to do what I want now." She walked down the crowded halls to her locker. Melinda Alice could be sweet; she could be witty. She could— The bell rang for homeroom. Melinda Alice stashed her books, slammed the locker shut, and just made it to her seat.

"Hey, Melinda Alice," whispered Fred. "You know that big math test next period?"

"Oh, no," grimaced Melinda Alice. Her thoughts raced; "That snail made me late, and I forgot to study."

"I'll blow it," she groaned aloud. "I wish I were dead."

---

3. **altruist** (al′troo·ist) *n*.: person who helps others without expecting anything in return.

1. The writer leaves no doubt about what Melinda Alice is like. Which word does *not* describe her?

   A   clever
   B   pretty
   C   nice
   D   cruel

2. Which word best describes what Melinda Alice *wants*?

   F   love
   G   friends
   H   knowledge
   J   power

3. Why is Melinda Alice walking alone to school?

   A   No one likes her.
   B   She prefers to be alone.
   C   She wants to study.
   D   She is enjoying nature.

4. Melinda Alice does *not* step on the snail because —

   F   it is so beautiful
   G   it is too yucky
   H   it offers her three wishes
   J   she wants to be kind

5. Melinda Alice's wishes form **parallel episodes** in this short story. How many wishes does she make?

   A   A thousand
   B   Three
   C   Four
   D   Ten

6. Melinda Alice uses her wishes —

   F   for herself
   G   to benefit humanity
   H   to get even with enemies
   J   all of the above

7. Melinda Alice wishes for all of the following *except* —

   A   a thousand wishes
   B   to be perfectly dressed
   C   pierced ears and earrings
   D   a stereo, tapes, and a TV

8. The **climax** of a story is its most exciting point, the moment when the outcome of the plot is decided. In "Those Three Wishes" the climax occurs when —

   F   the snail gives Melinda Alice three wishes
   G   Melinda Alice wishes for a thousand more wishes
   H   Melinda Alice wishes she were dead
   J   Fred reminds Melinda Alice of the math test

9. The **resolution** of the story —

   A   is described by the writer in great detail
   B   is left undecided
   C   happens after the story ends
   D   never happens

10. Which of the following *best* sums up the **message** of this story?

   F   Be careful what you wish for. You may get it.
   G   Goodness wins in the end.
   H   You always get what you want.
   J   Mean people always triumph.

DIRECTIONS

Read this excerpt from an autobiography. Then, read each question that follows on page 312 and circle the best response.

This excerpt from an autobiography takes place in Sweden soon after World War II. The narrator, a Polish Jewish girl, and her younger brother had been in Nazi concentration camps. There they both contracted tuberculosis, a lung disease. The children were rescued from the camps and taken to a sanitarium in the Swedish countryside. The narrator has now recovered from her illness and is on her way to a shelter for Polish children in Stockholm, the capital of Sweden.

from No Pretty Pictures: A Child of War

Anita Lobel

It had been explained to me that I had recovered from my illness. I couldn't stay at a house for sick people anymore. When Herr[1] Nillson came to gather me up at the sanitarium, I had to accept that I was going with him alone. My brother was still sick. Lucky, I thought, to be allowed to stay for a little while longer at the sanitarium.

Herr Nillson was taking me to a shelter for Polish refugee kids. "You will like being with people from your own country again," he said. He must have sensed instantly that he had not reassured me.

"It is a fine place," he said quietly. "You will see. And it is only temporary," he added. "Don't be frightened."

The trip to Stockholm had taken several hours. My recovery to good health was sending me into unwanted exile, but the journey did not feel like a deportation[2] or a flight. I loved sitting on a train with upholstered seats and watching the winter landscape rush by through the pristinely[3] polished window. In the January cold of Sweden there had been no possibility of sticking my head out an open window and letting the wind whip my face and hair. The hair that had grown to shoulder length and was at last braided into two thick, stubby braids. They were still too short. But there was no more concentration camp stubble to be ashamed of.

---

1. **Herr:** Swedish for "Mr."
2. **deportation** (dē′pôr·tā′shən) *n.:* forcible removal; banishment.
3. **pristinely** (pris′tēn′lē) *adv.:* here, to the point of perfect cleanliness.

We came to a quiet street away from the tramways and neon lights. After a ride to the third floor in a small cage elevator, we stood in front of a door with a brass plaque with "A. Nillson" engraved on it. Herr Nillson rang the bell. The door was opened by a gaunt lady, in a prim white apron over a brown dress. Except that her gray hair was tightly wound into a bun and her head was not covered in a wimple, she made me think of a Benedictine nun. She curtsied to Herr Nillson. I curtsied to her. She took my little suitcase and my coat and scarf.

"If Miss Stina would be so kind," Herr Nillson said, "our young traveler will have some tea and sandwiches."

I was twelve years old that late January afternoon when I was ushered into A. Nillson's elegant apartment in Stockholm, Sweden. For seven years, in or out of danger, I had lived and slept in hovels[4] or public rooms with many other people. The convent. The concentration camp barracks. The sanitarium. Institutions. Since we had fled with Niania[5] away from Kraków,[6] I had not been in a private place where people had properly arranged tables and chairs and rugs and lamps. And servants.

"You may sit down," Herr Nillson smiled. In the beautiful sitting room I eased myself cautiously onto the edge of a wooden chair that stood by the door. There were pots with plants by the windows. There were lace curtains. Several paintings on twisted silk cords hung from moldings. There was a rug on the floor that made me think of the old kilim in my parents' apartment in Kraków. One whole wall was covered with books. I heard the sounds of piano music from somewhere in the building.

"No, sit here," Herr Nillson said, pointing to an elegant chair covered in a silky blue striped fabric.

I wished I had been a doll or a puppet. I wished someone would come and bend my arms and legs into the right angles so that I knew how to fit myself properly into the seat of the beautiful chair I had been asked to occupy. I had seen a movie one afternoon in the big hall in the sanitarium. It took place in France. The people moved and posed gracefully in splendid rooms. Ladies in gowns of silk sat on silk sofas and took little sips of tea out of pretty porcelain cups and delicate bites of little cakes. Gentlemen bowed and kissed the hands of the ladies.

---

4. **hovels** (huv′əlz) *n.*: small, miserable dwellings; huts.
5. **Niania:** the writer's nanny (a person who cares for young children).
6. **Kraków** (kra′kou′): city in Poland.

I knew my body was clean. There were no lice in my newly grown hair. Or in the seams of the skirt and blouse and sweater that had come out of a freshly donated bundle. When I carefully eased myself down onto the seat, I could feel my wool stockings pull around my thighs as the home-sewn garters with the buttons dug into my buttocks. I sat on Herr Nillson's silk chair, still fearing that shameful dirt would seep through. In my head there were echoes of the Nazis' shouts.

Herr Nillson sank easily into a large upholstered chair with curved arms.

Stina brought buttered bread and ham and tea on a tray. And cups and linen napkins. I took little bites of my sandwich and held my teacup as delicately as I could. I wanted to stay there with Herr Nillson forever.

Behind him I saw a half-opened door to a small room with a bed. Herr Nillson followed my gaze. "For tonight that is your room," he said. "Early tomorrow we will continue our journey." We both sipped from our teacups.

Herr Nillson told me about the work he did with refugees who had come to Sweden after the war. And about the interesting times I could expect at the Polish shelter and beyond. When it was time to go to bed, Herr Nillson took down a book from his crowded bookshelf. "This is for you," he said. "You may keep this."

Safely tucked in my suitcase were some catechism magazines that had been given out during Sunday school lessons at the sanitarium. And my miniature copy of the New Testament with pages thin and delicate and filled with beautiful pictures of the Holy Family, the gift from Sister Svea. Now I would add another book to my belongings. I thanked Herr Nillson for the volume of Selma Lagerlöf stories. I thanked the stern-looking Stina for the food. Everyone said, *God natt.*

I went into my private room and closed the door. Tomorrow I was going to a place that would have no barbed wire around it. There would be no Nazis with guns. There would be no shooting. But again I would be living in an institution. Under the large soft bolster with my head on a pillow edged with lace, I fell asleep reading a tale by Selma Lagerlöf.

1. In this selection from an **autobiography,** the narrator visits —

   A a shelter for Polish refugees
   B Herr Nillson's apartment
   C a Nazi concentration camp
   D a tuberculosis sanitarium

2. The narrator of this story is grateful for the special attention she receives. A character from another autobiography in this book is also appreciative of special attention. That **character** is —

   F Harriet Tubman
   G Barbara Frietchie
   H Mrs. Flowers
   J Marguerite

3. The narrator of this story fled with her brother and nanny to escape from the Nazis. Another character in this book also ran away from tyranny. That **character** is —

   A Harriet Tubman
   B Barbara Frietchie
   C Mrs. Flowers
   D Marguerite

4. The narrator of this story and Marguerite in "Mrs. Flowers" have similar reactions when they receive a book as a gift. Both girls —

   F are pleased with the gift
   G wish they were able to read
   H refuse to accept the book
   J spill their drinks on the book

5. Although they lived in different times, the narrator of this story and Barbara Frietchie have an experience in common. Both —

   A told off a general
   B protected their flag
   C lived through a war
   D recovered from tuberculosis

6. The writer doesn't tell you what a *sanitarium* is. The word is mentioned twice in the first paragraph. Re-read the surrounding sentences, and use **context clues** to determine which of the following definitions means *sanitarium.*

   F Shelter for Polish children
   G Place for sick people
   H Train
   J Concentration camp

7. Which of the following sentences *best* expresses the **main idea** of this extract from an autobiography?

   A An act of kindness helps a child in many ways.
   B The Swedes are very kind people.
   C Children cannot accept change easily.
   D Children need their parents.

8. Both "Mrs. Flowers" and this extract from a book called *No Pretty Pictures* feature all of the following characters *except* a —

   F kind adult who helps a child
   G child who cannot talk
   H child who has suffered from violence
   J child who loves books

DIRECTIONS

Read the passage. Then, read each question that follows on page 315 and circle the best response.

In the novel The Cay, *Phillip, an eleven-year-old boy who is blind, is shipwrecked on a very small island, or cay, with a West Indian seaman named Timothy and a cat. Timothy dies while protecting Phillip during a hurricane. In this part of the story, Phillip is trying to make it on his own.*

from The Cay
Theodore Taylor

The sun came out strong in the morning. I could feel it on my face. It began to dry the island, and toward noon, I heard the first cry of a bird. They were returning.

By now, I had taught myself to tell time, very roughly, simply by turning my head toward the direct warmth of the sun. If the angle was almost overhead, I knew it was around noon. If it was low, then of course, it was early morning or late evening.

There was so much to do that I hardly knew where to start. Get a campfire going, pile new wood for a signal fire, make another rain catchment for the water keg, weave a mat of palm fibers to sleep on. Then make a shelter of some kind, fish the hole on the reef, inspect the palm trees to see if any coconuts were left—I didn't think any could be up there—and search the whole island to discover what the storm had deposited. It was enough work for weeks, and I said to Stew Cat, "I don't know how we'll get it all done." But something told me I must stay very busy and not think about myself.

I accomplished a lot in three days, even putting a new edge on Timothy's knife by honing it on coral. I jabbed it into the palm nearest my new shelter, so that I would always know where it was if I needed it. Without Timothy's eyes, I was finding that in my world, everything had to be very precise; an exact place for everything.

On the fifth day after the storm, I began to scour the island to find out what had been cast up. It was exciting, and I knew it would take days or weeks to accomplish. I had made another cane and beginning with east beach, I felt my way back and forth, reaching down to touch everything that my cane struck; sometimes having to spend a long time trying to decide what it was that I held in my hands.

I found several large cans and used one of them to start the "time" can again, dropping five pebbles into it so that the reckoning would begin again from the night of the storm. I discovered an old broom, and a small wooden crate that would make a nice stool. I found a piece of canvas, and tried to think of ways to make pants from it, but I had no needle or thread.

Other than that, I found many shells, some bodies of dead birds, pieces of cork, and chunks of sponge, but nothing I could really put to good use.

It was on the sixth day after the storm, when I was exploring on south beach, that I heard the birds. Stew Cat was with me, as usual, and he growled when they first screeched. Their cries were angry, and I guessed that seven or eight might be in the air.

I stood listening to them; wondering what they were. Then I felt a beat of wing past my face, and an angry cry as the bird dived at me. I lashed out at it with my cane, wondering why they were attacking me.

Another dived down, screaming at me, and his bill nipped the side of my head. For a moment, I was confused, not knowing whether to run for cover under sea grape, or what was left of it, or try to fight them off with my cane. There seemed to be a lot of birds.

Then one pecked my forehead sharply, near my eyes, and I felt blood run down my face. I started to walk back toward camp, but had taken no more than three or four steps when I tripped over a log. I fell into the sand, and at the same time, felt a sharp pain in the back of my head. I heard a raging screech as the bird soared up again. Then another bird dived at me.

I heard Stew Cat snarling and felt him leap up on my back, his claws digging into my flesh. There was another wild screech, and Stew Cat left my back, leaping into the air.

His snarls and the wounded screams of the bird filled the stillness over the cay. I could hear them battling in the sand. Then I heard the death caw of the bird.

I lay still a moment. Finally, I crawled to where Stew Cat had his victim. I touched him; his body was rigid and his hair was still on edge. He was growling, low and muted.

Then I touched the bird. It had sounded large, but it was actually rather small. I felt the beak; it was very sharp.

Slowly, Stew Cat began to relax.

Wondering what had caused the birds to attack me, I felt around in the sand. Soon, my hand touched a warm shell. I couldn't blame the birds very much. I'd accidentally walked into their new nesting ground.

They were fighting for survival, after the storm, just as I was. I left Stew Cat to his unexpected meal and made my way slowly back to camp.

1. What details tell you that the **setting** of this story is a tropical island?

   A Palm trees and coconuts

   B Warm sun

   C A wooden crate

   D Returning birds

2. Being blind and alone on a small island is scary enough for Phillip, but what detail of the setting adds horror to the **mood**?

   F Timothy's knife

   G Stew Cat

   H A signal fire

   J Attacking birds

3. Which sentence shows that Phillip is optimistic in spite of his troubles?

   A "There was so much to do that I hardly knew where to start."

   B "It was enough work for weeks, and I said to Stew Cat, 'I don't know how we'll get it all done.'"

   C "I accomplished a lot in three days, even putting a new edge on Timothy's knife. . . ."

   D "I found a piece of canvas, and tried to think of ways to make pants from it, but I had no needle or thread."

4. Which of the following **conclusions** can you reasonably make about Phillip's character?

   F Phillip is self-pitying.

   G Phillip is brave and intelligent.

   H Phillip is fun-loving and lazy.

   J Phillip lacks self-esteem.

5.

Phillip hears birds screeching.		Stew Cat kills a bird.

   If you were arranging the events of this passage in **chronological order,** which of the following events would you place in the empty box?

   A Birds attack Phillip.

   B Birds lay eggs in the sand.

   C Stew Cat eats the bird.

   D Phillip returns to camp.

6. Phillip says he accomplished a lot, "even putting a new edge on Timothy's knife by honing it on coral." *Honing* probably means —

   F breaking

   G sharpening

   H coloring

   J ruining

7. What does Phillip discover was the **cause** of the bird attack?

   A The birds hate humans.

   B The birds were hungry.

   C The birds were protecting their eggs.

   D The birds wanted to eat the cat.

8. What **inference** can you make at the end of the story?

   F Stew Cat eats the eggs.

   G The birds take the eggs to a safer place.

   H Phillip packs the eggs in his sack.

   J Stew Cat eats the bird.

DIRECTIONS

Read the story. Then, read each question that follows on page 317 and circle the best response.

Gil's Furniture Bought & Sold

Sandra Cisneros

There is a junk store. An old man owns it. We bought a used refrigerator from him once, and Carlos sold a box of magazines for a dollar. The store is small with just a dirty window for light. He doesn't turn the lights on unless you got money to buy things with, so in the dark we look and see all kinds of things, me and Nenny. Tables with their feet upside-down and rows and rows of refrigerators with round corners and couches that spin dust in the air when you punch them and a hundred T.V.'s that don't work probably. Everything is on top of everything so the whole store has skinny aisles to walk through. You can get lost easy.

The owner, he is a black man who doesn't talk much and sometimes if you didn't know better you could be in there a long time before your eyes notice a pair of gold glasses floating in the dark. Nenny who thinks she is smart and talks to any old man, asks lots of questions. Me, I never said nothing to him except once when I bought the Statue of Liberty for a dime.

But Nenny, I hear her asking one time how's this here and the man says, This, this is a music box, and I turn around quick thinking he means a *pretty* box with flowers painted on it, with a ballerina inside. Only there's nothing like that where this old man is pointing, just a wood box that's old and got a big brass record in it with holes. Then he starts it up and all sorts of things start happening. It's like all of a sudden he let go a million moths all over the dusty furniture and swan-neck shadows and in our bones. It's like drops of water. Or like marimbas only with a funny little plucked sound to it like if you were running your fingers across the teeth of a metal comb.

And then I don't know why, but I have to turn around and pretend I don't care about the box so Nenny won't see how stupid I am. But Nenny, who is stupider, already is asking how much and I can see her fingers going for the quarters in her pants pocket.

This, the old man says shutting the lid, this ain't for sale.

1. Cisneros writes: "Me, I never said nothing to him" and "I hear her asking one time how's this here." She uses **dialect** to do all of the following *except* —

   A give her characters a voice
   B make her characters come alive
   C make fun of her characters
   D show how her characters really speak

2. The narrator of this story says, "It's like all of a sudden he let go a million moths all over the dusty furniture and swan-neck shadows and in our bones." She uses these **figures of speech** to describe —

   F the magical power of music
   G how dirty the owner keeps his store
   H how creepy she thinks insects are
   J the animal shadows on the walls of the store

3. When the narrator says that the music is "like drops of water," she is using —

   A a simile
   B a metaphor
   C personification
   D irony

4. This little story is told by —

   F Nenny
   G Gil, the store owner
   H a young narrator who speaks as "I"
   J Carlos

5. The narrator turns around "so Nenny won't see how stupid I am." She is embarrassed —

   A because she has no money for the music box
   B by how much she likes the music
   C to be in such a dusty junk shop
   D to be seen with Nenny

6. When the narrator says that Nenny is "stupider" than she is, she is using **verbal irony.** What she really means is that —

   F Nenny is as moved by the music as she is
   G she's mad because Nenny has enough money to buy the box
   H she doesn't think Nenny is smart
   J she is embarrassed to be seen with Nenny

7. The **situational irony** in this story involves the fact that —

   A the girls are in an uncomfortable situation
   B the girls find beauty in a dirty, messy junk store
   C the junk store is dirty and crowded
   D the junk store is full of moths

8. For the narrator, the store owner, and Nenny, the music box is a **symbol** of —

   F joy that can come from surprising places
   G the store owner's inability to sell anything
   H how old things are just junk
   J the girls' love of shopping

DIRECTIONS

Read the story. Then, read each question that follows on page 319 and circle the best response.

This excerpt is from a story that takes place during Hanukkah, the Jewish Festival of Lights, which usually begins in December. Hanukkah celebrates the rededication of the Temple in Jerusalem in 165 B.C. Another Jewish holiday, Purim, mentioned in the first paragraph, is a spring festival that honors Queen Esther.

from Just Enough Is Plenty: A Hanukkah Tale

Barbara Diamond Goldin

Malka's family lived in a village in Poland. They were poor, but not so poor. They had candles for the Sabbath, noisemakers for Purim, and spinning tops for Hanukkah.

Mama was busy preparing for tonight, the first of the eight nights of Hanukkah. She peeled onions and grated potatoes for the latkes, the potato pancakes.

Malka's younger brother Zalman carved a dreidel, a spinning top.

"This dreidel will spin the fastest of all," he boasted.

Papa was working long hours in his tailor shop so they could buy more food for the holiday. More potatoes, more onions, more flour, more oil.

For on the first night of Hanukkah, Malka's family always invited many guests. But this year only Aunt Hindy and Uncle Shmuel were coming to visit.

"Only two guests?" Malka asked. "Last year, we had so many guests that Papa had to put boards over the pickle barrels to make the table big enough."

"That was last year," Mama said gently. "This year has not been a good one for Papa in the shop. People bring him just a little mending here, a little mending there. He cannot afford to buy new material to sew fancy holiday dresses and fine suits."

"But it's Hanukkah," Malka reminded Mama.

Mama patted Malka's shoulder. "Don't worry, Malkaleh. We know how to stretch. We're poor, but not so poor. Now go. Ask Papa if he has a few more coins. I need more eggs for the latkes."

Meet the Writer

When she wrote this story, **Barbara Diamond Goldin** was a preschool teacher and storyteller who lived with her husband and two children in Northampton, Massachusetts.

Three of her grandparents came from Poland. It was only in doing research for this book that she learned how they probably lived before coming to America. Perhaps this fictional story could be *their* true story!

---

1. The setting, a village in Poland, reflects the writer's **heritage** because —
   - A Poland is where she was born
   - B some of her grandparents came from Poland
   - C many Americans came from Poland
   - D Poland is a good place for a story

2. "She peeled onions and grated potatoes for the latkes, the potato pancakes." **Context clues** in this sentence tell you that *latkes* are —
   - F peeled onions
   - G grated potatoes
   - H potato pancakes
   - J Polish lakes

3. Hanukkah **traditions** mentioned in this excerpt include —
   - A eating potato pancakes
   - B working long hours
   - C blowing loud noisemakers
   - D living in Poland

4. This story excerpt mentions all of the following Hanukkah **traditions** *except* —
   - F latkes
   - G dreidels
   - H eight nights
   - J menorahs

5. When Mama says, "We're poor, but not so poor," she is expressing the **belief** that —
   - A they have enough
   - B they are really rich
   - C poverty doesn't matter
   - D it's better to be poor

6. In doing research for this book, the writer learned more about —
   - F teaching preschool
   - G life in Massachusetts
   - H Polish immigration
   - J her Polish heritage

DIRECTIONS

Read the two stories. Then, read each question that follows on page 321 and circle the best response.

The Dog and the Wolf

Aesop (sixth century B.C.)

One cold and snowy winter the Wolf couldn't find enough to eat. She was almost dead with hunger when a House Dog happened by.

"Ah, Cousin," said the Dog, "you are skin and bones. Come, leave your life of roaming and starving in the forest. Come with me to my master and you'll never go hungry again."

"What will I have to do for my food?" said the Wolf.

"Not much," said the House Dog. "Guard the property, keep the Fox from the henhouse, protect the children. It's an easy life."

That sounded good to the Wolf, so the Dog and the Wolf headed to the village. On the way the Wolf noticed a ring around the Dog's neck where the hair had been rubbed off.

"What's that?" she asked.

"Oh, it's nothing," said the Dog. "It's just where the collar is put on at night to keep me chained up. I'm used to it."

"Chained up!" exclaimed the Wolf, as she ran quickly back to the forest.

Better to starve free than to be a well-fed slave.

The Puppy

Aleksandr Solzhenitsyn (twentieth century)

In our backyard a boy keeps his little dog Sharik chained up, a ball of fluff shackled since he was a puppy.

One day I took him some chicken bones that were still warm and smelled delicious. The boy had just let the poor dog off his lead to have a run round the yard. The snow there was deep and feathery; Sharik was bounding about like a hare, first on his hind legs, then on his front ones, from one corner of the yard to the other, back and forth, burying his muzzle in the snow.

He ran toward me, his coat all shaggy, jumped up at me, sniffed the bones—then off he went again, belly-deep in the snow.

I don't need your bones, he said. Just give me my freedom. . . .

—*translated by* Michael Glenny

1. In the fable "The Dog and the Wolf," the Wolf decides to go to the village with the House Dog because she —

   A is hungry
   B wants an easier life
   C wants to be chained up
   D likes children

2. What does the Wolf notice on the way to the village?

   F Children playing happily
   G Well-fed people
   H A ring on the Dog's neck
   J The Dog limping

3. In "The Puppy," where is the little dog, Sharik, usually kept?

   A Chained in the yard
   B In a doghouse
   C In the living room
   D In the boy's bedroom

4. What do the House Dog and Sharik have in common?

   F They both are chained at times.
   G They both run away from home.
   H They both are starving.
   J They both hate their masters.

5. What do both the Wolf and Sharik want more than food?

   A Love
   B Freedom
   C Security
   D Fame

6. Which of the following sentences *best* expresses the **theme** that both the fable from ancient Greece and the story from modern-day Russia have in common?

   F Nothing is worth more than freedom.
   G Playing is more fun than eating.
   H It is worth being chained up in order to be fed.
   J One can never have both food and freedom.

7. In the first paragraph of "The Puppy," the writer uses the word shackled. Using context clues, you can guess that *shackled* means —

   A punished
   B chained up
   C fed
   D fenced in

DIRECTIONS

Read the poem and the summary. Then, read each question that follows and circle the best response.

Oranges
Gary Soto

The first time I walked
With a girl, I was twelve,
Cold, and weighted down
With two oranges in my jacket.
5 December. Frost cracking
Beneath my steps, my breath
Before me, then gone,
As I walked toward
Her house, the one whose
10 Porch light burned yellow
Night and day, in any weather.
A dog barked at me, until
She came out pulling
At her gloves, face bright
15 With rouge. I smiled,
Touched her shoulder, and led
Her down the street, across
A used car lot and a line
Of newly planted trees,
20 Until we were breathing
Before a drugstore. We
Entered, the tiny bell
Bringing a saleslady
Down a narrow aisle of goods.
25 I turned to the candies
Tiered like bleachers,
And asked what she wanted—

Light in her eyes, a smile
Starting at the corners
30 Of her mouth. I fingered
A nickel in my pocket,
And when she lifted a chocolate
That cost a dime,
I didn't say anything.
35 I took the nickel from
My pocket, then an orange,
And set them quietly on
The counter. When I looked up,
The lady's eyes met mine,
40 And held them, knowing
Very well what it was all
About.

     Outside,
A few cars hissing past,
Fog hanging like old
45 Coats between the trees.
I took my girl's hand
In mine for two blocks,
Then released it to let
Her unwrap the chocolate.
50 I peeled my orange
That was so bright against
The gray of December
That, from some distance,
Someone might have thought
55 I was making a fire in my hands.

"Oranges": A Summary

The poem "Oranges" by Gary Soto is about the bittersweet experience of a first date. As the boy walks to the girl's house, with a nickel and two oranges in his pocket, his breath is visible in the December chill. A dog barks at him till the girl appears; then all is well. They walk together to the drugstore. Offered her choice, the girl picks a chocolate that costs a dime. The boy pays for the candy with his nickel, which is all the money he has, and offers an orange as well. The saleslady understands, her eyes holding his for a moment. Back on the street again, the boy takes his girl's hand for two blocks and then releases it so she can unwrap her chocolate. He peels his orange, which is so bright in the darkness he says someone might have thought I was making a fire in my hands. The brightness of that moment will live in his memory like a flame.

---

1. Which phrase from the summary contains a **critical detail?**

   A "As the boy walks"

   B "with a nickel and two oranges in his pocket"

   C "his breath is visible"

   D "Back on the street again"

2. Which item below contains a less important detail, one that could have been omitted from the summary?

   F "A dog barks at him. . . ."

   G "They walk together to the drugstore."

   H "The saleslady understands. . . ."

   J "The boy takes his girl's hand. . . ."

3. Which of the following passages from the summary suggests the poem's **underlying meaning,** or **main idea**?

   A "The poem . . . is about the bittersweet experience of a first date."

   B "The saleslady understands, her eyes holding his for a moment."

   C "As the boy walks to the girl's house, with a nickel and two oranges . . ."

   D "The brightness of that moment will live in his memory like a flame."

4. Which passage from the summary is a **direct quote** and should be in quotation marks?

   F the bittersweet experience of a first date

   G all is well

   H The saleslady understands

   J someone might have thought I was making a fire in my hands

DIRECTIONS

Read the following two passages. Then, read each question that follows on page 325 and circle the best response.

Fragment on Slavery, 1854

Abraham Lincoln

If A can prove, however conclusively, that he may of right enslave B—why may not B snatch the same argument, and prove equally that he may enslave A?

You say A is white, and B is black. It is color, then, the lighter having the right to enslave the darker? Take care. By this rule you are to be slave to the first man you meet with a fairer skin than your own.

You do not mean color exactly? You mean the whites are intellectually the superior of the blacks and, therefore, have the right to enslave them? Take care again. By this rule, you are to be slave to the first man you meet with an intellect superior to your own.

But, say you, it is a question of interest; and, if you can make it your interest, you have the right to enslave another. Very well. And if he can make it his interest, he has the right to enslave you.

from What to the Slave Is the Fourth of July?

From an oration at Rochester,
July 5, 1852
Frederick Douglass

Would you have me argue that man is entitled to liberty? that he is the rightful owner of his own body? . . . To do so, would be to make myself ridiculous, and to offer an insult to your understanding. There is not a man beneath the canopy of heaven that does not know that slavery is wrong for him.

What! am I to argue that it is wrong to make men brutes, to rob them of their liberty, to work them without wages, to keep them ignorant of their relations to their fellowmen, to beat them with sticks, to flay[1] their flesh with the lash, to load their limbs with irons, to hunt them with dogs, to sell them at auction, to sunder[2] their families,

---

1. flay *v.*: strip the skin off, as by whipping.
2. sunder *v.*: drive apart; separate.

to knock out their teeth, to burn their flesh, to starve them into obedience and submission to their masters? Must I argue that a system, thus marked with blood and stained with pollution, is wrong? No; I will not. . . .

At a time like this, scorching irony, not convincing argument, is needed. . . . We need the storm, the whirlwind, and the earthquake. The feeling of the nation must be quickened; the conscience of the nation must be roused; the propriety[3] of the nation must be startled; the hypocrisy[4] of the nation must be exposed; and its crimes against God and man must be proclaimed and denounced.

---

3. **propriety** (prə·prī′ə·tē) *n.:* sense of correct behavior.
4. **hypocrisy** (hi·päk′rə·sē) *n.:* pretense of virtue or goodness.

---

1. The passage by Abraham Lincoln presents an argument —
   A for light skin
   B against personal interest
   C for slavery
   D against slavery

2. Which of the following statements *best* expresses what Frederick Douglass is saying?
   F Arguments won't work against slavery; passions must be aroused.
   G We should sit down and talk calmly about the evils of slavery.
   H We don't need to do anything; everyone knows slavery is wrong.
   J The world needs more stormy weather and earthquakes.

3. The passage by Abraham Lincoln was intended as a —
   A personal narrative
   B persuasive argument
   C newspaper advertisement
   D poetic description

4. Douglass's passage was intended to do all of the following *except* to —
   F convince
   G rouse to action
   H work on listeners' feelings
   J amuse

5. The **treatment** of ideas in the passage by Douglass is —
   A detached
   B emotional
   C unfeeling
   D silly

6. The **treatment** of ideas in the passage by Abraham Lincoln is —
   F humorous
   G emotional
   H unfeeling
   J logical

7. The **subject** of both texts is —
   A the Union
   B the Civil War
   C slavery
   D the Fourth of July

DIRECTIONS

Read the article. Then, read each question that follows on page 327 and circle the best response.

Blasting Through Bedrock: The Central Pacific Railroad Workers

Flo Ota De Lange

① In the winter of 1866–1867, blizzards gripped the Sierra Nevada. Dwellings were buried in blowing, shifting, drifting, driving snow. Men who were building the western portion of the country's first transcontinental railroad had to tunnel from their camp to the mountainside, where they spent long, cold days digging out rock so tracks could be laid. The Central Pacific Railroad was building east from California to meet the Union Pacific Railroad, which was working west from Omaha, Nebraska.

② Who were these hardy workers who survived the blizzards and helped build the nation's first transcontinental railroad? Most of them were immigrants from China. When other railroad hands saw the newly hired Chinese workers, they were scornful. How could these young men, averaging about four feet ten inches in height, heave a large shovelful of rock?

The other workers either didn't know or had forgotten that the ancestors of these men had built one of the Seven Wonders of the World—the Great Wall of China—which was begun in 221 B.C. The wall extends more than four thousand miles and averages about twenty-six feet high and twenty feet wide!

③ At the start the Central Pacific Railroad hired fifty Chinese laborers. These men knew little about railroad grading, but they learned quickly. Eventually the Chinese labor force grew to between ten thousand and twelve thousand workers. These men dug, blasted tunnels, and laid track up the Sierra Nevada, over the Donner Pass, and down through the deserts of Nevada.

④ People often credit the transcontinental railroad to men of vision—engineers, financiers, and politicians—without acknowledging the way their vision became a reality. As the president of the Central Pacific Railroad and former governor of California, Leland Stanford, wrote to President Andrew Johnson on October 19, 1865, "The greater portion of the laborers employed by us are Chinese. . . . Without them it would be impossible to complete the western portion of this great national enterprise within the time required by the Acts of Congress."

5 Complete it these workers did! Cannons roared in New York City and San Francisco when the telegraph lines carried the news: The Union Pacific and the Central Pacific Railroad lines had met at Promontory, Utah, on May 10, 1869.

---

1. Which statement *best* expresses the **main idea** of this article?

   A The winter of 1866 is famous for its terrible snowstorms and blizzards.

   B Chinese workers were important in building the transcontinental railroad.

   C The Great Wall of China is one of the Seven Wonders of the World.

   D Cannons were set off to celebrate the completion of the transcontinental railroad.

2. Which of the following details would be consistent with the **unity** of paragraph 1?

   F The Great Pyramids are also among the Seven Wonders of the World.

   G The Great Wall of China ascends steep ridges angled at seventy degrees.

   H Many people died from cave-ins and avalanches during the blizzards.

   J Building model trains is a rewarding and enjoyable hobby.

3. Read these sentences from paragraph 1. Which of the transition words that follow could be used to connect the two sentences **coherently**?

   "Dwellings were buried in blowing, shifting, drifting, driving snow. Men . . . had to tunnel from their camp to the mountainside. . . ."

   A before

   B however

   C although

   D therefore

4. Which of the following sentences could be added to this article without destroying its **internal consistency**?

   F During blizzards, people cannot see in front of them, and so they bump into things.

   G Chinese workers did backbreaking work from sunup to sundown six days a week.

   H Asa Whitney was the first to see the importance of a transcontinental railroad.

   J It took fourteen train lines to get Lincoln's body from Washington, D.C., to Illinois.

DIRECTIONS

Read the article. Then, read each question that follows on pages 329–330 and circle the best response.

The Smelly Skunks

"How do you keep a skunk from smelling?"—the old joke goes—"Put a clothespin on its nose." No bigger than a housecat, the skunk is avoided by much larger animals such as bears, wolves, and mountain lions, as well as by humans. That's because skunks have the ability to produce and spray a foul-smelling liquid— the worst-smelling liquid produced by any animal. No wonder the skunk has few natural enemies—except for the occasional bobcat and great horned owl, which seem to be *immune* to the skunk's odor.

Skunks belong to the family of mammals known as mustelids, which includes weasels, ferrets, minks, wolverines, badgers, and otters. Skunks are small, furry animals that have distinctive black-and-white markings. A fully grown skunk weighs about eight pounds. It has short legs and a long, flexible backbone. Skunks move with a characteristic waddle.

Skunks are peaceful creatures who use their foul-smelling spray only when threatened. Before a skunk releases the yellowish, oily liquid, it will issue a series of warnings. First, it will stamp with its front feet; next, it will rake the ground with its claws. If these early-warning signals don't work, the skunk will arch its back, hiss, and raise its tail.

A skunk's defensive spray is stored in two glandular pouches beneath its tail. When it sprays, the skunk tightens the muscles around each pouch to force the liquid through the openings, which resemble the nozzles of small water hoses. Skunks can spray accurately as far as fifteen feet, and, if necessary, they can spray several times in a row.

An animal or human who has been unlucky enough to come within spraying range of a skunk that considers itself in jeopardy may wear a distinctive odor for days or even weeks. Household bleach can be effective in removing the musky odor from clothes. Vinegar or tomato juice helps remove the odor from hair or skin.

There are three main types of skunks: striped, hog-nosed, and spotted. The striped skunk, whose scientific name is *Mephitis mephitis,* is the most common species in the United States. *Mephitis* means "evil smelling," and *Mephitis mephitis* means "double the stink."

Skunks tend to live underground in dens lined with dry leaves. They are *nocturnal* animals, preferring to sleep during the day. Female skunks usually give birth to four or five young in a litter. Skunks are solitary, self-sufficient, and independent.

Skunks eat caterpillars, insects such as beetles and crickets, and small rodents. They will also eat snakes. Frequently, skunks will prowl highways, feeding on insects, snakes, turtles, and other creatures killed by passing cars. Thus, the automobile is one of the skunk's deadliest enemies.

1. What causes large animals to avoid skunks?

   A Skunks are fierce fighters.
   B Skunks produce a foul-smelling spray.
   C Skunks put on a frightening display.
   D Skunks produce a powerful poison.

2. In the seventh paragraph, which of these is a clue to the meaning of the word *nocturnal*?

   F Give birth to four or five young
   G Live underground
   H Solitary, self-sufficient, and independent
   J Preferring to sleep during the day

3. In this article, *immune* means —

   A lacking the ability to smell
   B having the ability to resist
   C having the power to attract
   D having the power to defeat

4. If you wanted to learn more about skunks, you should —

   F read a book about mustelids
   G visit a botanical garden
   H read a book about badgers
   J look in an encyclopedia under "Insects"

5. Which sentence supports the author's statement that skunks are peaceful creatures who spray only when threatened?

   A "No bigger than a housecat, the skunk is avoided by much larger animals. . . ."
   B "Before a skunk releases the yellowish, oily liquid, it will issue a series of warnings."
   C "Skunks can spray accurately as far as fifteen feet. . . ."
   D "They are nocturnal animals, preferring to sleep during the day."

6. Which *opinion* is expressed in this article?

    F Skunks have few natural enemies.

    G Skunks spray only when threatened.

    H Skunks have the worst smell of any animal.

    J Skunks are solitary animals.

7. This article is *mainly* about —

    A why skunks smell

    B skunks and their relatives

    C the striped skunk

    D facts about skunks

8. The chart below shows some important ideas from the article.

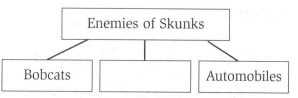

Based on the article, which of these belongs in the empty box?

    F Mountain Lions

    G Great Horned Owls

    H Bears

    J Wolves

DIRECTIONS

Read the article. Then, read each question that follows on page 333 and circle the best response.

Enter the Paper-Sculpture Contest

The Old-Town Sculpture Society is seeking entries for the Biannual Paper-Sculpture Contest. The group hopes to promote interest in and appreciation for sculpture. You might recall that last year the Society raised funds for a sculpture wing at the art museum. That project was a huge success. All museum visitors now enjoy the beautiful artwork in the new wing. Perhaps the winner of the Paper-Sculpture contest will find her or his work displayed there.

Sculptures are three-dimensional works of art. Unlike paintings, which present only one side to the viewer, sculptures can be viewed from all sides. They can be made from many different materials. Perhaps the finest sculptures are carved from marble. Others are made of plaster. Some sculptors even use objects other people have thrown away to make their art.

For the purposes of this contest, all sculptures will be made from a material that is easy to find and work with—paper.

By using the process described below, you can create your own sculpture.

The first thing you will need is an idea. What do you want to show? It can be something you have seen in nature, like an animal. It might be something you have designed, such as an original assortment of shapes. The possibilities are endless.

Once you have an idea, you can begin assembling materials. You will need a supply of newspaper and a bowl of thin paste made by mixing white glue and water. You will also need to make an *armature,* or frame. This will be the skeleton for your sculpture. It can be made of wire, craft sticks, or other such materials.

To begin making your sculpture, tear the newspaper into thin strips. One by one, dip the strips into the glue mixture. Then, drape each wet strip over the armature. Press the strips firmly into place. Continue in this manner until you have completely covered the frame. At this point, you should stop and allow the sculpture to dry overnight. Then you can add more strips to make the form appear as you had planned.

Now it is time to finish your artwork. Once the sculpture is completely dry, you can paint it with tempera paint. You may use realistic colors, or you might choose colors that are wild and imaginative. Add details by gluing objects such as buttons, sequins, or fabric scraps into place. For example, you might glue button eyes and felt ears onto an animal sculpture. When the paint and glue have dried, it is time for the final step: carefully sign your name on the base of the sculpture. Now you can fill out your entry form. A copy of the form is included below.

Paper-Sculpture Contest Entry Form

Please fill in all the spaces. Print neatly and use a ballpoint pen.

Name: _____

Address: _____

Phone number: _____ Age: _____

School: _____

Teacher: _____

Name of sculpture: _____

Description of sculpture: _____

_____

Bring this form with your sculpture to Oak Street Library by February 18. The library will display all sculptures for two weeks. Judging will take place on March 4.

1. This selection would *most* likely be found in —

   A   an encyclopedia
   B   a science magazine
   C   a local newspaper
   D   an art textbook

2. The author organized this selection by —

   F   presenting causes and effects
   G   comparing and contrasting
   H   describing events in the order they happen
   J   describing steps in a process

3. The second paragraph is *mostly* about —

   A   defining what sculpture is
   B   describing different types of art
   C   listing some famous sculptures
   D   discussing the importance of recycling

4. After you have completely covered the frame, you should —

   F   add more strips
   G   paint it with tempura paint
   H   assemble your material
   J   stop and allow the sculpture to dry

5. All of these are required on the entry form *except* your —

   A   school name
   B   teacher's name
   C   e-mail address
   D   phone number

6. Based on the entry form, you can assume that *most* people entering the contest will be —

   F   teachers
   G   students
   H   retired adults
   J   librarians

7. Here is a step-by-step chart that shows part of the process described in the selection.

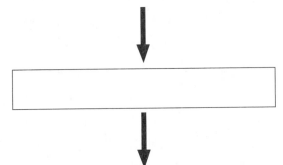

Get an idea.

Tear paper into strips.

Dip strips into glue and water mixture.

Which of these belongs in the empty box?

   A   Paint the sculpture.
   B   Drape wet strips over the armature.
   C   Assemble the materials.
   D   Fill out the entry form.

DIRECTIONS

Read the article. Then, read each question that follows on page 335 and circle the best response.

After the discovery of gold at Sutter's Mill in 1848, people swarmed to California to strike it rich. Within two years, more than 40,000 prospectors, called "forty-niners," had arrived there. Forty-niners used a variety of methods to comb rivers and riverbeds for nuggets of gold. In the following article you will learn about some of these methods.

How Gold Rush Miners Found Gold

Panning   Prospectors used a large tin or iron pan with slanted sides to wash gravel in water. They panned in streams, near sandbars, and along low-lying gravel banks. They stooped or squatted in freezing water, swirling and shaking the pan so that sand washed over the rim and gold flecks sank to the bottom.

Dry washing   Miners threw soil from dry streambeds onto a sheet and tossed the contents into the air. The lighter particles of *debris* blew away and gold flakes remained on the sheet.

Rocking   A rocker, or cradle, was an improvement over the pan. The rocker was a wooden box, open at one end, that was mounted on rockers. It resembled a baby's cradle. Miners shoveled gold-bearing gravel onto a metal sieve atop the box and poured in water while vigorously rocking the cradle. The tiny gold particles collected behind grooves (or riffles) at the bottom of the box.

Using toms   A tom was a long wooden box, from eight to twenty feet long, with riffles on the bottom and a metal screen on top. Miners would dump large amounts of dirt and gravel into the tom. Then they would pour water over the dirt and gravel, washing most of it away and leaving behind the gold. A tom used a huge amount of water, and two or three people were needed to manage one.

Hydraulic mining   In hydraulic mining, hillsides were blasted with thousands of gallons of water forced through large hoses. The water pressure blasted away tons of earth, which was then washed into sluices—troughs with ridges along the bottom to catch gold flakes.

River damming   Miners diverted whole rivers with heavy timbers and boulders on the chance that gold could be found in the exposed riverbed.

1. Prospectors used water as they panned for gold because —

   A the water cleaned the gold
   B the water washed the sand out of the pan
   C gold is more easily spotted when it is damp
   D the gold would float

2. After miners blocked whole rivers with dams, they —

   F blasted the hillsides with water pressure
   G threw soil from the banks of the river onto sheets
   H used expensive equipment to find gold in the water
   J looked for gold in the exposed riverbed

3. Which of these techniques would a miner working alone *most* likely use?

   A Rocking
   B Using a tom
   C River damming
   D Hydraulic mining

4. In a rocker, the gold collects —

   F on a sheet held in the air
   G at the front of the box
   H on heavy timbers or boulders
   J behind grooves at the bottom of the box

5. The purpose of this article is to —

   A persuade readers to look for gold
   B explain techniques once used by miners
   C entertain readers with a story about the gold rush
   D describe how miners used a rocker

6. If you wanted to find out more information about rockers, which keyword would be *most* helpful?

   F Rivers
   G Mining
   H Timbers
   J Dams

7. The title of this article helps readers by —

   A introducing a new vocabulary word
   B providing details about the first paragraph
   C telling what the article is mainly about
   D using words from the article

8. In this article, the word *debris* means small pieces of —

   F dirt
   G gold
   H wood
   J boulders

DIRECTIONS

Read the article. Then, read each question that follows on page 337 and circle the best response.

Water from the Sky

Fog, dew, hail, sleet—water, or precipitation, falls in many different forms. Two of the most common forms are rain and snow.

Rain is made up of drops of water. These drops can range in size from 0.02 to 0.25 inches. The larger the raindrop, the faster it falls. Smaller drops are mostly round in shape. Larger drops flatten as they fall.

Yearly rainfall amounts differ from place to place on Earth. Places near the equator can get as much as 400 inches of rain in one year. In fact, rain falls almost every day in parts of western Africa and in parts of South America. Other areas of Africa and South America are some of the driest places on Earth. Rain is rare in Africa's Sahara Desert. The Atacama Desert in Chile has gone for as long as 14 years with no rain at all.

Many things affect the amount of rainfall in an area. Rain falls more frequently in areas near the equator. Because of evaporation, areas near large bodies of water get more rain than inland areas. Wind direction and mountains also affect the amount of rainfall an area gets.

Snow is made up of tiny ice crystals that stick together. Although every snowflake has six sides, snowflake shapes vary greatly. In fact, some people claim that no two snowflakes have exactly the same shape. Flakes also vary in size, from very small to larger than 1 inch in diameter.

Snow does not contain as much water as rain. It takes 6 inches of wet snow or up to 30 inches of dry snow to equal 1 inch of rain. Snowfall rates, like rainfall rates, are affected by various factors. Temperature is the most obvious factor. Snow can fall all year in cold polar regions. However, the greatest amounts of snow fall during the winter in mountains that are not near the poles. The Rocky Mountains and the Alps are two areas that receive large amounts of snow.

Both rain and snow clean the air of dust and other pollutants. However, too much rain or snow can be dangerous. Avalanches can occur when snow piles too deeply on steep slopes. Strong rains and melting snows can both produce flooding.

Rain and snow are both important sources of fresh water. There is almost certainly a link between the human population and precipitation. Water for drinking, cleaning, growing crops, and recreational uses comes from rainfall and snowfall. People tend to live where there is enough water to support their needs.

---

1. **Snow is made up of tiny ice crystals that <u>stick</u> together.**

   Which sentence uses *stick* in the same way as above?

   A The walking <u>stick</u> had a carved handle.

   B If you <u>stick</u> the balloon with a pin, it will pop.

   C Glue helps the stamp <u>stick</u> to the envelope.

   D Did you see the lizard <u>stick</u> out its tongue?

2. This essay *mainly* compares —

   F types of raindrops

   G wet areas and dry areas

   H rain and snow

   J cold places and warm places

3. All of these belong in an outline of the third paragraph *except* —

   A rain is made up of drops of water

   B rainfall amounts are different from place to place

   C it rains almost every day in parts of western Africa

   D the Atacama Desert has gone 14 years without rain

4. The author organizes each of these paragraphs in a compare-contrast pattern *except* —

   F the third

   G the fourth

   H the fifth

   J the eighth

ACKNOWLEDGMENTS

For permission to reprint copyrighted material, grateful acknowledgment is made to the following sources:

Miriam Altshuler Literary Agency, on behalf of Walter Dean Myers: "The Treasure of Lemon Brown" by Walter Dean Myers from *Face to Face: A Collection of Stories by Celebrated Soviet and American Writers,* edited by Thomas Pettepiece and Anatoly Aleksin. Copyright © 1983 by Walter Dean Myers.

Susan Bergholz Literary Services, New York: "Gil's Furniture Bought & Sold" from *The House on Mango Street* by Sandra Cisneros. Copyright © 1984 by Sandra Cisneros. Published by Vintage Books, a division of Random House, Inc., and in hardcover by Alfred A. Knopf in 1994. All rights reserved.

Chronicle Books: "Oranges" from *New and Selected Poems* by Gary Soto. Copyright © 1995 by Gary Soto.

Don Congdon Associates, Inc.: "There Will Come Soft Rains" by Ray Bradbury. Copyright © 1950 by the Crowell-Collier Publishing Co.; copyright renewed © 1977 by Ray Bradbury.

Doubleday, a division of Random House, Inc.: From *The Cay* by Theodore Taylor. Copyright © 1969 by Theodore Taylor.

Farrar, Straus & Giroux, LLC: "Charles" from *The Lottery* by Shirley Jackson. Copyright © 1948, 1949 by Shirley Jackson; copyright renewed © 1976, 1977 by Laurence Hyman, Barry Hyman, Mrs. Sarah Webster, and Mrs. Joanne Schnurer. "The Puppy" from *Stories and Prose Poems* by Alexander Solzhenitsyn, translated by Michael Glenny. Translation copyright © 1971 by Michael Glenny.

Judith Gorog: "Those Three Wishes" from *A Taste for Quiet and Other Disquieting Tales* by Judith Gorog. Copyright © 1982 by Judith Gorog.

Harcourt, Inc.: "Broken Chain" from *Baseball in April and Other Stories* by Gary Soto. Copyright © 1990 by Gary Soto.

HarperCollins Publishers: From *No Pretty Pictures: A Child of War* by Anita Lobel. Copyright © 1998 by Anita Lobel.

The Estate of Martin Luther King, Jr., c/o Writers House as agent for the proprietor: "I Have a Dream" by Martin Luther King, Jr. Copyright © 1963 by Martin Luther King, Jr.; copyright renewed © 1991 by Coretta Scott King.

Little, Brown and Company: Excerpt (retitled "Camp Harmony") from *Nisei Daughter* by Monica Sone. Copyright © 1953 and renewed © 1981 by Monica Sone.

National Geographic Society: From "Destination: Mars" by Aline Alexander Newman from *National Geographic World,* January 2000, p. 14–18. Copyright © 2000 by National Geographic Society.

Dwight Okita: "In Response to Executive Order 9066" from *Crossing with the Light* by Dwight Okita. Copyright © 1992 by Dwight Okita. Published by Tia Chucha Press, Chicago.

Random House, Inc.: Excerpts (retitled "Mrs. Flowers") from *I Know Why the Caged Bird Sings* by Maya Angelou. Copyright © 1969 and renewed © 1997 by Maya Angelou. "Raymond's Run" from *Gorilla, My Love* by Toni Cade Bambara. Copyright © 1971 by Toni Cade Bambara. From *The Diary of Anne Frank* by Albert Hackett, Frances Goodrich Hackett, and Otto Frank. Copyright © 1956 by Albert Hackett, Frances Goodrich Hackett, and Otto Frank. CAUTION: *The Diary of Anne Frank* is the sole property of the dramatists and is fully protected by copyright. It may not be acted by professionals or amateurs without written permission and the payment of a royalty. All rights, including professional, amateur, stock, radio broadcasting, television, motion picture, recitation, lecturing, public reading, and the rights of translation into foreign languages are reserved. All inquiries should be addressed to the dramatists' agent: Leah Salisbury, 234 West 44th Street, New York, N.Y.

PHOTO CREDITS

AUTHOR AND TITLE INDEX